T0205414

Wireless Networks

Series Editor

Xuemin Sherman Shen, University of Waterloo, Waterloo, ON, Canada

The purpose of Springer's Wireless Networks book series is to establish the state of the art and set the course for future research and development in wireless communication networks. The scope of this series includes not only all aspects of wireless networks (including cellular networks, WiFi, sensor networks, and vehicular networks), but related areas such as cloud computing and big data. The series serves as a central source of references for wireless networks research and development. It aims to publish thorough and cohesive overviews on specific topics in wireless networks, as well as works that are larger in scope than survey articles and that contain more detailed background information. The series also provides coverage of advanced and timely topics worthy of monographs, contributed volumes, textbooks and handbooks.

Kui Ren • Cong Wang

Searchable Encryption

From Concepts to Systems

 Springer

Kui Ren
Zhejiang University
Hangzhou, Zhejiang, China

Cong Wang
City University of Hong Kong
Kowloon Tong, Kowloon, Hong Kong

ISSN 2366-1186   ISSN 2366-1445   (electronic)
Wireless Networks
ISBN 978-3-031-21379-3   ISBN 978-3-031-21377-9   (eBook)
https://doi.org/10.1007/978-3-031-21377-9

This Springer imprint is published by the registered company Springer Nature Switzerland AG
The registered company address is: Gewerbestrasse 11, 6330 Cham, Switzerland

Abstract

The prosperity of cloud infrastructures has motivated individuals and enterprises to store their massive data remotely, such as outsourced storage backups and in-the-cloud databases. The benefits of using cloud infrastructures to host various datastores have been well understood since its inception in the early 2000s. Yet, with the expanding demand for data ownership globally and the frequent data breach incidents, massive concerns have been raised regarding the security and privacy of remotely stored data. In such settings, off-site servers are usually beyond the data owner's physical control and often the high-valued attacking targets. They are subject to internal threats, e.g., sysadmins with root access, and external attacks, e.g., financially motivated hackers with system break-ins. To better safeguard private data, it has been increasingly regarded as a must that sensitive data be encrypted throughout its life cycle: at rest, in transit, and in use. Today's data encryption practices mainly focus on encryption at rest and in transit. How to secure the data in use, as one of the most active research topics recently, has evolved from theoretical research proposals a few decades ago to powerful cryptographic tools capable of driving real systems today. This book provides a comprehensive review of a specific line of research in this direction, namely searchable encryption, which allows data owners to securely outsource always-encrypted data without sacrificing the ability to search over it efficiently. Being able to selectively retrieve data of interest through queries over an outsourced encrypted database is arguably among the most critical functionalities for secure cloud applications. Yet, straightforward data encryption hinders direct computation and utilization over encrypted data, rendering (especially) information retrieval a challenging task. We will introduce searchable encryption basics, including motivations and objectives, general architecture frameworks, and security and performance measurements, followed by a comparative overview of different cryptographic primitives and algorithms that are building blocks for searching over encrypted data. We will then go through several milestone like searchable encryption schemes to improve the system's functionalities, performance, and security. Besides the broad overview of the field, we will discuss the current research trend of searchable encryption, particularly on the leakage-abuse attacks and their countermeasures, to give audiences more insights about different threat models, assumptions, and the related security guarantees, when using searchable encryption in the real-world settings. Furthermore, we will overview the latest efforts in building full-fledged encrypted database systems that draw insights from searchable encryption constructions. We will also discuss how building such encrypted systems with complex nature and versatile functionalities might be possible, with the emerging proliferation of hardware-assisted secure enclaves. Finally, we foresee challenges and opportunities ahead for future encrypted database systems, and call for broader engagement of researchers and practitioners to jointly pave the way for more practical in-the-cloud database services over encrypted data with guaranteed security and privacy.

Preface

After working in the areas of cloud data security for more than 15 years, we decided to take a systematic look back at this field through this book to review and present in easy-to-understand languages the classic results in this field. This book provides a broad introduction to searchable encryption, from theories to applications. It gives the vast majority of searchable encryption topics, introducing the underlying principles, and providing security and performance analysis. We have tried to keep our explanations as elementary as possible without compromising completeness and depth. We have also offered figures and examples, when possible, to illustrate how mechanisms or systems work.

This book is intended primarily for advanced undergraduates, graduate students, and practitioners who want an initial but extensive understanding of searchable encryption. The book requires only a basic knowledge of mathematics, cryptography, and computational complexity theory. Rigorous descriptions and formal security proofs are kept to the minimum, as they are sophisticated, requiring mathematics maturity. Materials for in-depth studies are provided at the end of each chapter for more self-driven audiences who want to know more about the field.

Our goal in writing this book was to make searchable encryption concepts and systems accessible to a broad audience who may not have relevant background knowledge. We would be grateful if you would let us know whether our efforts have been successful. In particular, feedback and constructive comments pointing out potential improvements in this book are always appreciated. We hope there are no errors or typos in this book. However, we would be grateful if you could let us know if you find any. You can email your feedback and errata to kuiren@zju.edu.cn or congwang@cityu.edu.hk; please put "Searchable Encryption: From Concepts to Systems" in the subject line.

Hangzhou, China   Kui Ren
Kowloon Tong, Hong Kong   Cong Wang

Acknowledgments

Kui Ren is deeply indebted to those who have believed, helped, and supported him throughout his career in both the USA and China. Since he started his research in this area (also his faculty career) in 2007, he has been very fortunate to have worked with a number of brilliant students and collaborators. He has also met a few great mentors and quite a lot of encouraging colleagues, and hence benefited tremendously from their guidance, discussions, and insights. This book would never have been possible without their contributions, and he is so grateful for that.

Cong Wang would like to thank Kui Ren and Qian Wang for introducing him to the world of security and privacy. Their influence can be felt until today and will no doubt continue into the future. He appreciates the constant guidance, support, and help from his mentors and colleagues since he started his faculty career in 2012 at the City University of Hong Kong. He is also very fortunate to have worked with many brilliant students and collaborators throughout his career, for which he is sincerely grateful.

Both authors wish to thank those who read earlier drafts of this book and offered constructive comments. They thank all the people from academia and industry who work in this field for their excellent ideas, profound insights, and all other inspirations. Special thanks go to Leqian Zheng, who has played a major assistive role in the development of this book by carefully reading the manuscript, preparing illustrative figures, and providing valuable feedback.

Kui Ren was supported in part by the National Natural Science Foundation of China (Grants No. 62032021) and the Leading Innovative and Entrepreneur Team Introduction Program of Zhejiang (Grant No. 2018R01005). Cong Wang was supported in part by the Research Grants Council of Hong Kong (Grant No. RFS2122-1S04, and CityU 11217620).

Contents

Chapter 1
Introduction

1.1 The Necessity for Always-Encrypted Data

Without doubt, we are in a data-driven economy today, where data is becoming increasingly more valuable than ever before [99]. Operations of various society sectors, such as healthcare [81, 294], business [96, 180], government [202, 226], individuals [267], etc., all heavily rely on the availability of data for various decision-makings. While the value of data is becoming universally recognized, there have been growing concerns regarding the security and privacy of important and sensitive data. Over the last decade, large-scale data breaches have occurred every now and then, affecting hundreds of millions of people and causing billion-dollar losses [65, 95, 255, 258]. The demands on controlling the ownership of the data are expanding globally. The importance of data ownership and privacy protection is underscored by the increasingly strict regulatory frameworks worldwide such as GDPR [264] and HK PDPO [237]. Yet, today's practices on data management and hosting services do not appear to provide sufficient guarantees to ease the growing concerns or make data owners worry-free.

For many individual and enterprise data owners, their data does not always reside on the devices entirely under their control. For example, the prosperity of cloud infrastructures over the past two decades has motivated both individuals and enterprises to store their data remotely, such as outsourced storage backups [69, 140, 142], cloud-based file hosting and syncing services [141, 189], in-the-cloud databases [119, 190], and various web applications running on top. But the lack of physical control of those remote machines and the lack of sufficient visibility inside the computing service providers have often put data owners in an inescapable dilemma. Either they have to blindly trust the remote machines to safeguard their data, which is not always the case, as evidenced by the surging growth of frequent data breach incidents, including many from noteworthy names [285], or they have to build the entire IT infrastructures in-house to host the data on-premise, but giving up the convenient benefits of using cloud infrastructures, such as service elasticity

© The Author(s), under exclusive license to Springer Nature Switzerland AG 2023
K. Ren, C. Wang, *Searchable Encryption*, Wireless Networks,
https://doi.org/10.1007/978-3-031-21377-9_1

and low entry bar, and accordingly bearing all the cumbersome computing and maintenance cost locally.

As more and more data are being generated, the dilemma mentioned above becomes more challenging to handle. When data gets bigger, it tends to be more privacy-sensitive. Thus, from the data ownership point of view, it seems more reasonable to host such sensitive data in-house at on-premise servers. But bigger data also demands more computing capacities to work with. For many individual and enterprise data owners, resorting to off-premise cloud-based solutions would seemingly be a more affordable choice [284]. So, the remaining question is: would it be possible for data owners to enjoy the benefits of using cloud infrastructures while always retaining the ownership of their important and sensitive data, as if it were stored at on-premise servers? As we're going to lay out in this book, we hope to convince our audiences that there will be a firmly positive answer to this question. The technical pathway is promising, but not without challenges ahead.

To protect sensitive data, using encryption is a necessary means. It has played a successful key role in securing the data at rest (aka data saved on disk), as adopted by many enterprise products and security practices [3, 115, 138, 192, 195, 203], and securing the data in transit (aka data en route through networks), like the Transport Layer Security (TLS) protocol suite [139]. These encryption practices have significantly raised the security bar of today's Internet. But the landscape of the surging cyber threats today is expanding, and there is an urgent call for keeping the data always-encrypted to protect the data not only at rest and in transit but also *in use* (aka confidential computing [90]). Conventional wisdom suggests putting important and sensitive data behind network firewalls, intrusion detection/prevention systems, and layers of access control mechanisms to keep attackers out. However, these traditional security measures alone are no longer sufficient, when attackers might manage to break into the system and gain administrative privileges, through rogue employees [205], carefully crafted social engineering [157], exploiting vulnerabilities in software or untrusted software supply chain [148, 241], and even human errors [146].

Keeping data always-encrypted helps obviate the need to deal with these thorny attack vectors, which are often unpredictable in practice, and guarantees the data confidentiality for owners, even if the data is out of their hands, e.g., hosted at in-the-cloud databases. It could also serve as an in-depth defense practice for data at on-premise devices. The challenge, however, is how to perform computation over the encrypted data. Computing over encrypted data has been a hot topic in the research community over the past decades, and there has been a plethora of works in the broadly defined area, such as multiparty computations (MPC) [8, 39, 79, 85, 160, 176, 183, 256, 260, 281], fully homomorphic encryption (FHE) [6, 25, 59, 62, 63, 72, 73, 76, 130, 185], searching over encrypted data [4, 7, 31, 31, 37, 38, 48, 74, 87, 153, 158, 194, 221, 224, 245, 254, 269, 290], and various security designs based on trusted execution environment (TEE), especially those leveraging the emerging hardware-assisted enclaves [7, 7, 11, 93, 227, 228, 239, 254, 254, 261, 265, 269].

These collective efforts from multiple domains have made tremendous advancements on how to secure the data in use. As one of the most active research topics recently, it has evolved from theoretical research proposals a few decades ago to powerful cryptographic tools capable of driving real systems today [89, 129]. This book comprehensively reviews a specific line of research in this direction, namely, searchable encryption. Being able to selectively retrieve data of interest, by searching, is universally needed, and even more so when data gets bigger. As search becomes ubiquitous, research on searchable encryption aims to address the conflict between data encryption and search. It covers the design and implementation of encrypted search algorithms, data structures, and systems that facilitate various forms of search over encrypted data. Given the fundamental role of search engines, the area of searchable encryption has attracted lots of interest from academia and industry. As we unfold in this book, its many exciting advancements have made searchable encryption one of the most potentially impactful topics that would influence all database systems and applications today and tomorrow.

1.2   Searching Always-Encrypted Databases

As a core pillar of modern computing underpinning the data-driven economy, databases provide indispensable means to organize, store, search, and retrieve data, among other functionalities. They are widely deployed in IT environments at different scales, penetrating every aspect of our daily lives. From the data management point of view, there are many functionalities a modern database provides, such as access control enforcement [224], transaction guarantee [99], storage engine [254], and rich analytics [301]. We consider them part of the broadly defined database management systems (DBMS). Throughout this book, we would like to explicitly distinguish our discussions from these DBMS functionalities for the betterment of presentation. Instead, we want to specifically focus on the core database functionalities of data indexing and search [99], about which searchable encryption designs are most concerned.

We have mentioned earlier that with the vital importance of databases comes the everlasting concern about their security. Keeping data always-encrypted seems an inevitable trend that the academic community and industry practitioners are pushing forward. Yet, ordinary encryption prevents efficient data indexing and search, as is done in the plaintext domain. Technically, enabling the indexing and search capabilities over always-encrypted data is quite different from the traditional encryption-based data protection practices adopted by existing database products, such as transparent encryption [82, 191, 203, 220].

The difference lies in the trust assumptions. For the former, the data owners generate and control the encryption keys to encrypt their data, and the keys are not supposed to be shared with anyone else, including the database servers. In other words, the database servers are untrusted, and all the indexing and search operations are done on encrypted data, which poses fundamental challenges and demands new technical advancements. For the latter, the database servers are entrusted to protect the data using encryption, which means they would hold encryption keys.

Essentially, transparent encryption achieves data encryption at rest. Whenever query processing demands access to specific encrypted data, the database servers will first decrypt the data on the fly to ensure that any subsequent database operations can be done over plaintext data transparently. Such a trust assumption, however, cannot cope with malicious attackers gaining administrative privileges or other memory scraping threats.

In light of the conflict between securing the data with always encryption and maintaining the ability to search over it, many encrypted search designs have been proposed [1, 7, 12, 20, 28, 34, 38, 56, 74, 87, 172, 173, 184, 211, 221, 224, 228, 235, 254, 268, 273, 278, 280, 287, 288, 290, 295], since the seminal work by Song et al. [245] in early 2000. Generally speaking, all these designs aim to transform a plaintext database to an *encrypted database*, through encrypted search algorithms and data structures, which enable confidential queries over always-encrypted data and confines information disclosure to well-defined leakage profiles. Despite the commonality of the design blueprint, the technical routes for achieving encrypted search are quite diverse. As we will delve into more details in Chap. 2, there are approaches based on property-preserving encryption [20, 28, 170], oblivious RAMs (ORAMs) [109], homomorphic encryption [104], and searchable symmetric encryption [74] (later known as the generalized structured encryption [56]).

Each of these approaches exhibits its strengths and weaknesses, and so far, no dominant solution stands out compared to others. The more practical viewpoint we would like to advocate is that building such encrypted database systems is a juggling act between security, performance, and functionality [99]:

- For security, it refers to the quantitative measurement of the well-defined leakage profiles throughout the setup, indexing and search, and other necessary maintenance procedures of the encrypted database (e.g., dynamic data update like deletion, insertion, etc.). Security is also intrinsically pertinent to adversary models and assumptions, as we uncover more in the next section and also in Chap. 3;
- For performance, it refers to how efficiently the indexing and search designs would operate. Performance would be majorly affected by the computation and communication workload and round efficiency. Typically, an encrypted search design with asymptotically sublinear search time would always be preferred than a design demanding a linear scan of the encrypted database;
- For functionality, it refers to the expressiveness of the query types that an encrypted search design can support. Intuitively, answering a more complex query, such as the conjunctive query with multiple keywords (e.g., search for "name = Alice AND major = CS"), would pose more challenges on the encrypted search algorithm and data structure design, which often leads to increased performance overhead and sometimes expanded leakage profiles [47], compared to a single-keyword search.

For researchers working in encrypted search, it is always about finding the right balance among security, performance, and functionality, and accurately characterizing the trade-offs of the design with rigorous definitions, thorough analysis, and reasonable assumptions. For security practitioners that want to adopt encrypted search designs, it is suggested that they precisely grasp the trade-offs among different technical routes and understand the associated risks accordingly, before making any deployment choices for their targeted application scenarios. Hopefully, this book will help in both regards.

1.3   Architecture and Operation Framework

We now turn to the general architecture and operation framework of encrypted database research to present a bird's-eye view of problem formulation, threat assumptions, and design goals. This section will provide the necessary background and context information when we delve into more technical descriptions in later chapters. Informally, an encrypted database can be considered a searchable data store that is supposed to respond to confidential queries for selected retrieval over encrypted data. The queries are often well defined in advance, e.g., through equality (commonly known as the keyword search in literature), range, etc., which can be combined to offer even more expressive search functionalities, such as Boolean expressions over multiple keywords [47].

From the security perspective, all the encrypted database designs want to make sure that the operation framework does not directly expose the query value or the plaintext of the encrypted data to the database server. Given any encrypted search algorithms, protocols, and related data structure designs, formally analyzing and assessing their security strength for the security goals, however, is a nontrivial task. It involves a formalized security definition proposal, followed by a rigorous analysis (e.g., through tight reasoning on how the claimed security can be reduced to some well-established assumptions). We will more frequently examine different security notions and the rationale for related security reasoning later in this book.

1.3.1   The Abstracted Scenario

Despite the different technical designs, most of the research on the encrypted database can be abstracted into a simplified client-server operation framework, including a "setup" phase and a "search" phase, as shown in Fig. 1.1. For easy illustration purposes, we adopt the typical scenario of a cloud-based encrypted data store, with the roles of different entities described below:

- The client: it encrypts the data before outsourcing them to the cloud server in the "setup" phase, and later issues encrypted queries to retrieve data of interest from the server in the "search" phase.
- The server: it hosts the encrypted data and answers encrypted queries over always-encrypted data without decryption in the "search" phase.

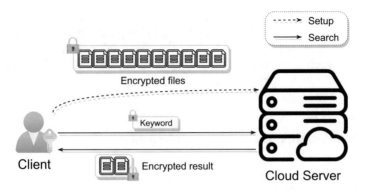

Fig. 1.1 Architecture of encrypted search in the typical cloud scenario

Note that the client, as shown in the figure, conducts two different tasks in operation:

1. Encrypt the data, often by following encrypted search algorithms and data structure designs, to set up (aka prepare) the encrypted database;
2. Generate the encrypted queries, with respect to the plaintext search request, for the server to conduct the encrypted search operation correspondingly.

Depending on different application contexts, the client's two tasks can be instantiated either by a single entity, data owner, or by two entities, data owner and data user, respectively. A data owner can be an enterprise or an individual, who owns the plaintext dataset. He can generate encrypted queries (aka search tokens) either for his own interests, according to requests from different data users [47], or even delegate the capability of encrypted query generation to multiple authorized users, upon proper key management and authorization control designs [74]. Unless explicitly mentioned, our focus in this book will be on settings with a single client and a single server. The client is assumed to combine the roles of both data owner and data users, respectively.

Figure 1.1 is intended to be a high-level illustration about the workflow of encrypted search designs. There are two additional points, on encrypted search indexes and dynamic data support, which are not shown in the figure, but we briefly elaborate below for completeness:

- The need for encrypted indexes that triggers additional data uploaded to server. To facilitate the encrypted search functionality, most of the modern encrypted search designs would need the client in the "setup" phase to also generate encrypted indexes (aka encrypted data structures with various auxiliary data in encrypted forms), which will be uploaded together with the encrypted dataset to the server for encrypted query processing. The design of encrypted indexes is one of the focal points in the literature of encrypted database research [23, 47, 48, 52, 74, 124, 151, 153, 217, 253, 300].

- The need for dynamic update that introduces additional client-server interactions. Many database applications demand dynamic data updates, such as modification, insertion, and deletion of the data records or document files in the dataset. While seemingly intuitive, supporting dynamic updates over encrypted data poses important yet challenging research problems. Not all encrypted search designs could support such encrypted updates explicitly. For the selected a few [37, 38, 48, 106, 128, 153, 249, 252, 270, 271, 302] that do, there are still many obstacles yet to be addressed from the security, performance, and functionality perspectives.

We hope that by now we have depicted a detailed enough picture about the operational framework for encrypted database research, with different entities and their respective roles, different phases of the operations, and the importance of encrypted indexes and dynamic data support that matter a lot in the encrypted database operations. Next, we will introduce threat assumptions and adversarial behaviors that are commonly considered in encrypted database research.

1.3.2 Threat Assumptions

We have already mentioned that in the context of always-encrypted databases, the server is untrusted, due to the possibility of both insider threats and external attacks. But to what extent do we "untrust" the server, such that we can still build our encrypted databases and make them operational as intended?

To answer the question, we must get concrete on the threat assumptions and the specific adversarial behaviors that most of the research on encrypted databases deals with. Firstly, we would like to clarify that in the encrypted search scenario, the client, who represents both data owners and authorized data users, as we have mentioned earlier, is fully trusted. This is easy to understand, since any misbehaving client could break the confidentiality guarantee of an encrypted database by revealing its secret key. Thus, we usually assume that the client is benign, and operating in a trusted context.

Semi-Honest vs. Malicious Model

As for the "untrusted" server, we follow the existing literature and introduce two commonly used threat assumptions: "honest-but-curious" and "malicious."

Honest-but-curious   is also known as "semi-honest" model. Under this assumption, we do not trust the server to see our data in plaintext. But we do put a reasonable amount of trust in the server's operations that would honestly follow our prescribed protocols to process encrypted data. Any adversary under this assumption can still "passively" observe and collect information while executing the protocols, in its "curious" attempt to learn more about the encrypted data.

Malicious   is a more severe scenario. In addition to all the adversarial capabilities derived from the "semi-honest" assumption, a "malicious" adversary can be intentionally non-cooperating. It can take "active" actions to disrupt the entire protocol operation or influence specific selected protocol steps, causing extra threats to the correctness of the system operation. Compared to the "honest-but-curious" assumption, the distinction here is the adversary's proactive actions that can willingly deviate from the prescribed protocols.

To our best knowledge, most of the encrypted database research [5, 99, 222, 242, 283] follow the "honest-but-curious" threat assumption on the untrusted server. They focus on how to measure, confine, and further mitigate the information (later defined as various leakage profiles) an adversary is allowed to observe and collect at the encrypted database passively.

Dealing with a "malicious" adversary would require additional enforcement techniques to ensure that the untrusted server is always behaving as intended, such as correctly answering queries. Different technical approaches have been proposed, such as the theoretical proposal on applying cryptographically verifiable designs [61], the adoption of multiple servers for robustness enhancement against individual dishonest behaviors [134], and developing the authenticated data structures [2, 16, 88, 107, 114, 212–214, 259]. Given the theme of this book on encrypted search designs, we would limit our attention to the "honest-but-curious" assumption that most of the active research has been considering. We recommend that interested audiences learn more from the references about dealing with "malicious" adversaries. But please keep in mind that due to the sophisticated nature of the problem, not all the proposals addressing "malicious" adversaries are coherent or compatible with all the encrypted search designs.

Snapshot vs. Persistent Adversary

Besides different levels of "untrust" assumptions, there are distinctions on the length of the attack window to be considered: How long would an adversary preside at the encrypted database server to (passively) observe and collect the information? This is a more fine-grained perspective following the "honest-but-curious" assumption. In this regard, we introduce notions of "snapshot adversary" and "persistent adversary," respectively, according to the literature [120, 121]:

Snapshot adversary   is the weaker version of the two. It is assumed to have a very short observation window to passively collect information at the compromised server. The name "snapshot" is self-explanatory: the adversary can only obtain a single "snapshot" of the encrypted database, including the encrypted dataset (e.g., tables or document files) and the encrypted indexes from memory, external storage, or even both, whereas the "snapshot" observation is static.

Persistent adversary   is the stronger version. It is assumed to have a long observation window, during which the adversary can stealthily observe all operations at the compromised server. The keyword "persistent" suggests that the adversary can preside at the server for long enough, obtaining not only many "snapshots" of the encrypted database but also step-by-step query executions, including how each query accesses encrypted data records or document files.

Encrypted database designs that are demonstrated to be secure against "snapshot" adversaries are not necessarily secure against "persistent" adversaries. This viewpoint gives us a very intuitive measurement to categorize the security strength of different encrypted database designs.

1.4 Balancing Among Security, Performance, and Functionality

As mentioned earlier, designing an encrypted database is a balancing act among security, performance, and functionality. In this regard, designs that put more priority on performance and functionality may leak a lot of sensitive information, such that even a "snapshot" attack can be devastating to break the confidentiality guarantee of the encrypted databases. For example, encrypted database proposals based on property-preserving encryption primitives, such as deterministic encryption [20] and order-preserving encryption [28], always exhibit or *leak* equality and order of ciphertexts from the ciphertext-only point of view. Thus, a "snapshot" adversary can conduct a simple frequency analysis over the ciphertext to partially recover the plaintexts [49, 198], with some reasonable background knowledge on the encrypted databases.

On the other hand, there are theoretical designs that put much more priority on security over performance, such as those based on generic cryptographic primitives like oblivious RAM (ORAM) [110] and fully homomorphic encryption (FHE) [104]. These proposals, by design, support query executions over encrypted data, and leak little observable information, naturally resilient against a long-lasting "persistent" adversary. Let us take ORAM-based designs as an example. In addition to the encrypted queries and encrypted data, the ORAM-based data retrieval protocols can even hide the access pattern against the server. Namely, a "persistent" adversary would not be able to infer which data records or files at the encrypted database have been queried and retrieved by the client.[1] From a security point of view, these designs are naturally stronger than those based on proper-preserving encryption primitives, but this is achieved at the cost of performance. Specifically, the ORAM-based designs [9, 86, 87, 113, 134, 194, 197, 230, 247, 301] would incur logarithmic or poly-logarithmic (in the total number of data records) amortized cost for each read and write. Currently, the consensus from the community is that none of these generic designs would be widely regarded as reasonable or practical enough

---

[1] ORAM-based designs do not hide the number of accesses [217], which is roughly equivalent to the number of responses (aka volume) per query. We will discuss more on this in Chap. 5.

for large-scale datasets. We will cover more about these different design choices in later chapters.

1.4.1 Encrypted Search with Controlled Leakage

Hopefully, our discussions so far have convincingly laid out the argument that more balanced encrypted search designs are desired. By being more balanced, we specifically refer to the following two aspects:

1. The designs should be at least secure against "snapshot" adversaries. In other words, they need to be stronger than designs based on property-preserving encryption primitives, and they must be able to deal with "persistent" adversaries that can observe all query execution steps at the server side for a sufficient long time.
2. The designs should be more performant than those based on the generic cryptographic primitives like ORAM and FHE. Among many performance indicators, such as round efficiency, communication overhead, data locality, extra storage overhead, etc., achieving the asymptotically sublinear search time is always much more preferred.

Is it possible to have a workable design blueprint that simultaneously meets the above "balance" requirements? The answer is positive, as witnessed by a line of research known as searchable symmetric encryption [74], the more generalized structured encryption [56], and their many follow-up work [23, 37, 38, 47, 48, 52, 106, 128, 151, 153, 217, 249, 252, 253, 270, 271, 300, 302]. The basic idea among this line of work is to trade off a small amount of well-defined information (aka leakage patterns) for significant performance speedup, such that sublinear or even optimal search time can be achieved. Here, the term "optimal" refers to the search time being linearly proportional to the number of data records or files matching the query.

At the first glance, this concept of trading off leakage for efficiency seems counterintuitive for security, as it implies that for any encrypted search construction (i.e., encrypted search algorithms and encrypted data structures) following this blueprint, the persistent adversary is very likely to collect and learn something about the encrypted database through the observation about encrypted query executions. Therefore, assessing its security must answer two key challenging questions that immediately follow:

How to formalize the security?   The goal is to formally establish an upper bound on the information leakage such that any given encrypted search construction would reveal no more than to any persistent adversary. Answering the question commonly demands nontrivial efforts at least on the following three aspects:

1. Identify the suitable leakage profiles;
2. Quantitatively model such leakages;

3. Capture the subtleties on how a persistent adversary might interact with the encrypted search designs through its chosen-keyword capability [74].

How to understand the leakage?   The goal is to accurately evaluate the risks associated with the allowed leakage [49]. Because information leakage is explicitly allowed and actually inevitable, understanding the risks would set up the guidelines, through both theoretical and empirical studies, to help concretely parameterize encrypted search solutions in practice. For example, given an encrypted dataset and some publicly available auxiliary information, how many encrypted queries are allowed to perform, before the accumulated leakage starts to pose a real threat for query or even data recovery?

Properly answering these questions is never an easy task. Up until the time we started to write this book, it has taken the community over two decades to evolve the knowledge on encrypted database designs, and gradually converge on how to define and analyze the security of any given construction through these two key questions. This is also the focus of later chapters in this book. From this controlled leakage perspective, we would like to point out that for almost all different encrypted database designs, the security strength, along with the richness of the query functionality support and the claimed performance, is largely separated by different choices of allowed information leakages.

1.4.2   Common Choices of Allowed Information Leakages

With the presence of a persistent adversary, all the design choices we have talked about so far exhibit certain kinds of information leakage. The spectrum of leakage can be very wide and comprehensive. Not all information leakages are easy to interpret, especially from a security standpoint. To give a tangible idea, below, we use one of the most widely accepted information leakages (aka leakage patterns), search pattern and access pattern leakage, as advocated by many searchable/structured symmetric encryption designs, to illustrate a concrete example. Our first goal is to demonstrate what a leakage pattern can be and further discuss how it might affect security under certain assumptions:

Search pattern   reveals whether two encrypted queries, issued at different times, are equal.

Access pattern   reveals which encrypted data records or files match the query, exposing the data identifiers per each query.

Note that none of these leakage patterns would give away the direct exposure of the plaintext in the encrypted database or the value or keyword in the encrypted queries. They are carefully chosen to be allowed to leak, such that one can build a very efficient (i.e., sublinear) encrypted search construction [74], opposing to the

ORAM-based designs that hide the access pattern (and also search pattern), but incur expensive costs.

So the benefits of allowing these leakage patterns are understood. How about the risks? The fundamental reason the risks exist is because leakage patterns are simply data dependent, with respect to the query and also the database. Take the access pattern as an example. What a persistent adversary can observe from the access pattern are the identifiers of all encrypted data records matching the encrypted query. To help gain more information from the access pattern, one strategy the adversary might try is to combine and correlate what it can observe with other publicly available auxiliary information. Access to such auxiliary information should not be unreasonable to justify. Related examples might include background of the database, e.g., electronic health records with sensitive attributes on age and/or disease severity; publicly released dataset, e.g., census data; or simply language-specific statistics.

From the observed (search) access pattern leakages, the adversary's objective is to identify any possibility of uniqueness, so as to recover the queried value (e.g., keywords in the case of document files), and later recover the (partial) plaintext of the database. For example, as demonstrated by one early result trying to empirically understand the access pattern leakage, even a simple counting attack that counts the number of data records or files returned by each query would help in this regard [49]. This is due to the observation that for certain datasets of document files, there exist lots of keywords that match a unique number of encrypted files, which might be known a priori by the adversary. We will elaborate on this aspect and some effective countermeasures in Chap. 5.

1.5   Early Results, Progress Today, and Challenges Ahead

We have set up all the necessary background on encrypted database research. Before we are about to go deeper into different technical aspects, we would like to briefly overview the advancements of encrypted database at different stages, from early results, progress today, to challenges ahead. In this way, we hope to better prepare the audiences for later chapters, when we introduce the development of encrypted search from concepts to systems in this book.

Over the past two decades of development, there have been many development on encrypted databases, covering the design and implementation of encrypted search algorithms, data structures, and systems. As the public knowledge on encrypted database evolves, the research focus has also been gradually shifting, including the following four perspectives:

Formalizing the security notion.   The notion of searchable encryption was first proposed by Song et al. [245] in 2000. Since then, several later constructions have been proposed [54, 108], with efforts trying to accurately understand and formalize the security notion of encrypted search. It was not until the landmark results by Curtmola et al. [74] in 2006 and Chase and Kamara [56] in 2010 that have essentially established the now standard notion on searchable/structured symmetric encryption. The definition formalizes leakage profiles and captures all the subtleties about a persistent adversary's chosen-keyword capability. These results have also, for the first time, given the encrypted index based constructions with sublinear search time on databases with encrypted document files and other encrypted structured data, like encrypted graphs.

Expanding the functionality and performance.   Following the security framework of searchable/structured symmetric encryption, many follow-up works have been proposed, trying to significantly expand the functionality and performance. For functionality, results have been proposed to enrich the expressiveness of the query, such as Boolean queries including conjunctive and disjunctive logic [47, 149, 218, 251, 282, 297, 302], supporting data updates [37, 38, 152, 153, 193, 302], supporting multiple-user authorizations [47, 74, 131, 147, 216, 231, 232, 234, 278, 297], and many more [44, 126, 174, 257, 272, 275, 276]. For performance, results on data locality [13, 35, 46, 48, 77], parallelization [152], distributed indexes [126, 246], etc. have also been proposed.

Understanding and mitigating the leakage.   The risks of leakage profiles had been overlooked for a long time until a line of research demonstrated some generic attacks [23, 49, 122, 124, 145, 159, 166, 206], through both theoretical and empirical studies. Note that these attacks leveraging leakage profiles do not contradict the security claims of searchable/structured symmetric encryption, as the leakage is explicitly allowed. Instead, they help deepen the community's understanding on the risks of leakage profiles, which indeed can reveal a lot on both encrypted queries and encrypted databases. As such, they have motivated many recent efforts [37, 38, 52, 106, 125, 151, 154, 272, 300], in thwarting specific attacks or generically mitigating the information leakage.

Toward full-fledged encrypted database systems.   With the advancement of encrypted search algorithms and data structures is the pressing demand for fully functional encrypted database management systems. Early attempts based on property-preserving cryptographic primitives, like [224], and more advanced cryptographic constructions, like [144, 215, 221], either do not exhibit strong security strength or incur prohibitive costs. The complexity of the problem motivates more recent attempts to leverage hardware-assisted secure enclaves that are based on different trust assumptions and techniques than cryptographic approaches [7, 87, 98, 194, 227, 254, 269, 280]. Despite much progress, we foresee that insights from encrypted search designs and leakage suppression techniques will play a key role in formalizing and assessing the security strength of these hardware-assisted secure systems.

Due to the space limitation, by no means we would be able to exhaustively list all the prior arts in the field of encrypted database research. Interested audiences, who want to learn more about the related works, are suggested to read these selected references we cover in this book first, and from there to find additional relevant results accordingly.

1.6   Summary and Further Readings

This chapter introduces the background and motivations of searchable encryption. It also provides the architecture, operational framework, threat assumptions, different design choices among security, performance, and functionality of typical representative encrypted search schemes. Because searchable encryption is a vibrant and active research area, we could only cover a small fraction of the most important work in this book. We mainly discuss private-key-based searchable encryption techniques, focusing mostly on the single-client scenario, and emphasize a setting where the server is assumed to be curious-but-honest. In the next chapter, we provide an comparative overview on the available cryptographic primitives that are useful for building an encrypted search system, including property-preserving encryption (also known as property-revealing encryption) and oblivious RAMs. We will share more technical details about their trade-offs in security, performance, and functionality, and demonstrate why a more balanced approach could be possibly achieved that leads to the line of research on searchable symmetric encryption.

Then in Chap. 3, we provide a formal definition of searchable symmetric encryption (later known as structured encryption), with a little history backdrop on earlier constructions and their security notions. We will also introduce the security models that are widely used in modern searchable symmetric encryption. We do not plan to delve into the detailed formal proofs in this book. But we believe it is still essential to provide logically clear explanations to these definitions and help audiences to better understand the security guarantees when using the searchable symmetric encryption in practice. Note that due to the design trade-offs among security, performance, and functionality, all constructions are expected to have leakage profiles.

In Chap. 4, we review recent advancements to bring enriched functionalities and performance to searchable encryption. We will discuss constructions that support data dynamics, with additional security requirement on forward/backward privacy. We will also overview efforts on dealing with rich queries, such as multi-keyword Boolean conjunctive search. Further, we will survey techniques on managing search rights of multiple users and discuss latest efforts in supporting possibly multiple writers to the encrypted database. On performance, we survey techniques that have been developed to enable efficient implementations of searchable encryption protocols. Constructions that take into account practical performance factors, such as data locality and I/O efficiency, space utilization, etc., will also be discussed.

In Chap. 5, we review the recent advancement in understanding the security impact of leakage profiles, particularly the access pattern and search pattern. We will go through the ongoing arms race among the newly identified leakage-abuse attack vectors and the new attack models/tools that essentially speed up the attacks, as well as the various leakage suppression efforts to mitigate such threats. As this area has quickly turned into an active subfield of searchable encryption, we expect to draw more insights, useful techniques, and guidelines from the discussions so as to better direct the future searchable encryption constructions and the related real-world deployment.

In Chap. 6, we overview more recent efforts that attempt to build full-fledged encrypted database systems. We will examine the key differences between full-fledged encrypted database systems and searchable encryption primitives, where the former are often highly optimized and complex systems in nature with strong transaction guarantees and expressive structured query support. These key differences demand much more than encrypted indexing and searching, which searchable encryption primitives are designed for. We will overview recent proposals that suggest to integrate searchable encryption and leakage suppression techniques with database systems and hardware-assisted security primitives (e.g., customized oblivious algorithms), to jointly push forward the vision of full-fledged encrypted database systems.

Finally, we conclude the book in Chap. 7, outlining the trajectory of searchable encryption research in a retrospective way, and suggesting possible directions for the future.

Chapter 2
Fundamental Cryptographic Algorithms and Technologies

In this chapter, we plan to introduce several fundamental cryptographic primitives that could be used to establish an encrypted search system. By briefly discussing these techniques' properties and design intuitions, we hope to build the necessary background to introduce the book's main focus on searchable/structured symmetric encryption schemes, their modern constructions, and the roadmap toward full-fledged encrypted databases in the following chapters. Moreover, we will cover the major limitations of these technologies from both security and efficiency perspectives.

Some searchable encryption constructions we will cover in the later chapters take specific primitives we introduce in this chapter as foundational building blocks. Thus, getting into the details of these primitives in this chapter would help understand more about the design intuitions and the pros and cons of later searchable encryption constructions. As we will discuss, some theoretically insurmountable barriers in these primitives may hinder their application to large-scale datasets. Some later searchable encryption schemes borrow the high-level ideas behind these cryptographic algorithms with adaptations, and propose their scenario-optimized implementations to achieve better performance. For interested audiences who want a better understanding of underlying principles and theories, we also append some reputed readings in each field in Sect. 2.5.

2.1 Property-Preserving Encryption

Ordinary encryption schemes such as DES, AES, and RSA aim to guarantee the confidentiality of data, where only individuals with the decryption keys can access the plaintext data. Roughly speaking, ciphertexts are (pseudo-)random bits from the perspective of the untrusted world. In many scenarios, however, we want the untrusted but computationally powerful server to help perform tasks (e.g., finding

K. Ren, C. Wang, *Searchable Encryption*, Wireless Networks,
https://doi.org/10.1007/978-3-031-21377-9_2

matches, sorting over plenty of data) with minimal information leakage. To fulfill this objective, a broad class of algorithms called *property-preserving* encryption (PPE) [1, 28, 29, 57, 158, 211] have been proposed to enable one to verify a property of plaintexts by performing a public test on the corresponding ciphertexts *without* any secrets. The untrusted server will then be able to run the desired tasks by leveraging the pre-defined property, e.g., searching for encrypted data with the property smaller than or equal to a given value. Below, we offer two PPE examples: deterministic encryption and order-preserving/order-revealing encryption.

2.1.1 Deterministic Encryption

Given the same plaintext and encryption key, a *deterministic* encryption (DTE) scheme always outputs the same ciphertext over separate executions. Typical examples include block ciphers in ECB mode or other modes with constant initialization vectors. On the contrary, a probabilistic encryption scheme introduces fresh randomness (aka nonce) into the ciphertext, with each execution generating a different ciphertext given the same plaintext and key.

The unique and fixed plaintext-ciphertext mapping in DTE schemes indicates the equality property, which is inherently suitable for any plaintext search functionalities directly over encrypted data [20], e.g., single-keyword search or conjunctive or Boolean keyword search. One trivial solution of searchable encryption is to first encrypt keywords in the dataset deterministically, and then send encrypted keywords (also through DTE) to the server, which will test the equality between ciphertexts for search. We will soon see that the seminal work [245] on searchable encryption leveraged the deterministic encryption schemes. However, the efficiency and flexibility advantage of preserving the same plaintext-ciphertext mapping in DTE is also its unavoidable weakness in security. When used in encrypted search, it may preserve the original keyword pattern and structure. In other words, if we encrypt a general text-document collection, the frequency of the plaintext keywords would remain the same after encryption. One may quickly recover some ciphertexts based on background knowledge of the dataset.

Despite this, a DTE scheme still finds application spaces due to its high efficiency, when the data collection does not have special patterns (technically speaking, drawn from space with high min-entropy [20]) and searched keywords are distributed uniformly over time. For instance, one may encrypt unique staff IDs with a DET scheme in a database table. However, suppose some specific staff is known to be popular recently (and thus might be frequently queried). In that case, an adversary can identify the corresponding ciphertext of the target staff ID by inferring from the frequent encrypted searches. Note that many latter searchable encryption designs leverage the flexibility of DET schemes but further introduce keyword-specific randomness, e.g., deterministically encrypting the keyword together with a counter for matching document.

2.1.2 Order-Preserving/Order-Revealing Encryption

The above DTE schemes are a special form of PPE which preserves the "equality" property. Another widely used type of PPE schemes is order-preserving/order-revealing encryption (OPE/ORE) [1, 28, 29], which *"ideally"* would have only leaked the order of ciphertexts. In particular, the order-preserving [1, 28, 162] encrypted ciphertexts *preserve* the numerical order of underlying plaintexts, i.e., the pseudorandom projection between the plaintext and ciphertext space will ensure that a numerically smaller plaintext will be always mapped to a numerically smaller ciphertext. Generally speaking, it is achieved by delicately mapping plaintexts of a small domain to ciphertexts of a larger range with the original order.

However, OPE tends to leak more information beyond the ciphertext order, such as top half of the bits [28], since the order comparison in OPE is limited to plaintext operators (i.e., "<," ">," etc.) which does not require extra computation. ORE schemes [50, 60, 170] are hence proposed to improve the security guarantees at the expense of slightly more complicated ciphertext comparison procedure, i.e., by executing a scheme-specific comparison function. We stress that the comparison function does not involve any secrets and an adversary thus still learns the exact order of ciphertexts but with extra computational efforts. With the help of extra but affordable computation during comparison, many ORE schemes [60, 170, 182] significantly reduce the undesirable leakage from first half bits to the most-significant differing bit or even less.

Moreover, one may also reduce the leakage information at the expense of ciphertext amplification [162], i.e., mapping the plaintext to a much larger range while preserving the original order. However, research on this line of work is still far from practical applications. From a security point of view, all existing OPE/ORE schemes leak other information beyond the total order of ciphertexts. From a performance point of view, OPE schemes suffer from either expensive encryption operations, large ciphertext amplification, or multiple-round interactions, while ORE schemes normally require a sophisticated comparison function with higher time complexity. Meanwhile, the lower bounds studied by Boldyreva et al. [28], Popa et al. [225], and Lewi and Wu [170] show that no efficient (stateless and non-interactive) OPE scheme can achieve best possible security even if the plaintext space consists of at least three elements.

We stress that even if there exists an ideal PPE scheme which reveals the target property only, one would still need to carefully choose whether or not to adopt the cryptographic primitive with respect to the specific confidential data collection, since the *property* itself sometimes could be harmful enough, as we have discussed above.

2.2   Homomorphic Encryption

Apart from testing various properties of ciphertexts, we will also briefly cover cryptographic primitives, namely, homomorphic encryption (HE) schemes, which support arithmetic operations over encrypted data. Such operations are among the most common workloads in encrypted databases, as demonstrated by the following SQL query asking for the average salary of all employees:

```
SELECT AVG(enc_salary) FROM employees;
```

There are different types of homomorphic encryption schemes focusing on different classes of computations over ciphertexts. Based on the supported types of mathematical operations and the total amount of allowed operations, they can be classified into the following three categories:

- Partially Homomorphic Encryption (PHE);
- Somewhat Homomorphic Encryption (SwHE);
- Fully Homomorphic Encryption (FHE).

For convenience, we denote the encryption of a message m as $E(m)$ in the following discussion. Partially homomorphic encryption supports only a specific operation type on encrypted values without any limit on the number of times to be performed. For instance, Paillier cryptosystem [209] supports additions over ciphertexts $E(m_1)$ and $E(m_2)$ as $E(m_1) \oplus E(m_2) = E(m_1 + m_2)$, where $\oplus$ denotes an algorithm-specific binary operator. Both unpadded RSA [229] invented in the summer of 1977 and ElGamal cryptosystem [102] support unlimited times of multiplications over ciphertexts.

However, limited arithmetic operation types allowed in partially homomorphic encryption restrict its applications, since it is common for a workload to involve both additions and multiplications. To overcome this limitation, some works named somewhat homomorphic encryption (SwHE) [91, 236, 266] have been proposed to support multiple operation types over ciphertexts, but only a limited number of times. Boneh et al. [32] proposed a well-known cryptographic system that supports unlimited times of additions and onetime multiplication.

Though still in development, fully homomorphic encryption provides rich functionalities while maintaining privacy by making data secure and accessible simultaneously. The obstacle that prevents unlimited times of both additions and multiplications in some SwHE schemes is mainly due to the noise integrated into the ciphertexts, which will grow along with adding and multiplying ciphertexts and result in indecipherable ciphertexts. Gentry [104] innovatively addresses this problem by bootstrapping a SwHE scheme and turning it into fully homomorphic. Roughly speaking, the FHE design intuition is to recursively self-embed a SwHE-encrypted ciphertext into a homomorphic decryption procedure. Doing so could effectively "refresh" the ciphertext and, as a result, obtain a newly SwHE-encrypted data of the same value but with lower noise. In this way, FHE can be achieved.

From the above discussion, it is not hard to verify that PHE schemes are more efficient than SwHE and FHE. Besides, we also note that multiplications are generally much more expensive than additions in FHE algorithms due to the sophisticated operations involved.

We will not go into details about how these schemes work since they involve advanced mathematical tools. Though theoretically appealing, the major limitation of FHE today is that it is still very inefficient. Though many efforts in the past decade have dramatically improved its performance millions of times, they remain far from satisfactory for practical employment. The work in [244] empirically compares different homomorphic encryption schemes. Their results indicate that PHE schemes are significantly faster at the specific mathematical operations they support than FHE, but relatively on par in encryption and decryption times. Nonetheless, PHE schemes are about 20,000–30,000 times slower than plaintext operations, and FHE schemes they evaluated are 1,600,000 times slower than plaintext for addition, and 19,000,000 times slower for multiplications. Concretely, a sum operation on 1 million records costing about 100 ms in plaintext would consume hours in PHE-encrypted data and even several days if they are FHE encrypted.

2.3 Oblivious RAM

From a pure security point of view, existing FHE and probabilistic encryption schemes eliminate almost all information leakage. However, semantically secure encryption schemes are sometimes insufficient to protect user privacy against strong adversaries who can persistently observe the data access procedure. Imagine a scenario where there is a popular item in an encrypted database, and a malicious administrator of the untrusted cloud server may observe that the client frequently queries a specific disk block. Though the ciphertext itself has a strong security guarantee, the adversary (e.g., the administrator) could easily figure out the plaintext of frequently accessed encrypted data with some background knowledge of the database. Therefore, it is of great importance to hide access patterns in confidential databases. Oblivious RAM (ORAM) is a security technique used to obfuscate access flows of the same length between trusted and untrusted domains. More formally, an ORAM will retain the input-output behavior of the original algorithms, but distort the distribution of memory accesses such that they are independent of the input. Therefore, no one can infer any meaning information according to memory access patterns (with all but negligible probability).

Oblivious RAMs could facilitate searchable encryption in its full generality and with strong security [110, 111]. Specifically, we can achieve any type of search query (e.g., conjunctive or disjunctive queries via the trivial solution in Sect. 4.3) without leaking access patterns to the server. However, this strong security guarantee and general framework come at the expense of a logarithmic number of interaction rounds or computational efforts for each search and update. Namely, the user stores some index data to help identify encrypted documents on the

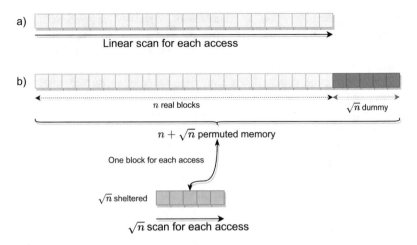

Fig. 2.1 The layouts of (**a**) the trivial ORAM scheme and (**b**) the square-root ORAM [110]

untrusted server, and fetches them by leveraging ORAMs with multiple rounds or performing extra computation. Note that network latency (tens of milliseconds or even seconds) usually is much higher than the computation efforts on the server side due to sophisticated network status in between them. Therefore, multiple-round mechanisms are typically unacceptable. In addition, even if we can reduce multiple rounds into one round trip, the extra computational efforts will significantly slow down the operations of large-scale databases.

Though the *direct* application of ORAMs to our topic of encrypted search is not very practical, we will still brief the high-level ideas behind different oblivious algorithms, considering that we may borrow some techniques here in the subsequent chapters. Firstly, a trivial but inefficient ORAM scheme as shown in Fig. 2.1 is to simply access every block in the untrusted memory and perform a *true* read/write if the block is the target. Otherwise, we will perform a dummy (i.e., just for hiding the true one) read/write. While it achieves the purpose of oblivious access, the approach scales very badly due to its linear time complexity $O(n)$, where n is the number of memory blocks.

Inspired by this linear-scan approach, [110] proposed the first sublinear ORAM scheme named the square-root ORAM, as shown in Fig. 2.1. The intuition is to access fewer blocks for each operation and shuffle the memory blocks regularly. The construction comprises two components: a permuted memory and a shelter. The former one is appended with $\sqrt{n}$ dummy blocks (i.e., blocks with meaningless bits) and will be regularly shuffled. The later one holds $\sqrt{n}$ blocks for short-term storage and will be linearly scanned in each operation.

In particular, the execution is divided into *epochs*. In each epoch, we first randomly shuffle the permuted memory part and then handle $\sqrt{n}$ user accesses. For each user access, we go through the shelter. If we do not find the target block, we will read from or write to the corresponding block in the permuted memory. Otherwise,

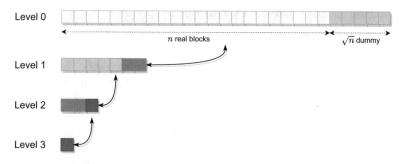

Level 0

n real blocks $\sqrt{n}$ dummy

Level 1

Level 2

Level 3

Fig. 2.2 Hierarchical ORAM design layout [110]

an appended dummy block in the permuted memory will be read or written. In both cases, there are precisely one block access to permuted memory, and $\sqrt{n}$ accesses to the shelter. Therefore, one cannot keep track of accessed memory blocks. We point out that the two-component ORAM construction achieves its optimal with the shelter size equal to $\sqrt{n}$, and one can refer to their paper [110] for concrete and formal analysis.

Goldreich and Ostrovsky [110] also offered a theoretical lower-bound $\Omega(n \cdot \log n)$ for ORAM schemes, in which n refers to the number of memory blocks. To get an asymptotically optimal solution, they proposed a hierarchical ORAM by leveraging the above square-root solution as shown in Fig. 2.2. The main idea is to treat the shelter as another permuted memory *recursively*. And we need a total of $\log n$ levels such that the shelter collapse into a constant size.

Instead of linearly scanning the array at each level, we will use a hash table to find the target block. However, it also brings other problems such as hash collisions and predictable hash functions. To solve these issues, we first use buckets of $O(\log n)$ capacity in each slot to prevent collisions with all but negligible probability. Besides, we also adopt a keyed hash function in each level to make it unpredictable against untrusted parties.

In addition to the above classical designs, there are other ORAM constructions with different focuses. For example, tree-based ORAMs [105, 243, 248] have the same asymptotic complexity but better practical performance. In partition-based ORAMs [247], the external storage is divided into a set of smaller partitions. Each of them is a fully functional ORAM (often called sub-ORAM or partition-ORAM), and the client uses a position map to identify which sub-ORAM the block belongs to. There are other ORAM schemes [14, 58] supporting parallel execution. Since they are not the focus of our book, we will not discuss them in detail.

2.4   Trusted Execution Environment

We observe that the majority of encryption requirements stem from insecure communication channels (data in transit), unprotected memory (data in use), or storage devices (data at rest), which can be eavesdropped or manipulated by malicious parties. Among these three scenarios, low-delay secure communication channels can be established via secure protocols like TLS. And high-performance symmetric encryption algorithms such as AES and DES can encrypt confidential data to external storage media with few overheads.

However, memory in between a CPU and external storage devices still requires theoretically secure protections. Section 2.1 introduces several classical cryptographic primitives to protect sensitive data with different functionalities. It is unfortunate, however, that they sometimes provide unsatisfactory security guarantees (e.g., property-preserving encryption) or inadequate performance(e.g., homomorphic encryption), or even both. Another observation we make is that a process (including its caches) is securely protected by its physical boundary. Adversaries may have physical access to disks or memory and steal data from them. However, it is infeasible for them to open an encapsulated CPU and steal data from the caches. From a software point of view, we also want to forbid any unauthorized parties, including the operating system and privileged users, to access sensitive codes or confidential data. But we can still trust the CPU to execute authorized codes over confidential data. With such a background and demand, the trusted execution environment (TEE) has thus been proposed.

There are several well-known TEE implementations by reputed vendors, such as Intel SGX [187], ARM TrustZone [136], and AMD SEV [80]. We will take Intel SGX as a concrete example to briefly introduce its principles and limitations due to its popularity and well-illustrated design. Intel SGX allows a user or OS codes to define a private region of memory called *enclave* which is inaccessible from all the other parties as shown in Fig. 2.3. It provides remote-attestation functionality to prove to the client that the running enclave is indeed the target identity.

Fig. 2.3 The architecture of Intel Software Guard Extensions [188]

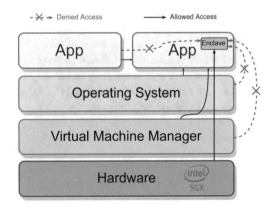

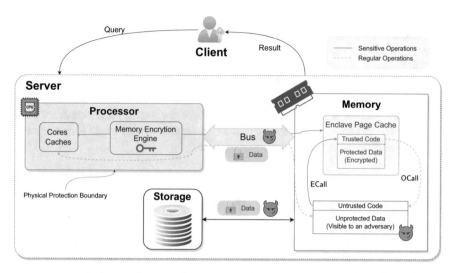

Fig. 2.4 The architecture of an enclave-based encrypted database design from [194]

In addition, a program needs ecall/ocall instructions to enter or exit its own enclave. We note that enclaves of different applications are independent and cannot access each other either. All data inside the enclave is automatically encrypted by a memory encryption engine sitting transparently between the caches and the enclave with a key burned in the CPU. All data leaving CPU caches will be protected by semantically secure encryption as shown in Fig. 2.4, which hence provides data confidentiality. Furthermore, Intel SGX also provides data integrity protection. SGX v1 offers a limited enclave page cache (EPC) size no greater than 256 MB. To support a larger EPC size, SGX v2 was thus proposed and provided in the third-generation Intel Xeon processors with up to 1 TB EPC support.

If trusted hardware is available, building a confidential computing system would seem relatively easier than developing advanced cryptographic primitives. We can simply use standard semantically secure encryption algorithms to encrypt confidential data in untrusted memory, move it into the EPC, decrypt it in the cache, and execute as if it were plaintext. It hence significantly improves the performance of many schemes. However, there remain the following limitations we must not overlook:

- First, we have to trust the manufacturers in their ability to correct implementation of the hardware without major security flaws. But this is not always the case, as shown by previous research [43, 238, 240]. On the contrary, building secure systems with cryptographic primitives *theoretically* does not require extending the level of trust as needed in trusted hardware.
- The memory access pattern and other potential side-channel leakage inside the trusted EPC are still exposed. An adversary may be able to infer sensitive data based on the access pattern together with auxiliary information as we

have illustrated in the ORAM section and what we will discuss in the later chapters. From this perspective, oblivious RAM tools or related techniques are still indispensable.

- There could be new engineering challenges while designing a secure system involving trusted hardware. For example, there are only 256 MB EPC available in the earlier versions of SGX, which poses difficulties when handling data-intensive secure applications. Besides, it is not always easy and bug-free, when converting a native program into an SGX-based one, which might introduce new vulnerabilities in the trusted computing base.

2.5   Summary and Further Reading

In this chapter, we introduce the typical fundamental crypto algorithms and technologies that can help build searchable encryption schemes and encrypted database systems. For space concerns, we have not been able to explain the concrete design details and formal correctness and security analysis. Below we introduce a few important references for interested audiences.

Bogatov et al. [26] explain and systematically compare several classical OPE and ORE schemes from the perspectives of security, implementation challenges, and experimental performance. In addition to the influential designs covered in [26], we recommend another ORE scheme called EncodeORE [182] that combines the advantages of two renowned constructions and achieves less information leakage and lower-performance overheads. Grubbs et al. [122] introduced attacks against some typical ORE schemes that can recover the approximate values of ciphertexts with high accuracy. Naveed et al. [198] and Bindschaedler et al. [22] proposed attacks against PPE schemes under the context of encrypted databases based on combinatorial optimization and statistical inferences.

Goldreich et al. [111] firstly introduced oblivious RAMs to hide the memory access pattern in an untrusted server. Goldreich and Ostrovsky [110] then showed a $\Omega(\log n)$ lower bound for ORAM access overhead, in which n is the data size. There are several attributes that we need to consider while choosing an appropriate scheme: (1) the client (i.e., trusted) storage, (2) the server storage, and (3) the time overhead while executing a memory access. Kushilevitz et al. [165] proposed an asymptotically optimal ORAM design regarding the client storage, i.e., the client only keeps $O(1)$ storage. Stefanov et al. [248] proposed an elegant ORAM construction with nearly optimal access overheads. Fletcher [94] comprehensively studied many well-known ORAM constructions from both theoretical and practical points of view. Chang et al. [55] provided a thorough evaluation of classic ORAM designs and gave their open source library, named SEAL-ORAM, on https://github.com/InitialDLab/SEAL-ORAM.

The paper [71] provides a summarized explanation of Intel SGX for beginners to get more familiar with the underlying principles. The official GitHub repository [143] presents a detailed manual on how to install Intel SGX (with an SGX-equipped processor). Meanwhile, there are also several code samples in that repository explaining how to achieve specific functionalities. In addition, the Awesome-SGX repository [177] collects various materials, including reputed papers, and well-written SGX-related codes for learning Intel SGX. We will cover more encrypted database systems using SGX techniques in future chapters.

Finally, beyond what we have covered so far, the encrypted search functionality can also be instantiated through a number of advanced public-key encryption designs, such as key-aggregate encryption [64], identity-based encryption (IBE) [30], attribute-based encryption [116] (ABE), and more generalized functional encryption [33]. We would refer interested audiences to those references and learn more about these primitives.

Chapter 3
Searchable Encryption Semantics

After acquiring adequate background knowledge, we are now about to advance to the world of searchable encryption, which has made prosperous progress since its first construction in the early 2000s. Since mainstream designs in searchable encryption focus on symmetric key-based primitives, we will focus on them in this chapter and only briefly discuss other designs when necessary.

Firstly, we provide an abstract of searchable symmetric encryption (SSE) schemes with a single client and an honest-but-curious server. We then give the correctness and security definitions guiding the subsequent designs. Although we omit many formal definitions and rigorous security proofs to avoid falling into tedious technical arguments, it is still crucial for us to precisely capture what properties the security notions aim to provide through those security definitions. All subsequent searchable encryption schemes we will cover in later chapters have been proven secure concerning these definitions.

Next, we introduce some early representative designs, which serve as entry points for new audiences into the field. We will illustrate how the literature on searchable encryption schemes evolves and finally reaches the modern construction of SSE. Notably, the now-standard framework of SSE is also the cornerstone of delicate designs we will discuss in later chapters.

Finally, we will briefly cover public key-based searchable encryption and discuss its pros and cons compared with the symmetric (private-key) ones.

3.1 Definitions for Searchable Symmetric Encryption

To establish a suitable definition, we first must clarify what tasks or functionalities a searchable symmetric encryption scheme targets to accomplish and what the entire process should look like. Informally, the initial goal of searchable encryption is to enable a data owner (i.e., the client) to outsource his/her encrypted data to

© The Author(s), under exclusive license to Springer Nature Switzerland AG 2023   29
K. Ren, C. Wang, *Searchable Encryption*, Wireless Networks,
https://doi.org/10.1007/978-3-031-21377-9_3

an untrusted third party and later *securely* search for encrypted data records or document files matching a given encrypted keyword. Ideally, this procedure should not reveal anything about the underlying document collection or searched keywords.

We begin by formally defining an SSE scheme in Definition 1, including all the generic functionalities it should support, rather than concrete implementations. Note that for the purpose of abstraction, we focus on the goal to support only single-keyword searches on an encrypted document collection DB $= (\mathrm{doc}_1, \ldots, \mathrm{doc}_D)$ over a dictionary or keyword space $\mathcal{W} = (w_1, \ldots, w_n)$.

Definition 1 (Searchable Symmetric Encryption [74]) An SSE scheme on a keyword space $\mathcal{W}$ is composed of 5 polynomial-time algorithms, SSE = (Gen, Enc, Trpdr, Search, Dec):

$K \leftarrow \mathsf{Gen}(1^\lambda)$ is a probabilistic algorithm run by the client to generate the secret key used in the scheme. It takes a security parameter λ as input and outputs a secret key K.

$(I, \mathrm{EDB}) \leftarrow \mathsf{Enc}(K, \mathrm{DB})$ is a probabilistic algorithm run by the client to encrypt the documents in DB. It takes a secret key K and a document collection DB $= (\mathrm{doc}_1, \ldots, \mathrm{doc}_D)$ as input and outputs an encrypted secure index I and a collection of ciphertexts EDB $= (c_1, \ldots, c_D)$. We sometimes refer to this as $\mathsf{Enc}_K(\mathrm{DB})$.

$t \leftarrow \mathsf{Trpdr}(K, w)$ is an algorithm run by the client to generate a trapdoor, or equivalently a search token, for a given keyword. It takes a secret key K and a keyword w as input and outputs a trapdoor t. We sometimes refer to this as $t \leftarrow \mathsf{Trpdr}_K(w)$.

$X \leftarrow \mathsf{Search}(I, t)$ is an algorithm run by the server to search for documents containing a keyword w in EDB with corresponding trapdoor t. It takes an encrypted index I and a trapdoor t as input and outputs a collection X of document identifiers.

$doc_i \leftarrow \mathsf{Dec}(K, c_i)$ is an algorithm run by the client to decrypt a document. It takes a secret key K and a ciphertext c_i as input and outputs a document doc_i. We sometimes refer to this as $doc_i \leftarrow \mathsf{Dec}_K(c_i)$.

Some works [151, 154, 217, 300] also merge the first two algorithms together for conciseness as follows:

$(K, (I, \mathrm{EDB})) \leftarrow \mathsf{Setup}(1^\lambda, \mathrm{DB})$ is a probabilistic algorithm run by the client. It takes the security parameter λ and document collection DB as input and outputs the secret key K to the client, and encrypted index I and document collection EDB to the server.

One of the most important metrics of searchable encryption is correctness of the results returned by the server. We could roughly distinguish SSE schemes into the following three categories based on the correctness [300]: perfectly correct, correct with all but negligible probability, and lossy. Before arguing for their respective necessities, we first give a formal definition for SSE correctness.

Definition 2 For all $\lambda \in \mathbb{N}$, all keywords $w \in \mathcal{W}$, all document collection DB $\in \{0, 1\}^{\mathcal{W}}$, we formally define the correctness of an SSE scheme as follows:

$$\Pr \left[\begin{array}{c} K \leftarrow \mathsf{Gen}(1^\lambda) \\ (I, \mathrm{EDB}) \leftarrow \mathsf{Enc}(K, \mathrm{DB}) \end{array} : \begin{array}{c} \mathsf{Search}(I, \mathsf{Trpdr}(K, w)) = \mathrm{DB}(w) \\ \bigwedge \mathsf{Dec}(K, c_i) = D_i, \ \forall i \in [n] \end{array} \right] = 1 - \nu(\lambda),$$

When $\nu(\lambda) = 0$, we say that the searchable encryption scheme is perfectly correct, i.e., the result set it returns contains *exactly all* documents containing the queried keyword. Meanwhile, it is able to successfully recover any encrypted document back to the plaintext form for any document collection and security parameter.

Sometimes, we may relax the correctness requirement such that $\nu(\lambda)$ to be a possibly non-negligible function to reduce information leakage or speed up the search process. Specifically, we normally demand that

$$\mathsf{Search}(I, \mathsf{Trpdr}_K(w)) \ominus \mathrm{DB}(w) \text{ is small with high probability,}$$

where $\ominus$ is symmetric difference between two sets A and B: $A \ominus B = (A \cup B) \backslash (A \cap B)$. When $\nu(\lambda)$ is negligible in λ, we call such SSE schemes correct with all but negligible probabilities as there are overwhelming chances that a perfectly correct result set will be returned.

We call the rest SSE schemes lossy since there are non-negligible (though possibly a small number, e.g., 0.1%) portion of mismatched results. And there could be false positives, i.e., $\mathrm{DB}(w) \subset \mathsf{Search}(I, \mathsf{Trpdr}_K(w))$, or false negatives, i.e., $\mathsf{Search}(I, \mathsf{Trpdr}_K(w)) \subset \mathrm{DB}(w)$, or even both.

Note that we use 1^λ as the input of the key generation algorithm because in theoretical computer science, we define a *polynomial-time* algorithm if its running time can be bounded by a polynomial of the input *size* rather than the input *value*. An algorithm whose running time is within a polynomial of the input value but out of the input size will be called pseudo-polynomial. We will use 1^λ as long as we would like to emphasize that the algorithm is polynomial in λ. And we will soon use it to denote a polynomial-time adversary.

3.1.1 Security Definitions

With a precise and formal description of an SSE scheme in place, we can then talk about its security—as one may naturally ask: *What is a "secure" searchable encryption scheme?* An intuitive answer would be that both encrypted documents and searched queries remain "well-hidden," even after seeing the search execution and ciphertexts. Nonetheless, just like other general cryptographic concepts, it is nontrivial to translate the intuition into a rigorous description while preserving its practical implications. Indeed, it took several years of research to refine the formalization of security definitions of SSE and finally reach the broadly accepted one today.

Before delving into formal definitions, let us first have a look at two general paradigms to define security for an SSE scheme as follows:

The Game-Based Definition An attack game involves two parities: an *adversary* (i.e., the untrusted server in our setting) and a benign entity called the *challenger* (i.e., the client). Both parties are probabilistic processes communicating with each other. Typically, the challenger will generate secrets owned by the client. And the adversary will have the right to generate *two* different versions of (partial) plaintext (e.g., documents and keywords) with some *constraints*, while the challenger will secretly pick *one* and encrypt it according to the aforementioned process, which may also involve other interactions between them.

Given those ciphertexts (e.g., trapdoors, documents) and the two plaintexts he chooses, the adversary needs to guess which one the challenger indeed processes. Our goal is to guarantee that any *probabilistic polynomial time* (PPT) adversary could only gain an advantage that is negligible in the security parameter λ in winning the game. The advantage here measures the gap between the probabilities of the adversarial guess and a purely random guess (i.e., $1/2$ as we have two candidates). In addition, the adversary's power is restricted to probabilistic polynomial time, similar to many other cryptographic primitives.

From a theoretical point of view, it is essential to restrict the PPT power and allow negligible advantages. Otherwise, there exists no practical scheme to satisfy any such security definition. To keep our introductory tone consistent throughout the book, we will not go further into the detailed explanations, and will redirect interested audiences to Sect. 3.4 for further readings.

In this setting, the constraints for the adversary on generating two different versions of plaintext are usually known as *leakages*. Recall that all searchable symmetric encryption designs intentionally trade off certain leakages for performance speedup. Such leakages are explicit, typically including the number of documents, the identifiers returned by each search, and the repetition of searched trapdoors. In order to set up a meaningful and fair game, the generated two versions of plaintext need to meet the same constraints as demanded by the explicit leakages. Otherwise, the adversary can simply generate one document collection containing only one document and another containing 1 million documents. Then, it will be quite hard or performance prohibitive to design a scheme to keep the adversary's advantage negligible. This is because the correctness requirement does not allow us to truncate 1 million documents. Thus, we would have to pad the smaller document collection to at least 1 million documents, which would inevitably result in substantial performance overheads.

Intuitively, the game-based definition says that no adversary can effectively *distinguish* between two encrypted document collections (and possibly tokens) of the challenger's choice (except a negligible chance). It then follows that an adversary cannot learn any information from them—otherwise, the adversary will be able to distinguish them with the learned information.

The Simulation-Based Definition For those new audiences to the security field, a natural question about the game-based security definitions might be: *what does indistinguishability mean? Or why does indistinguishability imply security?* On the one hand, the fact that no adversary can tell any difference between two given ciphertexts is an intuitive interpretation of security, as the ciphertexts could be encrypted by any two copies of plaintexts from an adversary's point of view. Thus, the adversary cannot learn any distinguishing information from the ciphertexts.

However, what precise information an adversary may learn is still somewhat obscure. An adversary may observe the size of encrypted data collection, as discussed above. But what else would an adversary learn? It seems any leakage an adversary would learn is specific to the concrete searchable encryption constructions. This observation leads to a follow-up question: would it be possible to formalize a security definition such that it would be invariant to the concrete information leakage, which can be abstracted by a leakage function $\mathcal{L}$? If yes, how? We now turn to the simulation-based security framework to properly answer these questions.

There are two worlds in simulation-based definitions as follows. Therefore, it is also known as the "real-ideal paradigm":

Real **world** depicts the real SSE process. The adversary generates a document collection and keywords to be searched, and acts as the server to execute the rest of the search process with a challenger (i.e., the client). The challenger will generate a secret key, encrypt data, and interact with the adversary by issuing encrypted trapdoors.

Ideal **world** is *secure by definition*. The adversary generates a document collection and keywords to be searched as well. And there is a *simulator acting like* the client. The difference is that the simulator will not take these documents and keywords as input, but the output of a *leakage function* $\mathcal{L}$. The function $\mathcal{L}$ captures the legitimate information allowed to be known by an adversary, which is similar to the *constraints* in the game-based definitions.

Note that the simulator has never been in touch with any plaintext. The "encrypted documents, indexes, and trapdoors" are purely simulated based on the information captured by $\mathcal{L}$.

In simulation-based definition, to argue for security for a given construction, the goal is to show that the outputs of the two worlds will distribute identically, except for a negligible difference. Alternatively, we say no PPT distinguisher (algorithm) can distinguish between them. Since no (PPT) adversary can tell the difference between a real world and an ideal world, we can conclude that the real world at most leaks the information as that of the ideal world, captured by $\mathcal{L}$. Note that the above two definitions are not always inherently equivalent unless proved so, as shown in the case of SSE [74].

Over the years, we have gained a lot of experiences when interacting with students about these definitions. The general feedback seems to suggest that it is relatively easier to write and understand proofs for game-based definitions, while simulation-based definitions often provide a more explicit description of security guarantee (included in the leakage function $\mathcal{L}$).

Note that we have already indicated that an SSE scheme explicitly allows controlled leakages for performance speedup. And it is almost impossible to eliminate those leakages, unless we can tolerate prohibitive performance penalties. Thus, a follow-up question regarding the leakages, captured by the leakage function $\mathcal{L}$, is: will the leakages compromise the client's privacy? This question has been overlooked for years, until [145] proposed the first study on leakage-abuse attacks by leveraging some auxiliary information (e.g., partial knowledge on the document collection, the distribution of keywords, etc.).

Subsequently, researchers have been trying to reduce leakage without significant penalties on performance. However, the arms race between the leakage-abuse attacks and leakage suppression tools is still going on. It is now an active searchable encryption subfield, producing valuable insights, helpful techniques, and guidelines to better direct future searchable encryption constructions and related real-world applications. We will elaborate on these attacks and discuss corresponding counter-measures in Chap. 5.

The Journey Toward the Adequate Notions In the seminal work of searchable encryption by Song et al. [245], the authors considered only the pseudorandomness (i.e., security) of indexes rather than the security of the whole system. Their model, therefore, is incomplete. After that, another definition of security has been proposed for SSE, i.e., indistinguishability against chosen-keyword attacks (IND2-CKA) [108]. It achieves the following security goal: Suppose an adversary can *choose* the keywords and documents, and persuade the client to generate encrypted indexes and search tokens on demand. Still, it cannot gain any more knowledge about the underlying encrypted *documents* beyond using those search tokens chosen by the adversary.

Note that the above statements only require that no adversary can learn any information about the documents but not the trapdoors (and corresponding keywords). One might try to remedy the situation by separately requiring trapdoors to be secure (i.e., they *alone* will not leak any information). However, it still fails to protect the security of queried keywords. A counterexample is given in the appendix in [74]. We omit it here, and refer interested audiences to their illustrations and explanations, along with the concrete security proofs in [74].

Regarding the previous deficiencies, [53] intended to present a stronger security definition for SSE by integrating secure trapdoors into their simulation-based definition. It is unfortunate that this seemingly "stronger" definition is actually unsatisfactory and can be easily satisfied by any SSE scheme, even for an insecure one. The technical details are also explained in [74]. Finally, [74] proposed broadly adopted security definitions for searchable symmetric encryption schemes, and we will discuss them in the following section.

3.1.2 Non-adaptive and Adaptive Semantic Security for SSE

We are now going to introduce the formal security definitions of SSE based on the real-ideal paradigm. We first introduce a simpler one, i.e., non-adaptive security, and then describe how it differs from an adaptive one and why we need an adaptively secure SSE.

Definition 3 (Non-adaptive Semantic Security [74]) Let $\mathsf{SSE} = (\mathsf{Gen}, \mathsf{Enc}, \mathsf{Trpdr}, \mathsf{Search}, \mathsf{Dec})$ be an SSE scheme. Consider the following probabilistic experiments:

$\mathsf{Real}_{\mathsf{SSE},\mathcal{A}}(\lambda)$	$\mathsf{Ideal}_{\mathsf{SSE},\mathcal{A},\mathcal{S}}(\lambda)$
$K \leftarrow \mathsf{Gen}(1^\lambda)$	$(st_{\mathcal{A}}, \mathrm{DB}, \mathrm{Q}) \leftarrow \mathcal{A}(1^\lambda)$
$(st_{\mathcal{A}}, \mathrm{DB}, \mathrm{Q}) \leftarrow \mathcal{A}(1^\lambda)$	$v \leftarrow \mathcal{S}(\mathcal{L}(\mathrm{DB}, \mathcal{W}))$
$(I, \mathrm{EDB}) \leftarrow \mathsf{Enc}_K(\mathrm{DB})$	**return** $st_{\mathcal{A}}, v$
for $1 \le i \le q$ **do**	
$\quad t_i \leftarrow \mathsf{Trpdr}_K(\mathrm{Q}_i)$	
$X = (t_1, \ldots, t_{|\mathrm{Q}|})$	
return $st_{\mathcal{A}}, v = (I, \mathrm{EDB}, X)$	

where $\lambda \in \mathbb{N}$ is the security parameter, $\mathcal{A}$ is a stateful PPT adversary, $\mathcal{S}$ is a simulator, and Q is a list of keywords to be searched. An SSE scheme is semantically secure if for all PPT adversaries $\mathcal{A}$, there exists a polynomial-size $\mathcal{S}$ such that for all PPT distinguishers $\mathcal{D}$, we have

$$| \Pr\left[\mathcal{D}(v, st_{\mathcal{A}}) = 1 : (v, st_{\mathcal{A}}) \leftarrow \mathsf{Ideal}_{\mathsf{SSE},\mathcal{A},\mathcal{S}}(\lambda) = 1\right]$$
$$- \Pr\left[\mathcal{D}(v, st_{\mathcal{A}}) = 1 : (v, st_{\mathcal{A}}) \leftarrow \mathsf{Real}_{\mathsf{SSE},\mathcal{A}}(\lambda) = 1\right] | \le \mathsf{negl}(\lambda).$$

For a standard SSE scheme, the leakage function $\mathcal{L}$ could be modeled as follows:

$$\mathcal{L}(\mathrm{DB}, \mathrm{Q}) = \left(|\mathrm{doc}_1|, \ldots, |\mathrm{doc}_D|, \left(\mathrm{DB}(w_1), \ldots, \mathrm{DB}(w_q)\right), M(\mathrm{Q})\right),$$

where M is a symmetric binary matrix such that $M_{ij} = 1$ if and only if $\mathrm{Q}_i = \mathrm{Q}_j$. Namely, it leaks the sizes of encrypted documents, document identifiers searched by each trapdoor, as well as the repetition of the searched keywords.

Since no adversary can differentiate the ideal and real worlds with all but negligible probability, and the simulator in the ideal world only knows little information $\mathcal{L}$ about the plaintext, we can claim that the target SSE scheme leaks at most $\mathcal{L}(\mathrm{DB}, \mathrm{Q})$ that amount of information. However, whether $\mathcal{L}$ may compromise user privacy is not related to the declaration of whether a SSE scheme satisfies Definitions 3 or 4. It only tells us that the scheme leaks no more than that amount of information—whether the explicit information will reveal other sensitive data is not captured by the definition.

Adaptive Semantic Security We observe that in Definition 3, the adversary needs to generate all documents and searched keywords at the very beginning. However, in a real situation, an adversary could *adaptively* choose the keywords during the process, i.e., he can select a keyword based on previous observations and convince the client to generate the trapdoor for it. It will be more demanding for an SSE scheme to defend against such a scenario, which leads to the *stronger* notion of adaptive semantic security as defined in Definition 4. For better illustration, we highlight differences to convert a non-adaptive definition into an adaptive one.

Definition 4 (Adaptive Semantic Security [74]) Let $\mathsf{SSE} = (\mathsf{Gen}, \mathsf{Enc}, \mathsf{Trpdr}, \mathsf{Search}, \mathsf{Dec})$ be an SSE scheme. Consider the following probabilistic experiments:

$\mathsf{Real}_{\mathsf{SSE},\mathcal{A}}(\lambda)$	$\mathsf{Ideal}_{\mathsf{SSE},\mathcal{A},\mathcal{S}}(\lambda)$
$K \leftarrow \mathsf{Gen}(1^\lambda)$	$(st_{\mathcal{A}}, \mathsf{DB}, \emptyset) \leftarrow \mathcal{A}(1^\lambda)$
$(st_{\mathcal{A}}, \mathsf{DB}, \emptyset) \leftarrow \mathcal{A}_0(1^\lambda)$	$v \leftarrow \mathcal{S}(\mathcal{L}(\mathsf{DB}, \mathcal{W}))$ //split into queries
$(I, \mathsf{EDB}) \leftarrow \mathsf{Enc}_K(\mathsf{DB})$	$(st_{\mathcal{S}}, I, \mathsf{EDB}) \leftarrow \mathcal{S}_0(\mathcal{L}(\mathsf{DB}))$
for $1 \leq i \leq q$ **do**	**for** $1 \leq i \leq q$ **do**
$\quad (st_{\mathcal{A}}, Q_i) \leftarrow \mathcal{A}_i(st_{\mathcal{A}}, I, \mathsf{EDB}, t_1, \ldots, t_{i-1})$	$\quad (st_{\mathcal{A}}, Q_i) \leftarrow \mathcal{A}_i(st_{\mathcal{A}}, I, \mathsf{EDB}, t_1, \ldots, t_{i-1})$
$\quad$ //(t_1, t_0) denotes empty for convenience	$\quad$ //(t_1, t_0) denotes empty for convenience
$\quad t_i \leftarrow \mathsf{Trpdr}_K(Q_i)$	$\quad t_i \leftarrow \mathcal{S}_i(st_{\mathcal{S}}, \mathcal{L}(\mathsf{EDB}, Q_1, \ldots, Q_i))$
$X = (t_1, \ldots, t_{|Q|})$	$X = (t_1, \ldots, t_{|Q|}))$
return $st_{\mathcal{A}}, v = (I, \mathsf{EDB}, X)$	**return** $st_{\mathcal{A}}, v := (I, \mathsf{EDB}, X)$

where the notations remain the same. An SSE scheme is adaptively semantically secure if for all PPT adversaries $\mathcal{A} := (\mathcal{A}_0, \ldots, \mathcal{A}_q)$, there exists a polynomial-size $\mathcal{S} := (\mathcal{S}_0, \ldots, \mathcal{S}_q)$ such that for all PPT distinguishers $\mathcal{D}$, we have

$$| \Pr\left[\mathcal{D}(v, st_{\mathcal{A}}) = 1 : (v, st_{\mathcal{A}}) \leftarrow \mathsf{Ideal}_{\mathsf{SSE},\mathcal{A},\mathcal{S}}(\lambda) = 1 \right]$$

$$- \Pr\left[\mathcal{D}(v, st_{\mathcal{A}}) = 1 : (v, st_{\mathcal{A}}) \leftarrow \mathsf{Real}_{\mathsf{SSE},\mathcal{A}}(\lambda) = 1 \right] | \leq \mathsf{negl}(\lambda).$$

The key idea behind this notion is that the adversary will generate keywords step-by-step with the knowledge of the index, encrypted document collection, and trapdoors until the current iteration. In addition, we also need to modify the simulator since the simulator has to generate trapdoors according to the adversary's actions. This wraps up the development of the modern security definition of SSE, which has become widely accepted in the community today.

3.2 Efficient and Secure Searchable Symmetric Encryption

After introducing the SSE scheme with different algorithms and what its security notions imply, we are now ready to present a non-adaptively secure construction called SSE-1 which achieves asymptotically optimal computation, communication, and storage complexity. Besides, one could easily transform it into an adaptively secure SSE scheme, as we will explain later. But until then, we would like to briefly describe designs before this one to observe the evolution of searchable encryption from the perspective of scheme designs.

3.2.1 The Evolutionary Process of SSE Schemes

One naive way to enable search on ciphertexts is simply substituting each keyword with a *deterministic* ciphertext, and then send the ciphertext of searched keyword to the server for checking matches. However, it will directly reveal where each encrypted keyword occurs, its frequency in each document, and the co-occurrence among different documents for any snapshot adversary who can access the encrypted document collection. Some statistical analysis, e.g., Zipf's law, indicates that keywords in articles may have a special distribution. The adversary will hence learn some sensitive information about the ciphertexts. Nonetheless, it is nontrivial to enable keyword search on *probabilistically* encrypted document collections, since encryption of the same plaintext at different time tends to result in independent ciphertexts (from the server's point of view).

Song et al. [245] showed a solution for searchable encryption by building two layers of encryption for each keyword as shown in Fig. 3.1. By assuming there are l words $W_1, W_2, \ldots, W_l$ in each document, the client first *deterministically* encrypts i-th keyword in each document as $X_i = E_k(W_i)$, which will then be split into $\langle L_i, R_i \rangle$ with $|R_i| = m$ and $|L_i| = n - m$. We use a pseudorandomly generated bit T_i to hide the ciphertext distribution by XORing with each X_i, i.e., the final ciphertext $C_i = X_i \oplus T_i$. Since T_is are different, the same W_i will be encrypted into different ciphertexts.

The remaining question is: why not generate T_i as a whole—the answer is to enable the server to check matches when given $E(W_i)$, i.e., the encrypted keyword W_i. We obtain T_i by XORing with the given trapdoor $E(W_i)$. However, the server cannot tell whether XORed results are indeed T_i since both matched and mismatched XORed results are meaningless (pseudo-)random bits. By splitting T_i into two parts S_i and $F_{k_i}(S_i)$, we can check matches by performing the same computation on the XORed results and the equality, i.e., $F_{k_i}\left(L_i'\right) \overset{?}{=} R_i'$, where L_i' is the first $n - m$ bits of $C_i \oplus E(W)$ and R_i' is the remaining m bits. We generate k_i by L_i as (1) we have to connect the underlying keyword with checking block and (2) only the first $n - m$ bits are exposed after XORing.

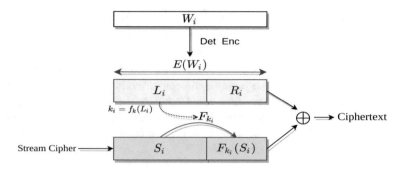

Fig. 3.1 Two-layered encryption construction from [245] with linear search complexity

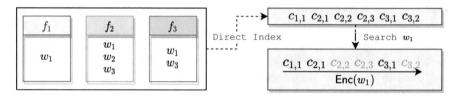

Fig. 3.2 Two-layered encryption construction example

In short, we use the outer layer of encryption to hide ciphertext distribution (security) and use the inner layer to check matches (search). As shown in Fig. 3.2, there are *three* documents containing totally *six* keywords and ciphertexts. Upon receiving a search request for w_1, the server has to *linearly* scan all the encrypted keywords to find matches with $\mathsf{Enc}(w_1)$, which severely limits its performance. Besides, only the encrypted keywords are proven to be secure, but not the entire *searchable encryption scheme*, the ciphertext frequency and co-occurrence patterns will be progressively revealed along with each search.

Goh [108] proposed a secure index scheme by using PRFs and Bloom filters [24]. A Bloom filter is a *probabilistic* data structure for membership testing, i.e., checking whether an element x belongs to a set S. There are possibly some false positives but no false negatives. Namely, it may report $x \in S$ but actually x does not belong to S, while for all x indeed belonging to S, it will always report truthfully. Their design creates a Bloom filter for each document by treating each keyword as the element x and each document as the set S, and then obfuscates the indexes and occurrences of each keyword w in different documents by independent PRFs. Upon searching for a keyword w, the client will issue obfuscated locations of w in each Bloom filter and masks to reveal its occurrence bits. Though it does not need to check every encrypted word in the collection, this scheme still has to go through *every* document to detect the presence of target keyword. Furthermore, there could be false positives, i.e., unmatched documents, in the returned result set.

As mentioned earlier, the security notion proposed by Goh [108] fails to protect the trapdoor from leaking information about queried keywords. Chang et al. [53]

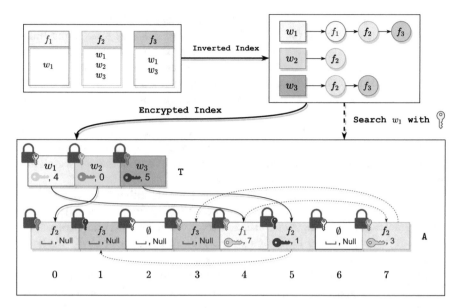

Fig. 3.3 The illustration of SSE-1 scheme [74]

proposed another construction trying to fix this problem. However, their notion still has limitations, and their construction requires amount of computation in proportion to the total number of documents in the collection. This is unfriendly to data collections where each file contains only several keywords. If each search only has a few matched results in the data collection, then this might result in a large performance penalty. For example, consider a photo collection in which each photo is tagged with several keywords only. Then the search time will be approximately proportional to the number of photos in the entire collection, while there are normally a small portion (e.g., 1% or even less) of matching photos for each search.

3.2.2   A Milestone Design

To make up for the above insufficiency, [74] proposed a construction SSE-1 with search time proportional to the number of *matching* documents and achieving perfect correctness. It creates an *inverted* index that maps each keyword to documents containing it (recall that we index the occurrences of keywords in each document in all previous approaches) as shown in Fig. 3.3. There is a list L_w storing document identifiers for each keyword w.

The SSE-1 scheme first randomly assigns nodes, including the id and a pointer to the next node (or NULL for the last node), in L to a search array A. After that, it encrypts each entry in A with independent but specially designed keys. However, the encryption will inhibit the server from "opening" the next node in the linked list L_w while searching for the keyword w. We thus implant the key to decrypt the next node in each of them before encryption. Hereafter, the server will be able to sequentially open nodes in L_w as long as he can open the first one. Therefore, we use another lookup table T to store encrypted keys and locations for the first node of each list L_w in A.

Upon searching for a keyword w, the client only needs to send the key for opening the corresponding entry in T to enable the server to sequentially open the list L_w and fetches encrypted documents accordingly. It is clear that the search time is proportional to the number of nodes in each list.

We also give a formal description of SSE-1 in Algorithm 1 to have a closer look at how to mathematically describe a searchable encryption scheme. Apart from the original algorithm designs, we also add some comments and brief explanations following "▷" sign to show the design intuitions behind that line or block, and hence help audiences better understand SSE-1 design.

Right before the formal definition, we first brief some notations here. Let l be the bit length of the longest keyword in $\mathcal{W}$ and s be the total "size" of the encrypted collection. We evaluate the size by unit of the smallest possible size for a keyword.

Security Proof Sketch We claim that SSE-1 is non-adaptively secure under Definition 3. We will not go into formal and detailed proof but just discuss the central idea. With the help of our explanations, the audiences would have a better idea of why it is secure and what processes a formal proof will need to go through.

The security definition requires that there *exists* a PPT simulator satisfying a set of conditions. Therefore, one key step is to present such a simulator. In general, the simulator behaves almost the same as the given scheme but with different parameters or inputs, since the simulator is actually fed with a list of features (i.e., the leakage) of the documents rather than the true document collection.

There are in total *three* sets of strings we need to simulate, i.e., the index $I^* = (A^*, T^*)$, the encrypted documents $EDB = (c_1^*, \ldots, c_D^*)$, and the trapdoors $(t_1^*, \ldots, t_q^*)$. Recall that a common leakage function is given as follows:

$$\mathcal{L}(DB, Q) = \left(|doc_1|, \ldots, |doc_D|, \left(DB(w_1), \ldots, DB(w_q)\right), M(Q)\right),$$

where $M(Q)_{i,j} = 1$ if and only if queries (trapdoors) i and j are identical.

We start with the easiest one—simulating c_i^*. Given the size of i-th document $|doc_i|$, S simply outputs a $|doc_i|$-bit string uniformly samples from $\{0, 1\}^{|doc_i|}$. Since SE_2 is a semantically secure symmetric cryptosystem, it will guarantee that c_i and c_i^* are indistinguishable with all but negligible probability.

To simulate A^*, S first sets $W = q$ and executes Line 2~10 (except for Line 4) of the Enc algorithm on the sets $DB(w_1)$ to $DB(w_q)$ by substituting $\phi(\text{ctr})$ with uniformly sampled strings of the same length $\log_2(s)$. S then fills the remaining $s - q$ entries with random strings of length $\log_2(D) + \lambda + \log_2(s)$. Note that from the adversarial point of view, he can open q lists of identical ids in both A^* and

---

Algorithm 1 A non-adaptively secure SSE scheme in [74]

Let SE_1 and SE_2 be two symmetric encryption schemes, f be a PRF, and π and ϕ be two PRP with the following parameters:

$$f : \{0, 1\}^\lambda \times \{0, 1\}^l \to \{0, 1\}^{\lambda + \log_2(s)};$$

$$\pi : \{0, 1\}^\lambda \times \{0, 1\}^l \to \{0, 1\}^l;$$

$$\phi : \{0, 1\}^\lambda \times \{0, 1\}^\lambda \to \{0, 1\}^{\log_2(s)}.$$

$Gen(1^\lambda)$:

1: $K_1, K_2, K_3 \overset{\$}{\leftarrow} \{0, 1\}^\lambda$; $K_4 \leftarrow SE_2.Gen(1^\lambda)$; **return** $K = (K_1, K_2, K_3, K_4)$.

$Enc(K, DB)$:

1: Allocate A with s entries, $\mathtt{T} \leftarrow \emptyset$ with W entries, initialize $\mathsf{ctr} \leftarrow 1$
2: **for** $1 \leq i \leq W$ **do**   ▷ w_i is the i-th keyword
3:     $K_{i,0} \leftarrow \{0, 1\}^\lambda$; $n_{w_i} \leftarrow |DB(w_i)|$
4:     $\mathtt{T}[\pi_{K_3}(w_i)] \leftarrow \langle \phi_{K_1}(\mathsf{ctr}) \| K_{i,0} \rangle \oplus f_{K_2}(w_i)$ ▷ Store the first entry for w_i in T
5:     **for** $1 \leq j \leq n_w - 1$ **do**   ▷ $id_{i,j}$ is the j-th document in $DB(w_i)$
6:         $K_{i,j} \leftarrow SE_1.Gen(1^\lambda)$; $\mathsf{ctr} \leftarrow \mathsf{ctr} + 1$
7:         $\mathtt{N}_{i,j} \leftarrow id_{i,j} \| K_{i,j} \| \phi_{K_1}(\mathsf{ctr})$ ▷ ID, decryption key and location of the next entry
8:         $\mathtt{A}[\phi_{K_1}(\mathsf{ctr} - 1)] \leftarrow SE_1.Enc_{K_{i,j-1}}(\mathtt{N}_{i,j})$
9:     $\mathtt{N}_{i,n_{w_i}} \leftarrow id_{i,n_w} \| 0^\lambda \| NULL$; $\mathsf{ctr} = \mathsf{ctr} + 1$ ▷ Process the last entry for w_i
10:     $\mathtt{A}[\phi_{K_1}(\mathsf{ctr} - 1)] \leftarrow SE_1.Enc_{K_{i,n_w - 1}}(\mathtt{N}_{i,n_w})$
11: Fill the remaining $s - \sum_{w \in \mathcal{W}} |DB(w)|$ entries of A with (pseudo-) random values of the same length.
12: **for** $1 \leq i \leq D$ **do**   ▷ Encrypt each document
13:     $c_i \leftarrow SE_2.Enc_{K_4}(doc_i)$
14: **return** (I, EDB), where $I = (\mathtt{A}, \mathtt{T})$ and $EDB = (c_1, \ldots, c_D)$.

$Trpdr(K, w)$:

1: **return** $t = (\pi_{K_3}(w), f_{K_2}(w))$.

$Search(I, t)$:

1: $(\gamma, \eta) \leftarrow t$; $\theta \leftarrow \mathtt{T}[\gamma]$ ▷ Fetch the head of the list if exists
2: **if** $\theta = \perp$ **then**
3:     **return** $\perp$
4: $\langle addr_{next} \| K_{next} \rangle \leftarrow \theta \oplus \eta$; $X \leftarrow \emptyset$
5: **do**   ▷ Decrypt and parse each entry in the list
6:     $addr_{cur} \leftarrow addr_{next}$; $K_{cur} \leftarrow K_{next}$
7:     $id \| K_{next} \| addr_{next} \leftarrow SE_1.Dec_{K_{cur}}(\mathtt{A}[addr_{cur}])$
8:     $X \leftarrow X \cup \{c_{id}\}$
9: **while** $K_{next} \neq 0^\lambda$ and $addr_{next} \neq NULL$
10: **return** X.

$Dec(K, c_i)$: **return** $doc_i = SE_2.Dec_{K_4}(c_i)$.

A but from different locations and with different keys. However, no PPT adversary can differentiate them, or distinguishing the remaining random strings in $\mathtt{A}^*$ and ciphertexts in A due to the semantic security of SE_1 and the pseudorandomness of ϕ.

To simulate T^*, S generates q pairs of random bits α_i of length l and β_i of length $\log_2(s) + \lambda$. By retrieving the addresses of q first nodes in each list from the previous step, S sets

$$T^*[\alpha_i] = \langle \mathrm{addr}_{A^*}(N_{i,1}) \| K_{i,0} \rangle \oplus \beta_i.$$

S then inserts random strings to the remaining entries in T^*. One can use the underlying $\mathrm{addr}_{A^*}(N_{i,1})$ to locate the first node in A^* and use $K_{i,0}$ to decrypt that entry, just like things happened in SE-1, but from different locations α_i^* or $\pi_{K_3}(w_i)$ and different keys β_i^* or $f_{K_2}(w_i)$. By the pseudorandomness of π and f, we can claim that no PPT adversary can distinguish between them with all but negligible probability.

S simulates $t_i^* = (\alpha_i^*, \beta_i^*)$ for $1 \leq i \leq q$, and similar arguments hold for the trapdoors. We then complete the proof sketch.

An Adaptively Secure Design Chase and Kamara [56] observe that one can easily convert SSE-1 into an adaptively secure scheme by demanding both SE_1 and SE_2 to be symmetric *non-committing* encryption schemes (as explained below). In fact, the simplest possible symmetric encryption scheme is a non-committing one. We thus gain adaptive security almost for free!

We briefly describe what a non-committing encryption scheme is as follows. In traditional schemes, the ciphertext may be used to commit to the plaintext and the encryption key. Namely, it may be impossible for the client to find another pair of plaintext and key which could be encrypted into the target ciphertext. However, in a non-committing encryption scheme, for any given ciphertext, the client can choose a plaintext string (with arbitrary combination of 1s or 0s) and an appropriate key correspondingly, and show that the plaintext can be encrypted into the given ciphertext. In short, it breaks a "strong" link between the ciphertext and the plaintext built by the secret key; the ciphertext hence cannot "commit" to any plaintext.

SSE-1 inspires many other designs, including what we will discuss in Chap. 4 and becomes a basic and standard SSE scheme or a building block serving many purposes, including dynamic searchable encryption, multi-user support, conjunctive search, etc.

3.2.3 Encrypted Multi-Map and Searchable Structured Encryption

An abstract data type called a *multi-map* (or multi-dictionary) allows more than one value to be associated with and returned for a given key.

In most programming languages, multi-maps are offered by either a self-balancing binary search tree or a hash table. The former implementation has a higher asymptotic complexity, $O(\log n)$ for both lookup (search) and insertion operations, where n is the number of key-value pairs. However, it has a lower constant multiplicative overhead and inherently preserves the order of the original data. The latter implementation (i.e., hash table based) has a constant time complexity $O(1)$ on average, but with higher constant overhead and worst-case complexity $O(n)$. Furthermore, we cannot expect any order in this implementation.

In Algorithm 1, there is a *logic* multi-map in which the keys are keywords and the corresponding values are the identifiers of documents containing the keyword. We encrypt the multi-map by pseudorandomly allocating key-value pairs into a search array and encrypting the entries with different keys. Therefore, literature afterward also calls this type of searchable encryption "encrypted multi-map." Variants based on encrypted multi-maps may differ in encryption methods with different performance and various functionalities. But there is always a *logic* multi-map in those approaches.

Chase and Kamara [56] also proposed several searchable encryption constructions, especially for queries on matrices and graphs, including adjacency queries and subgraph queries on graphs. However, all those schemes take advantage of the encrypted multi-map. Sometimes, people may also use the term Searchable Structured Encryption (STE) to refer to SSE. Unless one would like to emphasize that they are focusing on encrypted searches over structured data collection, we will use two terms (SSE and STE) alternatively.

3.3 Public-Key Encryption with Keyword Search

The previous section and the next chapter concentrate on searching over data collection encrypted by symmetric encryption, since the data is owned by, *encrypted by,* and searched by the same individual in many real-world scenarios. However, sometimes people may also want others to help *encrypt* data owned by him, and also *build* an encrypted index for him for future searches. For instance, email senders encrypt emails which are sent to Alice and will be stored on an untrusted email server. Meanwhile, Alice also wish the server could help test (i.e., a special kind of search) if the encrypted email contains the keyword "urgent" such that the email could be routed accordingly. Clearly, this scenario is a natural fit for public-key encryption, as different senders do not want to share a symmetric key with the others. Boneh et al. [31] then proposed the concept of public-key encryption with keyword search (PEKS) for this scenario.

We note that PEKS schemes are generally used in multi-writer situations. One may argue that the writer could first establish a secure channel with the querier and then transmit the encrypted data to the querier, which is then converted to a searchable symmetric encryption problem. However, we notice that the querier (i.e., the private-key owner) is not always online and may not be able to receive and process the private data in time. It then demands a writer to directly upload the encrypted data to an untrusted server, and the querier may search for a keyword with a token generated by its private key afterward. Therefore, PEKS is also an integral part of searchable encryption.

Almost all current solutions [31, 278, 291, 296] take the advantage of bilinear maps on elliptic curves to build a PEKS scheme. In particular, a bilinear map $e : G_1 \times G_1 \mapsto G_2$ takes as input two elements in the group G_1 of the order p, outputs an element in the group G_2 of the same order p. In addition, the map has to satisfy the following three properties:

Bilinearity   we have $e(g^x, g^y) = e(g, g)^{xy}$ for any integers $x, y \in [1, p]$;

Symmetry   we have $e(g^x, g^y) = e(g^y, g^x)$ for any $g \in G_1$ and integers $x, y \in [1, p]$;

Non-degeneracy $e(g, g)$ is a generator of G_2 if g is a generator of G_1.

Next, we will brief the construction proposed by Boneh et al. [31] due to its elegance. First of all, suppose Bob sends an encrypted email msg with keywords $w_1, \ldots, w_W$ to Alice; he will send the following messages:

$$\left[E_{A_{pub}} (email) , \text{PEKS}_{A_{pub}} (w_1) , \ldots, \text{PEKS}_{A_{pub}} (w_W) \right],$$

where A_{pub} is Alice's public key and **PEKS** is an scheme defined as follows.

Definition 5 (PEKS [31]) A public-key encryption with keyword search (PEKS) scheme is composed of four polynomial algorithms as follows:

$\text{Gen}(1^\lambda)$ is a probabilistic algorithm which takes a security parameter λ as input and outputs a public-private key pair A_{pub}, A_{priv}.

$\text{PEKS}(A_{pub}, w)$ is a probabilistic algorithm which takes the public key A_{pub} and the keyword w as the input and output a searchable encryption of w. Sometimes, we also refer to this as $\text{PEKS}_{A_{pub}}(w)$.

$\text{Trpdr}(A_{priv}, w)$ is an algorithm which takes the private key A_{priv} and a keyword w as input and outputs a trapdoor t_w. Sometimes, we also refer to this as $\text{Trpdr}_{A_{priv}}(w)$.

$\text{Test}(A_{pub}, s, t_w)$ is an algorithm which takes the public key A_{pub}, a searchable encryption produced by **PEKS**, and a trapdoor t_w as input and outputs a bit $b \in \{0, 1\}$ indicating whether s is an encryption of w. Sometimes, we also refer to this as $\text{Test}_{A_{pub}}(s, t_w)$.

The correctness requires that for any searchable encryption and trapdoors, the Test algorithm should produce a correct bit showing whether they are indeed from the same keyword w or not.

We then give a formal description of the PEKS scheme proposed by Boneh et al. [31] as follows. Besides, we also need two hash functions $\pi : \{0, 1\}^* \rightarrow G_1$ and $\phi : G_2 \rightarrow \{0, 1\}^{\log p}$.

Gen(1^λ) : We chooses two groups G_1 and G_2 according to the security parameter λ. It then selects a random $\alpha \in \mathbb{Z}_p^*$ and a generator $p \in G_1$. It returns $A_{priv} = \alpha$ and $A_{pub} = (g, h = g^\alpha)$.

PEKS(A_{pub}, w) randomly samples an integer $r \in \mathbb{Z}_p^*$, computes $t = e(\pi(w), h^r) \in G_2$. It returns $s = (g^r, \phi(t))$.

Trpdr(A_{priv}, w) outputs $t_w = \pi(w)^\alpha \in G_1$.

Test(A_{pub}, s, t_w) parses s as (X, Y), and returns a bit indicating $\phi(e(t_w, X)) \overset{?}{=} Y$.

It is easy to verify the correctness as for a matching pair of t_w and s, we have $\phi(e(t_w, g^r)) = \phi(e(\pi(w)^\alpha, g^r)) = \phi(e(\pi(w), g)^{r\alpha}) = \phi(e(\pi(w), g^{r\alpha})) = \phi(e(\pi(w), h^r)) = Y$. If t_w does not match the searchable encryption s, we will have two different hashed values, $\pi(w)$ and $\pi(w')$ with all but negligible probabilities and thus fail to establish the equality. Furthermore, the non-degeneracy as well as other computational hardness assumptions (e.g., computational Diffie-Hellman problem) guarantees the security of a PEKS system.

Note that the above construction requires expensive public-key encryption operations and has to scan all the searchable encryptions to find all documents containing the target keyword, which may result in some performance concerns for large-scale data collections. It is in general hard to jointly build a search index to narrow down the search scope for efficient search since writers do not share any secrets during the encryption process. In the past two decades, almost all the PEKS solutions [31, 291] have to scan the entire encrypted keyword collection to filter out the matches, while ideally we do not want to waste time on checking for mismatched results. Wang and Chow [278] were the first ones who proposed a *hybrid* searchable encryption scheme that still scans all updated keywords of each writer but runs a searchable symmetric encryption within each writer's data collection. It then successfully removes redundant checks within the encrypted data collection of each writer. However, the inherent expensive public-key encryption operations (e.g., pairing on elliptic curves) still prohibit their application to large-scale datasets.

3.4 Summary and Further Reading

In this chapter, we go through the world of searchable symmetric encryption from its basic definitions and security notions to a mature construction fulfilling various requirements. We also introduce other security definitions and constructions along developing searchable encryption. We solve a quite basic problem in which the client can securely search for one keyword on an encrypted document collection. It significantly raises the attacking bar against adversaries who can only access the server at some moments or against data breaches.

However, it remains to upgrade our construction to support the user to insert files into or delete files from the encrypted document collection. Besides, most of the modern search engines support conjunctive queries with multiple keywords and many other functionalities. Furthermore, will the "features" of trapdoors and encrypted documents used in our security notions compromise the user's privacy? We will soon be answering those questions in the following chapters.

If you find difficulties in understanding the security definitions or proofs, we strongly recommend a tutorial on game-based proof techniques [201] and simulation-based proof techniques [179]. The research work of [56] will also help us learn how to formally and precisely define the security of various constructions as well as their leakage functions. Moreover, you could also find the experimental performance of aforementioned constructions done by Li and Liu [175].

As we have discussed before, there are other multi-writer schemes utilizing public key encryption with keyword search techniques. In particular, [31] first explicitly considered the searchable encryption with public-key encryption primitives, which are inherently suitable for multiple-writer scenario but suffering from expensive encryption operations. Xu et al. [291] further improve the PEKS scheme from a security point of view. Wang and Chow [278] firstly proposed a PEKS scheme achieving sublinear search time by integrating the searchable symmetric encryption approaches for each writer.

Chapter 4
Recent Advancements on Functionality and Performance

In this chapter, we will continue our journey to introduce recent advancements of searchable encryption on functionality and performance. We will first show how to construct a *dynamic* searchable symmetric encryption, i.e., supporting data insertions, deletions, and updates in Sect. 4.1. After that, we will extend our scope to other common functionalities, i.e., multi-user supports in Sect. 4.2 and Boolean queries over encrypted data in Sect. 4.3. Next, Sect. 4.4 will discuss some practical optimizations to SSE schemes to an appropriate depth. Finally, some selected in-depth and distinguished readings will be given in Sect. 4.5.

4.1 Toward Dynamic Data Support with Scalability

As we have learned from the previous chapter, searchable symmetric encryption (SSE) enables one to search for documents or records matching a keyword, which are previously outsourced to an untrusted cloud server while maintaining user privacy. In addition to its security and efficiency, another crucial property of a *practical* SSE scheme is the ability to add and delete documents efficiently. Although there had been two schemes [108, 178] supporting updates of the encrypted data, both of them have limitations from a practical point of view. The former one [108], which has been discussed in the previous chapter with lower security guarantees, requires impractical search time and results in false positives. The latter one [178] demands a potentially large encrypted index size. Besides, it has rigorous conditions on updates either, such as rare occurrences of updates, a limited number of updates, or the necessity of being interleaved with searches.

Therefore, we will elaborate on four carefully selected dynamic SSE schemes from their constructions to their performance and leakage profiles. The first scheme is an elegant one built on top of the SSE-1 that we have discussed in the previous chapter. We will then show its limitations from both security and performance

K. Ren, C. Wang, *Searchable Encryption*, Wireless Networks,
https://doi.org/10.1007/978-3-031-21377-9_4

perspectives. The second one is hence proposed to effectively mitigate drawbacks of
SSE-1 with a slightly different design. We note that this design will actually serve
as the fundamental building block of many other advanced SSE schemes due to its
high efficiency and elegance. However, there remains a notable security defect in
the second construction named *non-forward private*; the third one and the fourth
one will help fix this issue efficiently and straightforwardly.

For convenience, we denote $n_w := |DB(w)|$ as the number of documents
containing keyword w, and $N := \sum_{w \in \mathcal{W}} n_w$ that is the number of document-
keyword pairs. The notion m_{id} is the number of unique keywords contained in
the document id, $D := |EDB|$ is the number of documents in the database, and
$W := |\mathcal{W}|$ is the number of keywords.

4.1.1   An Intuitive SSE Extension Supporting Data Dynamics

To address the limitations discussed at the beginning of this section, [153] proposed
the first SSE scheme which simultaneously satisfies the following four properties:

*   *Optimal* search time;
*   Security against *adaptive* chosen-keyword attacks;
*   Compact indices, i.e., reasonable index size;
*   The ability to add and delete documents *efficiently*.

Their design is based on the *inverted index* approach of [74] which we have discussed in the previous chapter. Recalling that the *static* scheme SSE-1 constructs a
list L_{w_i} for each keyword $w_i \in \mathcal{W}$. Each list consists of n_{w_i} nodes $(N_{i,1}, \ldots, N_{i,n_{w_i}})$
randomly stored in the search array A_s. The node $N_{i,j}$ is composed of the identifier
id of the corresponding document containing the word w_i, $\mathsf{addr}_s(N_{i,j+1})$ indicating
the location of next node $N_{i,j+1}$ in A_s, and a corresponding key to decrypt the next
node.

The pointer to the head of the list L_{w_i} is then inserted into the search table T_s
under search key $F_{K_1}(w_i)$, in which K_1 is the key of the PRF F. Meanwhile, the
list is encrypted using SE under another key generated as $G_{K_2}(w_i)$, where K_2 is the
key of the PRF G.

To search for a keyword w, the client only needs to send two search keys $F_{K_1}(w)$
and $G_{K_2}(w)$. It suffices for the server to recover the pointer to the head of L_w and
decrypt the list as well as the identifiers of the targeting documents. By instantiating
the search table T as a hash table with $O(1)$ lookup complexity, the search time for
the server could achieve the optimal n_w.

Making SSE-1 Dynamic   As we discussed in the previous chapter, there are two
major limitations in SSE-1: (1) it is non-adaptively secure and (2) it is not explicitly
dynamic. As observed in [56] and explained in Sect. 3.2, the adaptive security could
be achieved by simply requiring *non-committing* SE.

The second limitation is, however, more challenging to overcome. The difficulty lies in the demands of adding, deleting, or modifying nodes in the encrypted lists stored in A_s. It is difficult for the server to do because:

- Upon deletion, it is hard to *reversely* locate nodes in each list.
- Upon insertion or deletion, it is difficult to modify the pointer of the previous encrypted node.
- Upon addition, it is not aware of the free entries in A_s either.

Kamara et al. [153] addressed the above issues as follows:

Document deletion. To solve the difficulty of reversely locating nodes corresponding to the document being deleted, we can offer an extra encrypted data structure A_d called the *deletion array* to preserve the connections of nodes in the same document in A_s. More precisely, the deletion array stores a list L_{id} of nodes pointing to the nodes in A_s which should be deleted for each document id. Therefore, we have a list for each word w consisting of document ids and a list for each document id containing the pointers of corresponding nodes in A_s.

Pointer modification. The pointers stored in a node are encrypted using a homomorphic encryption scheme. By providing an appropriate value, the server can modify the pointer without decrypting the node. Meanwhile, the location of previous nodes in both arrays is stored in the deletion array as well.

Memory management. The server maintains an encrypted *free list* consisting of free entries in both arrays to help add new nodes.

An Illustrative Example

We use Fig. 4.1 to demonstrate how a fully dynamic SSE scheme works for a specific index.

We build the index on three documents named f_1, f_2, f_3 over three keywords w_1, w_2, w_3. Keyword w_1 is contained in all three documents, keyword w_2 is only contained in document f_2, and keyword w_3 is contained in both documents f_2 and f_3. In addition, Fig. 4.1 also shows the respective search (deletion) table T_s (T_d) and the search (deletion) array A_s (A_d). We omit padding for simplicity, which does exist in a real DSSE index to hide the number of keyword-document pairs.

Searching Consider a client who wants to search for all documents containing the keyword w_1. He first prepares the search token containing $F_{K_1}(w_1)$ and $G_{K_2}(w_1)$, where the first value $F_{K_1}(w_1)$ tells the server where to find the corresponding entry in the search table T_s. In our example, this value is $x = (4\|1) \oplus G_{K_2}(w_1)$. The server then locates the right entry in the search array by computing $x \oplus G_{K_2}(w_1)$, i.e., 4 in our example, and "unmask"s the stored pointers to the target documents f_1, f_2, and f_3.

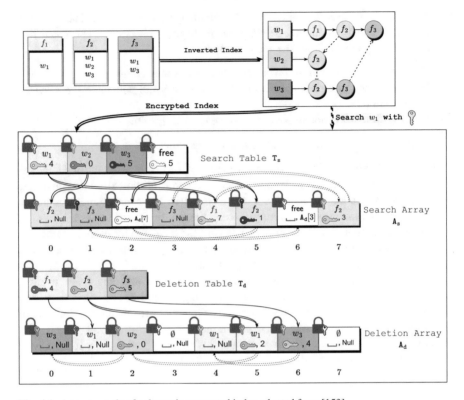

Fig. 4.1 A toy example of a dynamic encrypted index adopted from [153]

Adding a Document If the client wants to add a document f_4 containing the keywords w_1 and w_2. The search table is the only data structure that remains unchanged since it stores the first entries of keywords in the search array, and f_4 will be appended as the last entry in the list of keywords w_1 and w_2. However, the rest of the data structures have to be updated as follows. Firstly, the server identifies available entries in the search array A_s with the free pointer, and stores the new information (w_1, f_4) and (w_2, f_4) in the corresponding locations. These positions are 6 and 2 in our example. After that, the server will connect newly added entries to the respective keyword lists: it retrieves the indices $i = 0$ and $j = 3$ with insertion tokens in the search array A_s, and homomorphically sets $A_s[0]$'s and $A_s[3]$'s "next" pointers to newly added entries, i.e., 2 and 6, respectively.

Note that the server will modify the deletion array accordingly. In our example, the server will store tuples (f_4, w_1) and (f_4, w_2) at the entries 3 and 7. Finally, it will update the deletion table by setting the entry $F_{K_1}(f_4)$ to position 3 in the deletion array, such that it can easily retrieve file f_4 for deletion later.

Deleting a Document Assume the client now wishes to delete document f_3, which contains two keywords w_1 and w_3. Informally speaking, the deletion is a "dual operation" to the addition. The server first locates the value $4 \oplus G_{K_2}(f_3)$ in the deletion table by using the value $F_{K_1}(f_3)$ in the deletion token. As with the addition process, it allows the server to access the remaining data structures that need to be updated. In particular, it will "free" the entries 4 and 6 in the deletion array A_d and the entries 1 and 3 in the search array A_s. Besides, it will homomorphically update the respective pointers of previous entries in the keyword lists w_1 and w_3 to the new entries, i.e., to the end of the lists in our example.

Performance and Leakage

Both search tables T_s and T_d are of size $O(W)$ as there is one entry for each keyword w. The search arrays are of size $O(N)$, since each list L_w has n_w number of nodes. Therefore, the encrypted indices cost totally $O(N + W)$ space.

Upon adding a document, the client has to send $O(|\mathcal{W}(\text{id})|)$-size messages to the server, where $\mathcal{W}(\text{id})$ is the set of *unique* keywords in the document id. Upon deleting a document, it suffices for the client to send only keys to recover corresponding lists as well as the document id to the server; thus, the communication complexity is only $O(1)$. Upon updating a document, the server needs to go through every word $w \in \mathcal{W}(\text{id})$ to modify corresponding nodes in the search and deletion arrays, thus incurring $O(|\mathcal{W}(\text{id})|)$ computation.

From the above example, we can observe that this scheme leaks the *structure* of the added document. In other words, it reveals the pattern of which (encrypted) keywords appear in which documents when they are added. For instance, suppose $\{w_1\}$ are added to id_1, $\{w_1, w_2\}$ are added to id_2, and $\{w_1, w_2, w_3\}$ are added to id_3. Then, the server could learn that three documents contain exactly one common keyword, and the latter two documents have exactly two common keywords. Subsequently, unexpected disclosures of any one of them will leak the information of the others. Or the adversary could perform some advanced statistical analysis on this leakage pattern to recover plaintext documents or trapdoors.

In addition, it is not hard to verify that the search operation reveals the search pattern—the equality of searched keywords, the access and response identity patterns, as well the response volume pattern.

4.1.2 A More Scalable Construction Considering Add-Only Updates

Due to the severe security drawback of the previous SSE design, [48] then proposed an SSE scheme achieving much smaller leakage, search computation time, and optimal server storage size with a generic dictionary structure. It could be viewed as generalizing and simplifying more ad hoc techniques in [47], which will be introduced in the future section. The scheme easily supports the additions to the data, as well as deletions via revocation lists, i.e., using a blacklist to filter out deleted documents rather than actually removing them.

We first formalize a dictionary data type in detail here for references. A *dictionary implementation* consists of four algorithms such that:

Create $\left((l_i, d_i)_{i=1}^m\right)$ takes a list of label-data pairs, where each label is unique, and outputs the data structure γ;

Get (γ, l) takes as input the data structure γ and a label l, outputs the data items associated with that label;

Insert $(\gamma, (l, d))$ updates γ such that it contains the new given pair.

The basic scheme as demonstrated in Algorithm 2 is very straightforward. Each keyword-record pair is associated with a pseudorandom label, and then a corresponding document id will be encrypted and tagged with this label. Afterward, the client will store those label-data pairs in a dictionary that we have described above. The labels are derived such that the client can efficiently compute two keyword-specific short keys K_1 and K_2 which allow the server to generate labels, retrieve, and decrypt the matching ids.

Extension for Updates

Add-Only Scheme We start with an extension that supports additions only, i.e., the client only adds document-keyword pairs during Update. It is simpler and perhaps more interesting in its own right.

Algorithm 2 The basic scheme in [48]

Setup(DB):

1: $K \xleftarrow{\$} \{0, 1\}^\lambda$ allocate list L;
2: **for** each $w \in \mathcal{W}$ **do**
3:     $K_1 \leftarrow F(K, 1\|w)$, $K_w \leftarrow F(K, 2\|w)$;
4:     Initialize counter $c \leftarrow 0$;
5:     **for** each id $\in \mathrm{DB}(w)$ **do**
6:         $l \leftarrow F(K_1, c)$, $d \leftarrow \mathrm{Enc}(K_2, \mathrm{id})$, $c++$;
7:         Add (l, d) to the list L (in lexicographic order);
8: Set $\gamma \leftarrow$ Create(L);
9: **return** the client key K and EDB $= \gamma$.

Trpdr(K, w):

1: Generate $K_1 \leftarrow F(K, 1\|w)$, $K_2 \leftarrow F(K, 2\|w)$;
2: **return** search token $= (K_1, K_2)$.

Search(token):

1: Parse $(K_1, K_2) =$ token;
2: Initialize counter $c \leftarrow 0$, result set $S \leftarrow \emptyset$;
3: **for** $d \leftarrow$ Get($\gamma, F(K_1, c)$), $d \neq \bot$ **do**
4:     $m \leftarrow \mathrm{Dec}(K_2, d)$, $c++$;
5:     Parse m as id, add into $S \leftarrow S \cup \{\mathrm{id}\}$;
6: **return** the matching result S.

We use an initially empty dictionary γ^+ dedicated to storing added label-data (i.e., keyword-id) (l, d) pairs. To allow for adding documents to the outsourced encrypted database, it is necessary for the client to compute (l, d) pairs to be inserted into the dictionary γ^+. We furnish the client with this ability by storing the count c for each newly added keyword locally in a dictionary δ; then, it can generate (l, d) pairs according to its key and the count c in the same approach as the **Setup** stage. We use another key for addition $K^+ \leftarrow F(K, 3)$, and the procedure is described as follows:

Update(add, id, $\mathcal{W}$(id)):
1: Initialize an empty list L;
2: **for** $w \in \mathcal{W}$(id) **do**
3:     Set $K_1^+ \leftarrow F(K^+, 1\|w)$, $K_2^+ \leftarrow F(K^+, 2\|w)$;
4:     Compute $c \leftarrow$ Get(δ, w); If $c = \perp$ then $c \leftarrow 0$;
5:     Set $l \leftarrow F(K_1^+, c)$; $d \leftarrow$ Enc(K_2^+, id);
6:     Insert $(\delta, (w, c + 1))$ to update the word count;
7:     Add (l, d) to L in lexicographic order;
8: Send L to the server.

On receiving the list L, the server adds each $(l, d) \in L$ to γ^+ and completes the update protocol. To reduce the storage burden on the client side, or make the client *stateless*, we can transfer the responsibility of storing the count dictionary δ to the server. By doing so, however, the client has to *download* δ, re-encrypt δ, and send it back to the server. In this variant, the communication cost becomes larger, and the server will learn how many *new* keywords are added by observing the size of δ without padding.

Upon searching for a keyword w, the client also generates tokens for the addition dictionary γ^+ as follows.

Trpdr(K, w):
1: Generate $K_1 \leftarrow F(K, 1\|w)$, $K_2 \leftarrow F(K, 2\|w)$;
2: $K_1^+ \leftarrow F(K^+, 1\|w)$, $K_2^+ \leftarrow F(K^+, 2\|w)$;
3: **return** search token $= (K_1, K_2, K_1^+, K_2^+)$.

And the server just repeats the original search procedure twice, one for the static dictionary γ, and the other for the addition dictionary γ^+.

Search(token):
1: Parse $(K_1, K_2, K_1^+, K_2^+) = $ token;
2: Initialize counter $c_1, c_2 \leftarrow 0$, result set $S \leftarrow \emptyset$;
3: **for** $d \leftarrow $ Get$(\gamma, F(K_1, c)), d \neq \perp$ **do**
4:     $m \leftarrow $ Dec$(K_2, d), c_1 + +$;
5:     Parse m as id, add into $S \leftarrow S \cup \{$id$\}$;
6: **for** $d \leftarrow $ Get$(\gamma^+, F(K_1^+, c)), d \neq \perp$ **do**
7:     $m \leftarrow $ Dec$(K_2^+, d), c_2 + +$;
8:     Parse m as id, add into $S \leftarrow S \cup \{$id$\}$;
9: **return** the matching result S.

The scheme does not support deletion in the true sense but maintains a filter or revocation list to *conceptually* delete documents. To delete a record-keyword pair (id, w) from the server, the client generates a pseudorandom *revocation* id and sent to the server as follows:

Update(del, id, $\mathcal{W}$(id)):   ▷ We derive the key $K^- = F(K, 4)$ at the Setup stage
1: Initialize an empty list L_{rev};
2: **for** $w \in \mathcal{W}$(id) **do**
3:     $K_1^- \leftarrow F(K^-, w)$, revid $\leftarrow F(K^-, id)$;
4:     Add revid to L_{rev} in lexicographic order;
5: Send L_{rev} to the server.

The server additionally maintains a set S_{rev} to store the deleted revid. After receiving L_{rev}, it adds each revid to S_{rev} and finishes the del operation.

The deletion operation complicates the addition protocol, as it has to compute revid in advance, such that for each keyword-document pair, the server can verify its corresponding revid. In code, the client executes as follows:

Update(add, id, $\mathcal{W}$(id)):
1: Initialize an empty list L;
2: **for** $w \in \mathcal{W}$(id) **do**
3:     Set $K_1^+ \leftarrow F(K^+, 1\|w)$, $K_2^+ \leftarrow F(K^+, 2\|w)$;
4:     $K_1^- \leftarrow F(K^-, w)$;
5:     Compute $c \leftarrow $ Get(δ, w); If $c = \perp$ then $c \leftarrow 0$;
6:     Set $l \leftarrow F(K_1^+, c); d \leftarrow $ Enc(K_2^+, id);
7:     revid $\leftarrow F(K_1^-, id)$
8:     Add $(l, d, $revid$)$ to L in lexicographic order;
9: Send L to the server.

The server needs to tell the client whether newly added documents have ever been deleted before, such that the client can update counter c correctly. It generates a response $r \in \{0, 1\}^{|L|}$ as follows. The i-th bit of r is set to 0 if revid $\in S_{\text{rev}}$ for $(l, d, \text{revid}) := L_i$, and revid is removed from S_{rev}. Otherwise, the bit is set to 1 and we add (l, d) to γ^+. The client now updates corresponding counters for keywords according to the 0/1 bit in the response r, which finally completes the protocol.

To generate a token for searching keyword w, the client also computes $K_1^- \leftarrow F(K^-, w)$ and sends token $= ((K_1, K_2, K_1^+, K_2^+, K_1^-)$ to the server. The server follows the exact Search procedure above, except that it computes revid $\leftarrow F(K_1^-, \text{id})$ and discards id if revid $\in S_{\text{rev}}$ before sending the result set back. The authors also provide some extensions for external storage, which will be discussed in Sect. 4.4.

Performance and Leakage

The scheme has asymptotically optimal encrypted index size $O(N)$, and the search complexity is $O(n_w + d_w)$, where d_w is the number of times the keyword w has been added/deleted. The scheme also achieves optimal update computation time and client storage space.

The comprehensive and formal leakage functions are described in [48]. We will informally describe the information leakage as follows. On updates, the server will learn when/whether the document id has had the same keywords added/deleted before, and when/whether the same keywords have been searched for. Information about whether the same keyword is added to or deleted from different documents will not be leaked until it is searched.

The dynamic scheme of [48] achieves almost optimal complexity, at the expense of non-forward privacy (which will be explained shortly), though it leaks much less than the previous one [153].

4.1.3 A Conceptually Forward Private Construction

Though the scheme in Sect. 4.1.2 [48] leaks much less information than the one in Sect. 4.1.1 [153], it is still vulnerable to an adaptive attack [299], which can recover the searched keywords by inserting as few as a dozen new documents.

Necessity of Forward Privacy

As we have mentioned above, there are some attacks targeting dynamic encrypted databases to break query privacy. For instance, [145] and [49] showed that even a small amount of leakage can be devastating and exploited by an adversary to compromise the client's privacy. They assume that the attacker can *adaptively* submit or induce the client to submit new documents produced by the adversary into the collection, such that they can reconstruct queries of the client. Zhang et al. [299] improve this *document injection attack* and demonstrated its devastating power.

The adaptive attack they described is extremely powerful but applies only to *non-forward* private schemes. Specifically, the adversary can recover a searched keyword w by inserting $\log 2T$ new documents if he knows parts of the database, or using $W/T + \log T$ if he doesn't, where T is the *threshold parameter* used to avoid non-adaptive document injection attacks. T should not be too large to make the SSE scheme inefficient and should not be too small to avoid large security losses. In their experiments [299], with $T = 200$, the adversary can easily reconstruct a queried keyword by injecting less than 10 new documents.

The above attack has shown the importance of forward privacy for any dynamic SSE scheme. On the other hand, a forward private scheme also allows the client to build their encrypted database online, which can shift the computation and space burden to the cloud server.

To explain what is forward privacy from another perspective, imagine that the server keeps an old search token issued by the client for keyword w at a timestamp t_w, and if the client inserts some new keyword-id pairs into the encrypted data collection of the same keyword w, the server will immediately learn that the client has indeed inserted a document containing a keyword which was searched at the timestamp t_w—it leaks extra unnecessary information to adversaries! One natural requirement is that the server should never learn whether the newly inserted file contains a keyword that has ever been searched before. This problem was explicitly considered by Stefanov et al. [249] at the earliest time and named solutions hiding such leakage pattern "forward private." We will then discuss how to achieve forward privacy.

Specifically, to add a document-keyword pair id − w into the collection, it stores an encryption of $(w, \text{id}, \text{add}, c)$ in a hash table, in which c denotes that id is c-th document containing w. To delete a document-keyword pair id − w from the encrypted database, the server just stores an encryption of $(w, \text{id}, \text{del}, c)$. During the encrypted search of a keyword w, the server retrieves all addition and deletion keys from the hash tables, filters out the deleted id, and sends the survived matching results back.

However, storing both addition and deletion entries may cause linear time complexity in the worst case. For example, suppose that we first add some documents containing the keyword w, and we then delete all such documents. After that, each search of keyword w will go through all addition and deletion entries. However, the result set is empty as there is actually no matching document.

To alleviate this problem, encrypted indices need to be periodically rebuilt so that the opposite entries could be canceled out. The rebuilding operation is again a linear cost. To reduce the cost to logarithmic, it adopts a multilevel structure, which is reminiscent of the algorithmic techniques used in the ORAM literature (e.g., [110, 112]). A *fresh* key is used to encrypt the entries within the new level to guarantee the forward privacy of the scheme, as the old tokens are no longer usable within the new level.

Performance and Leakage

The server storage is $20\times$ larger than that of the previous scheme [48] according to the experiments in [37]. It costs much more space for the client to store the local states. However, it is still affordable on many mobile devices—only about hundreds of megabytes in practice. Another minor shortcoming of this scheme is its nonconstant update communication cost, which is $O(\log N)$ and N is the total number of keyword-document pairs in the encrypted document collection—although it is only several kilobytes for each keyword-document pair update in practice.

Upon updates, the protocol leaks the operation type op (i.e., addition/deletion), the document identifier id being updated, the volume, or the number of keywords $|m_{\mathsf{id}}|$, as well as the time t of the update. In contrast to the previous protocol [48], it does not leak *which* keywords are contained in the updated document.

Upon searches, it leaks the search patterns and response identity patterns, i.e., whether a search repeats and ids of matching documents. We emphasize that the above leakage captures *forward privacy*, in the sense that the set of matching identifiers does not leak future documents. However, it is not *backward private* (will be discussed shortly) as the set of matching identifiers also reveals ids that were deleted.

4.1.4 An Efficient Dynamic SSE Achieving Forward Privacy

In this section, we will describe the design intuitions of an optimal forward private dynamic SSE regarding the security and performance trade-off. The interesting scheme name $\Sigma_{o\phi o\varsigma}$ pronounced as "sophos" stands for "Scalable Optimal FOrward Secure Searchable Encryption" [37]. It also refers to the ancient Greek for "wise" as the author strongly believes that using a forward private SSE scheme is a wise choice.

The previous design in Sect. 4.1.3 uses nontrivial ORAM-related techniques, which brings a large bandwidth overhead on updates. $\Sigma_{o\phi o\varsigma}$ is a forward private SSE scheme achieving optimal computation and communication complexity, for both search and update operations. It depends only on some simple cryptographic tools—PRFs and trapdoor permutations. Hence, the scheme could be easily understood and implemented. The author also provided a well-written and open-source implementation of his scheme [36].

The author gave the formal definition of forward privacy as follows.

Definition 1 (Forward Privacy [37]) A $\mathcal{L}$-adaptively secure SSE scheme Σ is *forward private* if the update leakage function $\mathcal{L}^{\mathsf{Updt}}$ can be written as

$$\mathcal{L}^{\mathsf{Updt}}(\mathsf{op}, \mathsf{in}) = \mathcal{L}'(\mathsf{op}, \{(\mathsf{id}_i, m_{\mathsf{id}_i})\}),$$

where op is the operation type and $\{(\text{id}_i, m_{\text{id}_i})\}$ is the set of updated documents together with the number m_{id_i} of modified keywords for that document id_i.

The above definition slightly extends the informal description of forward privacy from the previous section Sect. 4.1.3, which puts attention only on *added* documents rather than both added and deleted documents.

General Ideas to Achieve Forward Privacy

Recall that we usually use an indexed list of matching documents $(\text{id}_0, \ldots, \text{id}_{n_w})$ for each keyword w. Then, every matching index id_c of this list is encrypted and stored at a (pseudorandom) location, which is denoted by $UT_c(w)$ as it is derived from c and w (and the client key). To add a document containing w, the client calculates the new location $UT_{n_w+1}(w)$ as the update token and then sends it together with the encrypted document to the server.

When the client searches for a keyword w, the server has to locate all the entries matching w via recomputing all the update tokens based on the search token sent by the client. To put it in another way, the update tokens of a given keyword w should be detached until a search token $ST(w)$ is given. In this case, the client generates the search token $ST_c(w)$ depending on the number c of matching documents. Meanwhile, he wants the search token $ST_c(w)$ to be detached to future update tokens, i.e., $UT_i(w)$ for $i > c$ due to the forward privacy requirement. Particularly, it also implies that the server is unable to produce $ST_i(w)$ from $ST_c(w)$ for $i > c$.

One simple way to achieve this goal is to generate all $ST_i(w) := F(w, i)$ where F is a PRF and sending them to the server. However, this approach is inadequate as it demands the client to send $O(n_w)$ tokens, which could be an issue on some mobile devices with limited communication resources. In [37], the author proposed an alternative way based on trapdoor permutations: the server can compute $ST_{i-1}(w)$ from $ST_i(w)$ via the public key, but only the client can compute $ST_{i+1}(w)$ from $ST_i(w)$ using his private key.

Figure 4.2 demonstrates the connections among those tokens and illustrates the high-level idea for the token generation. In short, only the client can apply the inverse of a one-way trapdoor permutation π to compute $ST_{c+1}(w)$ from $ST_c(w)$. Given the public-key PK, the server can do the opposite, i.e., computing all the tokens ST_i for $0 \leq i < c$ from the search token $ST_c(w)$. Finally, the server will derive the update tokens from the search tokens via a keyed hash function. Upon deletion, $\Sigma_{o\phi o\varsigma}$ uses a revocation data structure as well, i.e., the server stores the deleted ids and filters them out while returning the matching results.

In particular, the basic construction requires the client to store both $ST_c(w)$ and c for each updated keyword w. However, for many concrete trapdoor permutation implementations, including RSA and Rabin's squaring, $ST_c(w)$ will be pretty large. For example, for a 5.25-GB size EDB in their experiments, there are about 2.1×10^6 keywords. And if we store the latest search token for each keyword on the client side,

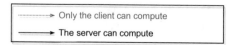

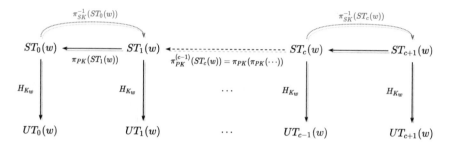

Fig. 4.2 Relations among tokens in $\Sigma_{o\phi o\varsigma}$ [37]

it will cost about 600 MB with a 2048-bit RSA scheme, which could be a problem in some constrained devices.

To reduce storage overhead, the client derives $ST_c(w)$ from the initial search token $ST_0(w)$. However, it looks very computationally expensive as it seems that the client has to iteratively compute π^{-1} for c times. Fortunately, in common trapdoor permutation constructions such as RSA, it is not the case. We can easily compute $ST_c(w)$ from $ST_0(w)$ according to its special properties. With this optimization, client storage can be reduced to 64 MB in the above example.

Performance and Leakage

The client storage is $O(W \cdot \log D)$ as each keyword could be contained in at most D documents, i.e., $c \leq D$. The computational complexity of $\Sigma_{o\phi o\varsigma}$ is optimal: $O(n_w)$ for search and $O(1)$ for update. All the dynamic SSE schemes we described are single round, which means that network latency will not affect their performance more than regular insecure protocols. The experiments in [37] showed that the server storage of $\Sigma_{o\phi o\varsigma}$ is only 12.5% of the forward private scheme in Sect. 4.1.3 [249] and 2.5 times more than the non-forward private scheme in Sect. 4.1.2 [48], which well balances the security and the performance of dynamic SSE.

For concise notation, [37] also defined the leakage function Hist(w) as all the modifications made to the set DB(w) over time, i.e., the *history* of keyword w. It consists of two elements DB(w) and UpHist(w), the former one is the set of document ids matching w at the setup stage, and the latter one is the set of updated documents matching w, called *update history*. For example, suppose we have two documents id_1 and id_2 containing the keyword w, and the document id_1 is added at the first update and deleted in the 11-th update, the document id_2 is added at the 4-th update. Then UpHist(w) = [(1, add, id$_1$), (4, add, id$_2$), (11, del, id$_1$)].

Upon a search operation, $\Sigma_{o\phi o\varsigma}$ leaks the search patterns $\mathsf{sp}(w)$ as well as $\mathsf{Hist}(w)$. Besides, $\Sigma_{o\phi o\varsigma}$ leaks nothing during the update stage.

Limitations Induced by Forward Privacy

With the introduction of forward privacy, there are also some downsides regarding efficiency.

On Storage Recall that all of the previous dynamic schemes we have described do not remove the keyword-document pairs from the encrypted index in the true sense, which is the absence of space reclamation in the searchable encryption. In such a case, the adversary will be able to determine that the deleted keyword has been searched in the past if the scheme reclaims space. One effective way to alleviate this problem is through rebuilding the encrypted indices periodically to cancel out those deleted items (e.g., the scheme in Sect. 4.1.3).

On Locality The study [46] has shown the impossibility of achieving minimal locality and optimal encrypted database $\Theta(N)$ at the same time. For dynamic schemes, forward privacy and locality are two conflicting notions. First, we note that locality only makes sense if the scheme does not access/modify a large part of EDB. Otherwise the accessing time for a large amount of data will become the dominant cost factor. We hence discuss SSE schemes whose search protocol will access a small amount of data. Under this assumption, forward privacy implies that the locations of inserted tokens will be independent of the locations of existing tokens matching the same keyword, which implies the independence of their locations. In other words, we cannot improve data locality unless we do some large modifications of EDB to regroup those index entries together, which in turn introduces a new performance overhead either during index updates or keyword searches.

Fortunately, the author [37] demonstrated that it is not a critical performance issue with modern SSDs without minimal locality. We will also cover the part of data locality shortly.

4.1.5 Handling Backward Privacy with Data Deletions

We note that all of the dynamic SSEs we have learned so far do reveal document indices that have been *logically* removed from the collection. Therefore, researchers have proposed another natural notion of security as *backward privacy*, i.e., matching entries after deletion will not be leaked.

It was initialized by Stefanov et al. [249] and later formalized by Bost et al. [38]. The authors proposed three formal definitions of backward privacy with different security levels as follows [38]:

I. Backward privacy with addition pattern. It leaks the documents *currently* matching w, when they were added, and the total number of updates on w.

II. Backward privacy with update pattern. Apart from the type I leakage, it additionally leaks when all the updates (including addition and deletion) on w happen (but not their content).

III. Weak backward privacy. Apart from the type II leakage, it additionally leaks which deletion operation canceled which addition operation.

Bost also built several schemes to satisfy different BP types. The high-level idea is to develop a cryptographic scheme that can revoke the master secrete key's ability to decrypt. With a revoked secret key on a tag list, the server can decrypt ids if the associated tags do *not* belong to the list. Otherwise, it fails. The design relied heavily on incremental puncturable encryption to achieve this functionality. The audiences can refer to [38] for the formal definitions and detailed constructions.

The strong security guarantees of backward privacy imply complicated and delicate scheme designs. There are numerous constructions [4, 38, 52, 78, 253, 271] focusing on different perspectives, including offering stronger security, eliminating extra round trips while executing a query, reducing computation or storage overhead, or extending its functionalities to other query types (e.g., range queries, Boolean queries). The means of providing backward privacy also varies. One line of works [38, 52, 78, 253] make use of powerful cryptographic primitives, e.g., symmetric puncturable encryption, ORAM, and homomorphic encryption; other approaches [4, 271] leverage the power of trusted hardware (e.g., Intel SGX) and rely on the security guarantee of trusted execution environments.

Because of their complexity, we just illustrate some well-known backward private DSSE designs in Table 4.1 for your reference. N denotes the total number of keyword/document pairs, D denotes the total number of documents, and W denotes the total number of distinct keywords in the document collection. For a keyword w, a_w denotes the total number of inserted documents containing w, d_w denotes the corresponding number of deletions, and $d = \max_{w \in W} d_w$. n_w is the size of search result matching w and $n_w = a_w - d_w$. $\tilde{O}$ notation hides poly-logarithmic factors, i.e., $f(n) \in \tilde{O}(g(n)) \Leftrightarrow \exists k : f(n) \in O\left(g(n) \cdot \log^k (g(n))\right)$.

4.2 Multiple-User Support

We then move to another important area in SSE—*multi-user searchable symmetric encryption* (MUSSE)—in which a data owner outsources the encrypted data to an untrusted cloud server, and then enables several other entities to execute specific queries on the encrypted data. This contrasts with the previous work we have discussed, where the data owner is the same as the data querier, and it extends the application range of searchable encryption to other fields, such as collaborative data sharing.

Table 4.1 Comparison of selected backward private dynamic SSE designs

Schemes	Communication			Computation		Client storage	Backward privacy
	#Rounds†	Search	Update	Search	Update		
Fort [4]	1	$O(n_w)$	$O(1)$	$O(n_w + \sum_w d_w)$	$O(\log^2 N)$	$O(W \log D)$	Type-I
Moneta [38]	3	$\tilde{O}(a_w \log N + \log^3 N)$	$\tilde{O}(\log^3 N)$	$\tilde{O}(a_w \log N + \log^3 N)$	$\tilde{O}(\log^2 N)$	$O(1)$	Type-I
Orion [52]	$O(\log N)$	$O(n_w \log^2 N)$	$O(\log^2 N)$	$O(n_w \log^2 N)$	$O(\log^2 N)$	$O(1)$	Type-I
Bunker-B [4]	1	$O(n_w)$	$O(1)$	$O(n_w)$	$O(1)$	$O(W \log D)$	Type-II
Fides [38]	2	$O(a_w + d_w)$	$O(1)$	$O(a_w + d_w)$	$O(1)$	$O(W \log D)$	Type-II
Mitra [52]	2	$O(a_w + d_w)$	$O(1)$	$O(a_w + d_w)$	$O(1)$	$O(W \log D)$	Type-II
SD_a [78]	2	$O(a_w + \log N)$	$O(\log N)$	$O(a_w + \log N)$	$O(\log N)$	$O(1)$	Type-II
SD_d [78]	2	$O(a_w + \log N)$	$O(\log^3 N)$	$O(a_w + \log N)$	$O(\log^3 N)$	$O(1)$	Type-II
Aura [253]	1	$O(n_w)$	$O(1)$	$O(n_w)$	$O(1)$	$O(Wd)$	Type-II
Bunker-A [4]	1	$O(n_w)$	$O(1)$	$O(a_w)$	$O(1)$	$O(W \log D)$	Type-III
Diana_{del} [38]	2	$O(n_w + d_w \log a_w)$	$O(1)$	$O(a_w)$	$O(\log a_w)$	$O(W \log D)$	Type-III
Janus [38]	1	$O(n_w)$	$O(1)$	$O(n_w d_w)$	$O(1)$	$O(W \log D)$	Type-III
Horus [52]	$O(\log d_w)$	$O(n_w \log d_w \log N)$	$O(\log^2 N)$	$O(n_w \log d_w \log N)$	$O(\log^2 N)$	$O(W \log D)$	Type-III
Janus++ [254]	1	$O(n_w)$	$O(1)$	$O(n_w d)$	$O(d)$	$O(W \log D)$	Type-III

†: The #Rounds here indicates the number of communication round trips required for the client to receive the document id

4.2.1 An Intuitive SSE Extension Supporting Multiple Users

The influential work [74] firstly took multi-user searchable symmetric encryption into account, and they also gave the formal definition and an efficient construction under this setting. Their construction takes the advantage of *broadcast encryption* to transfer a single-user SSE scheme to a multi-user one. Let $\mathcal{U}$ be the user space, i.e., the set of all possible user Us.

Definition 2 (Broadcast Encryption [92]) A broadcast encryption scheme BE is composed of the following four polynomial-time algorithms:

$mk \leftarrow$ Gen(1^λ) run by the data owner takes a security parameter λ as inputs and generates a master key mk;

$uk_U \leftarrow$ Add(mk, U) run by the data owner takes the master key mk and a user $U \in \mathcal{U}$ as inputs, adds the user U into valid user set G, and returns a user key uk_U;

$c \leftarrow$ Enc(mk, G, m) run by the data owner takes the master key mk, a set of users $G \subseteq \mathcal{U}$, and a plaintext m as inputs, and returns c as a ciphertext of m;

$m \leftarrow$ Dec(uk_U, c) run by the other entities (i.e., queriers or users and the server) takes a user key uk_U and a ciphertext c as inputs, decrypts and outputs either the plaintext m or the failure symbol $\perp$.

If no useful information about the message can be derived from its ciphertexts by any user not in G, then a broadcast encryption scheme is considered secure.

The multi-user construction is formally described in Algorithm 3 in detail. During the setup stage, it first generates the owner key, which consists of a key K for the underlying single-user scheme, a master key mk for the broadcast encryption scheme, and a key r for the PRP π. Then, the owner encrypts the database with a single-user SSE, which results in a secure index I and an encrypted document collection $\mathbf{c}$. After that, it generates a server state st_S composed of the broadcast encryption of r. Finally, the owner uploads the secure index I, encrypted documents $\mathbf{c}$, and the server states to the cloud server.

To authenticate a user to query on the encrypted data, the owner simply adds the user by generating a user key uk_U of the broadcast encryption scheme, and then shares uk_U together with the underlying single-user SSE key and the key r for the PRP function π.

To perform a keyword search, an authorized user first retrieves the server states st_S and tries to decrypt it, resulting in either an empty symbol $\perp$ or the key r of PRP π. The user then generates the search token t' of the single-user SSE with shared keys. Finally, it encrypts the token t' as t with the PRP π and its key r.

Upon receiving a search token t, the server first retrieves the key r, which is used to decrypt the wrapped search token using the PRP π, and then runs the underlying single-user SSE scheme to obtain the matching results.

To revoke a user from the authorized list, the owner randomly picks a new key r for encrypting search tokens and updates corresponding states in the server. Without

---

Algorithm 3 A multi-user SSE scheme [74]

Require: A broadcast encryption scheme BE $=$ (Gen, Add, Enc, Dec), a single-user SSE scheme SSE = (Gen, Enc, Trpdr, Search), a pseudo-random permutation π.

Setup(1^λ, G, DB):   ▷ Run by the data owner

  1: Generate $K \leftarrow$ SSE.Gen(1^λ), $mk \leftarrow$ BE.Gen(1^λ), $r \xleftarrow{\$} \{0,1\}^\lambda$;
  2: Set $G \leftarrow \{U_1, \ldots, U_m\} \bigcup \{S\}$ as the initial user group and the server;
  3: Compute $(I, \mathbf{c}) \leftarrow$ SSE.Enc$_K$(DB) and $st_S \leftarrow$ BE.Enc(mk, G, R);
  4: The data owner keeps $K_o = (K, mk)$, $st_O = r$ and sends EDB $= (I, \mathbf{c}, st_S)$ to the server.

Add(K_O, st_O, U):   ▷ Run by the data owner

  1: Compute $uk_U \leftarrow$ BE.Add(mk, U);
  2: **return** $K_U = (K, uk_U, r)$ to the user.

Revoke(K_O, st_O, U):   ▷ Run by the data owner

  1: Sample $r \xleftarrow{\$} \{0,1\}^\lambda$, $st_S =$ BE.Enc(mk, $G \backslash U$, r);
  2: The data owner updates $st_O = r$ and sends st_S to the server.

Trpdr(K_U, w):   ▷ Run by the querier

  1: Retrieve st_S from the server.
  2: **if** BE.Dec(uk_U, st_S) $= \perp$ **then**
  3:     **return** $\perp$;
  4: Compute $r \leftarrow$ BE.Dec(uk_U, st_S), $t' \leftarrow$ SSE.Trpdr$_K$(w);
  5: **return** $t \leftarrow \pi_r(t')$ to the server.

Search(st_S, I, t):   ▷ Run by the server

  1: Compute $r \leftarrow$ BE.Dec(uk_S, st_S), $t' \leftarrow \pi_r^{-1}(t)$;
  2: **return** $X \leftarrow$ SSE.Search(I, t').

---

the proper key r, a user cannot encrypt or wrap the search token correctly, and the server will not obtain any useful search token.

Performance and Security

The performance overhead of the search operation on the server side is relatively small, since only a pseudo-random permutation evaluation is necessary to determine whether the querier has been revoked or not. However, the interaction between the data owner and the users could be potentially costly due to the broadcast encryption scheme. Under this scheme, it is also difficult to allow a per-query-based interaction between the data owner and each individual user, where the owner only wants to grant a onetime search token to the user. Another possible downside is that once a corrupted user colludes with the adversarial server, then the entire secure index will be hurt and thus compromise the privacy of the data owner.

4.2.2   Multi-User Support with Search Token Distribution

Chase and Kamara [56] proposed a model for structured encryption which involves some complex structures such as labeled graph data. Besides, they also considered a multi-user setting with the concept "controlled disclosure," namely, the data owner provides another party the search token to reveal necessary information for the querier but nothing else. One potential application scenario is in the data analysis over a large-scale social network, the user can disclose only "pieces" of the entire network to help the server perform this task. It does not involve any user addition and revocation operations inherently, and thus saves the corresponding communication and computation costs. Due to structured data collection, they considered only single-keyword queries, and they were incapable of efficiently supporting more complex queries such as Boolean queries.

4.2.3   Multi-Writer Searchable Encryption Schemes

In addition to multiple readers (queriers) against one writer (data owner), researchers also proposed several searchable encryption schemes in which there are multiple writers and one reader by leveraging cryptographic primitives including public-key searchable encryption (PKSE), identity-coupling key-aggregate encryption, and homomorphic encryption.

In multiple-writer settings, the writer should be unable to decrypt ciphertexts encrypted by others. Otherwise, a "spy" or a compromised writer can easily recover all confidential documents by colluding with the server.

Generally speaking, public-key searchable encryption is inherently suitable for multiple writers, since each writer will take the public key of the reader to generate searchable ciphertexts. And the reader asks the cloud server to search over encrypted document collections to find matching keywords. It is nontrivial to design a sublinear (in the database size) search time PKSE scheme since each writer independently generates their ciphertexts, which forces the server to individually check each writer's encrypted document collection.

Xu et al. [291] derive the secret key for PKSE by noninteractive key exchange while searching for a keyword. As a result, it takes expensive pairing operations for each traversal during a keyword search, though it takes only u_w such operations with u_w denoting the number of updates on the keyword w. Furthermore, it is not forward private, i.e., an authorized search token over an old database version may be employed by an adversary to compromise the privacy of the newly submitted data by other honest writers.

Wang and Chow [278] proposed another multi-writer searchable encryption scheme achieving better search time by integrating a DSSE scheme into a PKSE scheme, which thus results in W public-key operations and u_w symmetric-key operations. Though the total operations are more than that of the scheme in [292],

W public-key operations here are less expensive and u_w symmetric-key operations are much cheaper. It also achieves epoch-based forward privacy by periodically rebuilding the encrypted document collection.

Aronesty et al. [12] also proposed another sublinear (potentially constant-time) PKSE scheme focusing on a different setting. In their setting, there is one secure but weak device (e.g., a phone) and one powerful but potentially insecure device (e.g., a desktop shared by several staffs). Each user/writer will generate large sensitive documents during their work. The writer may want to index them separately and encrypted, with the secret key kept on the trusted phone. In addition, each user may check whether a keyword w belongs to a document by obtaining a token from the desktop. But the phone (i.e., the user) should not learn anything else, and the desktop should not fool the phone by giving the wrong token. Their scheme can be distributed among n servers in a noninteractive, verifiable, and resilient way. Furthermore, their solution has been deployed in a commercial complication by Atakama.

Since the above constructions involve other advanced cryptographic primitives and other intricate techniques, audiences interested in the concrete designs can refer to their papers accordingly.

4.3 Boolean Query Support

Another one of the most common functionalities in a search system is Boolean search, namely, to find documents satisfying a given (possibly) complex keyword conditions. Before introducing how to support arbitrary Boolean search, we first delve into conjunctive search supports, i.e., to find documents containing *all* given keywords rather than a particular keyword. Obviously, we can reduce this problem to the single-keyword case by combining the intersection of resultant sets returned by each single-keyword search. However, this trivial solution has two major drawbacks:

1. Inefficient search complexity, e.g., if one of the conjunctive terms is "gender = female," then it will return about half of the entire data collection;
2. Significant information leakage, e.g., it will reveal the access pattern and the number of matching documents for *each* keyword.

Other searchable encryption solutions (using FHE or ORAM) supporting conjunctive search and eliminating those leakages require computation linear in the total number of documents in the encrypted database, which is impractical and inflexible in large-scale databases. In addition, none of the above constructions support general Boolean queries or free-text search. Namely, all of them work only for structured key-value type databases.

Cash et al. [47] proposed the first SSE design, the OXT protocol, which efficiently supports conjunctive searches as well as arbitrary Boolean queries on arbitrarily structured data, by allowing a much better leakage profile than the naive solution as described above.

In addition to the rich functionality, the OXT protocol can be extended to the *multi-user* setting, and users thus can perform more complex queries on the encrypted data with the search tokens provided by the data owner.

We will then elaborate on how to support arbitrary Boolean queries as well as the multi-user setting via the OXT protocol [47]. The authors first introduced an abstract data structure called a tuple set, or *T-set*. The intuition behind T-set is to associate each keyword with a list of fixed-size data tuples, and later use a token generated by the corresponding keyword to retrieve the list. It is used as an "expanded inverted index." Particularly, a T-set instance is composed of a tuple of three algorithms as follows:

TSetup(T)   takes as input an array $\mathbf{T}$ of lists indexed by the keyword $w \in \mathcal{W}$. Namely, $\mathbf{T}[w]$ is a list $\mathbf{t} = (t_1, \ldots, t_{n_w})$. It will output a tuple (TSet, K_T), i.e., the underlying data structure TSet and its key K_T.

TSetGetTag(K_T, w)   takes as input the key and a keyword w and outputs a tag stag used in retrieval.

TSetRetrieve(TSet, stag)   takes as input the TSet and a tag stag, and returns the list $\mathbf{t}$ corresponding to the keyword w.

In fact, prior SSE schemes we have learned can be treated as instantiating the T-set as the inverted index to enable search. More specifically, it uses each keyword $w \in \mathcal{W}$ as keywords in the T-Set, and encode identifiers (ids) of documents containing w as the list $\mathbf{t}$ corresponding to w. The details are illustrated as the black text in Algorithm 4 together with some intuition and brief explanations following "▷" sign. We note that the basic design is almost the same as the one in Sect. 4.1.2.

4.3.1 Extension Basis

To enable conjunctive keyword search, we first begin with a straightforward extension. To perform a conjunctive search $\overline{w} = (w_1, \ldots, w_n)$, the user first chooses a term w_i with an (estimated) least frequency among $\overline{w}$, namely, with the smallest $|DB(w_i)|$; w.l.o.g., we assume it is is w_1. Then, we aim to reduce both computation complexity and leakage function to a quantity connected with the least frequent term w_1. Note that it is common to have such terms in classical Boolean queries: in relational databases, users can use statistics about attributes to choose the least frequent term; or in the free-text setting, one may use Zipf's law or a small state stored in the user devices. The evaluation in [47] has shown that a state less than 100 KB suffices for the user to keep that information.

A naive solution is to retrieve all documents matching w_1 from the server, and then search for the remaining conjunctive words on the user side. It is not efficient, since it may retrieve many more documents than the actual results. The intuition here is to ask the server to retrieve TSet(w_1) and then find the intersection of conjunctive

---

Algorithm 4 BXT: Basic Cross-Tags Protocol

Text in blue indicates changes from a single-word case to a conjunctive query

Setup(DB):
1: Select keys K and K_X for PRF F and f;
2: Initialize **T** to an empty array; Initialize XSet as an empty set;
3: **for** each $w \in \mathcal{W}$ **do**   ▷ Build the list **T**[w] and XSet
4:     Initialize **t** as an empty list, and set $K_e \leftarrow F(K_S, w)$, xtrap $\leftarrow F(K_X, w)$;
5:     **for** each id $\in$ DB(w) **do**   ▷ In random order
6:         Compute $e \leftarrow$ Enc(K_e, id) and append e to **t**;
7:         Compute xtag $\leftarrow f$(xtrap, id) and insert xtag to XSet;
8:     **T**[w] $\leftarrow$ **t**;
9: (TSet, K_T) $\leftarrow$ TSetup(**T**);
10: **return** The key $K = (K_S, K_X, K_T)$ and EDB = (TSet, XSet).

Trpdr($K, w_1, w_2, \ldots, w_n$):
1: Parse K as (K_S, K_X, K_T), and compute $K_e \leftarrow F(K_S, w_1)$, stag $\leftarrow$ TSetGetTag(K_T, w_1);
2: For $i = 2, \ldots, n$, set xtrap$_i \leftarrow F(K_X, w_i)$;
3: **return** token = (stag, K_e, xtrap$_2, \ldots,$ xtrap$_n$).

Search(token):
1: Parse token as (stag, K_e, xtrap$_2, \ldots,$ xtrap$_n$);
2: Initialize the matching set $S \leftarrow \emptyset$, and set **t** $\leftarrow$ TSetRetrieve(TSet, stag);
3: **for** each ciphertext $e \in$ **t do**
4:     Compute id $\leftarrow$ Dec(K_e, e);
5:     If f(xtrap$_i$, id) $\in$ XSet, $\forall i = 2, \ldots, n$ **then** $S \leftarrow S \cup \{$id$\}$; ▷ Check if id containing w_i
6: **return** the matching results S.

---

terms at the server as well, who will then send the documents matching all keywords back only. To achieve this, we improve in the following ways.

We first explain the terminology *s-term* and *x-term*. The authors use s-term (small term) to refer to the estimated least frequent keyword, and x-term (cross term) to refer to the other terms in the conjunction $\overline{w}$. During the setup stage, we build another set XSet to include encrypted tags for each keyword-id pair. Specifically, it first computes a value xtrap $= F(K_X, w)$ for each keyword w, and then computes a tag xtag $= f$(xtrap, id) for each id $\in$ DB(w), where both F and f are PRFs. The server cannot infer the original ids and keywords based only on xtrap or xtag.

To perform a conjunctive search $\overline{w}$, the user chooses the estimated least frequent keyword w_1 and computes the key K_e and the tag stag as normal. In addition, it also computes values xtrap$_i \leftarrow F(K_X, w_i)$, and sends them all together to the server. Upon receiving the search token, the server uses stag to retrieve the encrypted id list matching w_1, and then decrypts id with the key K_e. After that, the server checks whether f(xtrap$_i$, id) $\in$ XSet for all the remaining keywords ($i = 2, \ldots, n$). Finally, it sends survived ids back to the user. The detailed modifications are shown as the blue text in Algorithm 4.

The intuition behind this protocol is to check if the keyword w_1 appears in a pair with another keyword w_i. If it holds for all the remaining keywords ($i = 2, \ldots, n$), then the document id contains all terms in the conjunction. Otherwise, it's not. It is easy to verify the correctness since any document id including a keyword w could be represented by xtag *if and only if* xtag $= f(\text{xtrap}, \text{id}) \in$ XSet.

The cost of search operation in the server side is proportional to $n \cdot |\text{DB}(w_1)|$, which is a significant improvement compared with either a linear scan of the entire index set or the total number of documents matching each keyword (i.e., $\sum_{i=1}^{n} |\text{DB}(w_i)|$ as $|\text{DB}(w_1)|$ is the least frequent term).

However, this solution directly reveals the set of ids matching the s-term (i.e., w_1). However, the server still learns statistics about x-terms by accumulating information revealed from different searches. For instance, if the server observed two queries (w_1, w_2) and (w'_1, w'_2), the server could then learn the results of (w_1, w'_2) (and (w'_1, w_2)). As it learns matching ids of w_1 as well as xtrap_2, it can then compute xtag $= f(\text{xtrap}_2, \text{id})$ and check if it exists in XSet.

We note that the above leakage is potentially harmful and it is still necessary to improve the security guarantee further. A simple method to fix the leakage is to add one more round, in which the user decrypts ids in the list **t** and then computes and sends xtags back to the server. This approach, in addition to increasing network latency, allows the server to cheat by sending other encrypted id values back, and is inappropriate with multi-user settings either (as the querier will learn extra ids matching the s-term but not the conjunction).

4.3.2 Oblivious Cross-Tags (OXT) Protocol

To solve the above issues, [47] used a form of *oblivious shared computation between user and server* to substitute the function $f(\text{xtrap}, \cdot)$. In particular, the protocol uses *blinded exponentiation* (inspired by Diffie-Hellman-based oblivious PRF) and some precomputation in the setup stage. It slightly increases the communication and computation costs, which are still affordable in practice. Meanwhile, it is a single-round protocol and the costs scale with $|\text{DB}(w_1)|$.

The benefit from the extra computation and communication efforts is the significant reduction of information leaked. With respect to intra-query leakage, if the user sends xtag_i in the same order for all $i = 2, \ldots, n$, then the server can infer the number of documents matching sub-conjunction including w_1 and any subset of $w_2, \ldots, w_n$. If the user applies a (pseudo-) random permutation for xtags, then the server will only learn the maximal number of satisfied terms per tuple in $\text{TSet}(w_1)$.

Regarding inter-query leakage, it is only possible for the adversary to learn the intersection between any two queriers only if they have the same x-terms but different s-terms, and both s-terms occur in the same document. The only other leakage (in addition to the single-keyword case) is whether two queries have the same s-term w_1 and the volume information $|\text{DB}(w_1)|$. For detailed and precise descriptions of the OXT protocol and corresponding leakage functions, audiences can refer to their research paper [47].

4.3.3 Processing Boolean Queries

We then describe how to extend the OXT protocol to handle *arbitrary* Boolean queries. Recall that the above conjunctive search procedure could be roughly divided into the following two steps:

1. Execute a classic SSE search algorithm to retrieve the document set **t** matching the first term, i.e., s-term;
2. Filter out unsatisfied documents in **t** *individually* with the help of xtraps.

A key observation is that whether a term satisfies the given Boolean formula is independent of the others except the first term. We can hence easily support any Boolean expressions as long as it can be expressed as $w_1 \wedge \phi(w_2, \ldots, w_n)$ where ϕ is an arbitrary Boolean formula. For instance, the user searches for documents matching the expression $w_1 \wedge (w_2 \vee \neg w_3)$. The first step retrieves five documents $\mathsf{id}_1, \ldots, \mathsf{id}_5$, which means that they contain the keyword w_1. And the second step shows that w_2 is contained in the documents id_1, id_3, and id_4, while w_3 is contained in id_5 only. Then, the server can easily verify that $\mathsf{id}_1, \ldots, \mathsf{id}_4$ satisfy the Boolean formula $w_2 \vee \neg w_3$, i.e., a document containing w_2 or not containing w_3. Finally, the surviving four documents will be returned to the user.

We are now able to solve all Boolean formulas that can be regrouped or re-expressed as the above form $w_1 \wedge \phi(w_2, \ldots, w_n)$, where ϕ is an arbitrary Boolean formula. If there are multiple w_1 candidates, the user will choose the least frequent one as the s-term to improve performance and reduce information leakage.

However, not all Boolean formulas could be expressed in the above form, e.g., $\neg w_1$, $w_1 \vee w_2$, etc. To handle those Boolean queries, we will treat them as $\mathrm{True} \wedge \phi(w_1, \ldots, w_n)$, which is converted to the above case and handled correspondingly, though the performance degrades to the case where all documents will be selected in the first step.

To enable multi-user search, one can ask the data owner to provide the search token, or use it as the underlying single-user SSE scheme in the first multi-user SSE scheme we have discussed.

4.4 Performance Optimizations

Searchable symmetric encryption schemes enable a client to store a database on an untrusted server while supporting keyword search securely. Despite people having built some asymptotically optimal SSE schemes, there are several directions to improve their practical performance, including spatial locality, parallelism, page efficiency, etc. An identical set of algorithms with different implementations will likely have different operational efficiencies. In this section, we will focus on optimizations based on the schemes we have learned, to investigate potential efficiency improvements.

4.4.1 Constructions Supporting Data Locality

In a hard disk drive (HDD), a magnetic head moves in an arc across spinning platters to read or write data. Compared with random accesses to the disk, which ask the heads and platters to *frequently* move and spin after each access to adjust to the correct physical address, sequential accesses do not demand the heads to move around except for the first move to the start address, and the platters only need to spin for a small range to offer successively stored data blocks. Therefore, random operations on an HDD are intrinsically slower than sequential operations.

Empirically, random accesses are several times (e.g., $5 \times -10\times$) slower than the sequential one. *Spatial locality* (also termed as data locality) refers to storing data elements within relatively close locations. To improve the performance of large-scale encrypted databases, it is important to improve the data locality of the inverted index (without increasing too much storage overhead).

Cash et al. [48] have shown that even an efficient dictionary instance will perform poorly when it is stored on a disk. Recall the basic scheme in Sect. 4.1.2 [48], each label-data (keyword-identifier) pair is (pseudo-)randomly distributed in a dictionary, which causes low data locality and significantly affects database efficiency when the index size exceeds the available memory space ($7\times$ slower according to their experiments). To better show the intuitions behind it, we split the entire locality optimization into three steps from a trivial one to a complete one as follows.

Reduce Dictionary Retrievals In the basic construction, we retrieve n_w (i.e., $|DB(w)|$) independent tags from the dictionary. To improve spatial locality, a simple idea is packing several identifiers ids into one block of ciphertext, which will be retrieved as a whole later. Specifically, we denote the block size as B, and we encrypt B identifiers into one encrypted block d with the same tag while building the result list. We pad the last block with dummy values up to the same size. Upon searching for a keyword w, the server works as normal except that it fetches and decrypts the results in blocks rather than individually.

Further Reductions with Pointers The above operation reduces the number of disk operations from n_w to $\lceil \frac{n_w}{B} \rceil$. However, there is a dilemma in choosing an appropriate block size B:

- If B is small, then it is still inefficient when processing a huge set $DB(w)$ as $\lceil \frac{n_w}{B} \rceil$ will not be reduced significantly.
- If B is large, then it will result in too much padding to small sets $DB(w)$ as $n_w \ll B$ and introduce many meaningless disk accesses.

We address this issue by introducing pointers into the scheme. In addition to compressing B identifiers into one block of B, we randomly store those blocks in another array instead of the dictionary. The dictionary now records encrypted blocks of b pointers to these external blocks. To perform a search, the server first fetches the encrypted pointers and then retrieves the inverted indices from the array accordingly.

Most Practical Version In real-world databases, the volume of documents matched by different keywords may vary dramatically, which complicates the optimization of data locality, since it is hard to find appropriate B and b giving acceptable trade-offs between the search time and index size (due to padding).

Therefore, [48] further modified their scheme to mitigate this issue. The key difference is to process and store sets $\mathrm{DB}(w)$ based on their sizes. The intuition behind this design is to distinguish $\mathrm{DB}(w)$ as *small*, *medium*, and *large*. For small $\mathrm{DB}(w)$, we directly store *packed* identifiers in the dictionary and thus reduce an unnecessary step of fetching blocks according to pointers. For $\mathrm{DB}(w)$ of medium size, we use blocks of pointers in the dictionary to locate identifiers in the external memory. Finally, for large sets, we adopted two levels of pointers: the dictionary holds pointers pointing to blocks of pointers that point to id blocks. The detailed description is given in Algorithm 5.

Algorithm 5 Locality optimization in [46]

Setup(DB):

1: $K \xleftarrow{\$} \{0, 1\}^\lambda$ allocate list L, array A;
2: **for** each $w \in \mathcal{W}$ **do**
3:     $K_1 \leftarrow F(K, 1||w), \ K_w \leftarrow F(K, 2||w)$;
4:     $T \leftarrow \lceil n_w/B \rceil$;
5:     **if** $n_w \leq b$ **then**   ▷ Small case: store ids in the dictionary as usual
6:         Pad $\mathrm{DB}(w)$ to b elements;
7:         $l \leftarrow F(K_1, 0), \ d \leftarrow \mathsf{Enc}(K_2, \mathrm{DB}(w))$;
8:         Add (l, d) to L;
9:     **else**   ▷ Medium or large cases
10:         Partition $\mathrm{DB}(w)$ into B-blocks $I_1, \ldots, I_T$;
11:         Pat I_T up to B elements;
12:         Choose random empty indices $i_1, \ldots, i_T$ in A;
13:         **for** $j = 1, \ldots, T$ **do**   ▷ Store ids in array
14:             $d \leftarrow \mathsf{Enc}(K_2, I_j); \ A[i_j] \leftarrow d$;
15:         **if** $T \leq b$ **then**   ▷ Medium case: store pointers in the dictionary
16:             Pad $\{i_1, \ldots, i_T\}$ to b elements;
17:             $l \leftarrow F(K_1, 0); \ d' \leftarrow \mathsf{Enc}(K_2, i_1 || \cdots || i_b)$;
18:             Add (l, d) to L;
19:         **else**   ▷ Large case: store pointers in the array and store pointer-to-pointers in the dictionary
20:             $T' \leftarrow \lceil T/B \rceil$;
21:             Partition $\{i_1, \ldots, i_T\}$ into b-blocks $J_1, \ldots, J_{T'}$;
22:             Pad $J_{T'}$ to B elements;
23:             Choose random empty indices $i'_1, \ldots, i'_{T'}$ in A;
24:             **for** $j = 1, \ldots, T'$ **do**
25:                 $d \leftarrow \mathsf{Enc}(K_2, J_j); \ A[i'_j] \leftarrow d$;
26:             Pad $\{i'_1, \ldots, i'_{T'}\}$ to b elements;
27:             $l \leftarrow F(K_1, 0); \ d'' \leftarrow \mathsf{Enc}(K_2, i'_1 || \cdots || i'_b)$;
28:             Add (l, d'') to L;
29: Set $\gamma \leftarrow \mathsf{Create}(L)$;
30: **return** the client key K and $\mathrm{EDB} = (\gamma, A)$.

Concretely, if we have fixed parameters b and B, then sets $DB(w)$ with $n_w \leq b$ are classified as small, sets $DB(w)$ with $b < n_w \leq b \cdot B$ are classified as medium, and the remaining sets are treated as large. Note that we always set b and B such that $n_w \leq b \cdot B^2$ for all n_w, since two levels of pointers will be efficient enough.

The experiments conducted by Cash and Tessaro [46] demonstrated dramatic performance improvements (over thousands of times) compared to previous basic designs. Furthermore, this kind of locality optimization also applies to other query types (e.g., conjunctive queries in Sect. 4.3). We leave concrete constructions and implementations to audiences for practice.

4.4.2 Some Impossibility Results Regarding Data Locality

We noticed that to achieve better data locality in the above example, we have to pay some costs in other dimensions; e.g., we may store extra dummy values in the last block, or use extra space to keep pointers (or two levels of pointers) in the dictionary. Both approaches increase the *storage overhead* of the original scheme. Another important dimension in evaluating the efficiency of an SSE scheme is its *read efficiency*, or in other words, the amount of data needed to answer each query. Therefore, one question arises naturally:

Can we build a searchable symmetric encryption scheme that
enjoys optimal locality, space overhead, and read efficiency at the same time?

Unfortunately, [46] have shown that it is impossible to simultaneously obtain the optimal results in three dimensions without revealing any information about keywords that the client has not searched for. Any secure SSE scheme must be suboptimal in either its locality, space overhead, or read efficiency. We will describe the sketch proof of the lower bound as follows.

Firstly, let's assume the SSE scheme has optimal locality and read efficiency, namely, the server always accesses only one consecutive region with exactly $\lambda \cdot n_w$ bits from EDB when searching for a keyword w (λ is the security parameter). One can easily verify that it is the minimum data to answer a query. Secondly, we assume all reads have no intersection (i.e., perfectly disjoint).

Then, two databases DB_0, DB_1 with the same size will be provided to the adversary, such that DB_0 has keywords matching a large portion of the database while DB_1 does not. After that, the adversary will search for tokens whose keywords match relatively few documents. By observing the access patterns, there will be large regions in DB_0 being not accessed due to its perfect locality. However, it could not be the case for DB_0 (e.g., the accessed regions are evenly distributed along with the storage). Therefore, the above scenario allows the adversary to distinguish two cases and thus break the security guarantees.

Fortunately, we could construct SSE schemes enjoying nearly optimal space overhead, locality, and read efficiency. In particular, [77] have proposed an SSE scheme with $O(N \log N / \log L)$ space, L locality, and $O(1)$ read efficiency which matches the lower bound proved by Asharov et al. [13], where the locality is quantified as the number of noncontiguous memory locations. Besides, to achieve optimal $O(N)$ space and $O(1)$ locality, [13] constructed an SSE scheme with $\omega(1) \cdot \epsilon(n)^{-1} + O(\log \log \log N)$ read efficiency, which only adds a $O(\log \log \log(N))$ overhead to the known lower bound $\omega(1) \cdot \epsilon(n)^{-1}$. Asharov et al. [13] have pointed out that $\omega(1)$ could be set to any super-constant function (e.g., $\log \log \log \log N$, which is pretty small even for large N).

4.4.3   Taking into Account Page Efficiency

The initial attention to the study of page efficiency in SSE [35] is that the locality is no longer a good indicator of practical performance due to the increasing prevalence of new storage media such as solid-state drives (SSDs). Instead of spinning disks or moving heads, SSDs use semiconductor chips to read and write data. These semiconductors are divided into pages that are operated as a whole. Since they do not contain any moving parts, their speed is far greater than that of a traditional HDD, and sequential accesses do not have an obvious advantage over random accesses. Therefore, SSD performance is primarily determined by *page efficiency*, that is, operating as few pages as possible. Or, more formally, the page efficiency of an SSE scheme is the number of pages accessed to perform a query, divided by the number of pages for an optimal plaintext solution. Bossuat et al. [35] have demonstrated the effectiveness of page efficiency as a predictor in SSDs by experiments as well.

Let's take the basic construction in [46] as an example again. For convenience, we denote the number of elements per page as p. *Page cost* $a \cdot X + b$ indicates that the discussed scheme needs to access at most $a \cdot X + b$ pages to perform a query, while that of an optimal plaintext solution is X. And the page efficiency is simply $\lceil \frac{a \cdot X + b}{X} \rceil$. To process a search for keyword w, the page cost for an plaintext database $X = \frac{n_w}{p}$. The page cost of their base scheme is $O(n_w)$ or $O(p \cdot X)$ since it is very likely to store each inverted index on different pages. And the page efficiency is thus $O(p)$.

The packing scheme we have learned in [46] optimizes the page efficiency to $O(1)$ by packing groups of indices of a keyword into one page. However, the worst case of their storage efficiency will be $O(p)$ if the vast majority of keywords match only few documents resulting in quite expensive padding, up to a factor p in storage in the worst scenario. Therefore, it raises a question: is it possible to offer both (nearly) optimal page efficiency and storage efficiency?

Bossuat et al. [35] gave a positive answer to this question by constructing a page-efficient SSE scheme, named **Tethys**, which achieves page cost $2X + 1$ or page efficiency 3, and storage efficiency $3 + \epsilon$ with a client stash of size $O(p \log \lambda)$. In addition, they also provided two variants to offer different trade-offs between page efficiency and server storage. Particularly, to have a smaller server storage $1 + (\frac{2}{e})^{t-1}$, the page efficiency will be amplified to $2t + 1$.

Their experiments have shown that the packing scheme with an appropriate pack size could achieve competitive throughput and page efficiency but at the huge expense of server storage—it costs more than one hundred times of the Tethys storage. Meanwhile, Tethys outperforms the schemes which achieve nearly optimal locality and storage, with over 170 times higher throughput. The averagely small client stash is independent of the size of the database, though the possible maximum stash size is about $100\times$ larger, which is still affordable in practice. Their designs mainly depend on a combinatorial problem, called *Data-Independent Packing* (DIP). For the detailed description and analysis, we recommend our audiences to their full paper [35].

4.4.4 Constructions Supporting Parallel Search Execution

Due to advances in multicore architectures, researchers have started to design explicitly parallelizable and dynamic searchable encryption schemes. Kamara and Papamanthou [152] proposed the dynamic and parallelizable SSE scheme achieving sublinear search time $O(\frac{n_w}{p} \cdot \log D)$, where p is the number of processors. However, their design is based on a tree-based multi-map data structure—the keyword red-black tree, which is complicated and requires large index space (i.e., $O(D \cdot W)$). The speedup of parallelism is limited if the database contains many documents, as $\log D$ may be greater than the number of processors available.

We again take the famous SSE construction [46] as an example. It is trivial to make the search process parallel with any number of processors as long as the dictionary allows parallel read accesses. Each thread simply starts from different counters c, computes $F(K_1, c)$, fetches, and decrypts the ciphertext independently. The main thread will merge those result sets after all threads are done. With the advantage of multicore architectures, the search complexity can be further reduced to $O(n_w/p)$.

However, the search process in Algorithm 1 based on "linked list" could not be easily parallelized since entries matching the keyword are sequentially arranged, and the key to decrypt the next entry is planted in the current one. Hence, one may not be able to fetch the i-th matching identifier by skipping the previous entries.

4.5 Summary and Further Reading

In this chapter, we aim to provide an easy-to-understand and exciting introduction to recent advancements in functionality and performance, so omit a lot of formalization and proofs. *Forward privacy* was for the first time explicitly considered by Stefanov et al. [249]. The authors built in their paper a dynamic, sublinear scheme achieving forward privacy. After that, [37] gave the formal definition of forward security, and [167] gave a generalized version [167]. Security (e.g., security against chosen keyword attacks, forward security) is established by formally confining the leakage.

Regarding updates, *backward security* guarantees that deleted results will be indeed inaccessible to the server afterward. Bost et al. [38] define three levels of backward security. The techniques for backward security are still evolving [52, 117]. In particular, [253] proposed the first non-interactive and practical Type-II backward-secure dynamic SSE scheme which does not rely on trusted execution environments.

The first security definition for multi-user searchable symmetric encryption was proposed by Curtmola et al. [74]. Since then there has been a plethora of follow-up works: [147] and [251] extended the protocol that supports Boolean queries with a single user [47] to the multi-user setting. They addressed problems of authorization in this scenario as well as hiding the query keywords from the data owner in addition to the server.

Most works, however, consider only the cloud server as the adversary that wishes to violate the privacy of data. The attack of [232] has shown a severe threat in MUSSEs where the users may collude with the adversarial server to compromise the privacy of the data owner. To eliminate the above threat, [131] modified the security definition in [223] and gave two constructions that achieve it. Meanwhile, constructions in [131] achieve an even stronger security notion, i.e., protecting the users against owner-server collusion where they wish to learn which keywords are being searched. Furthermore, [216] constructed another MUSSE to avoid storage blowup and achieve better efficiency with small cross-user leakage. Rompay et al. [231] proposed a scheme combining private information retrieval and bilinear pairings. Subsequently, [234] proposed a more efficient construction based on Bloom filters and oblivious transfer techniques. They further improved its efficiency in [233] by leveraging a Diffie-Hellman key exchange protocol.

Another large domain in searchable encryption we omit in this book is the support of various types of queries. Order-preserving encryption was first proposed by Agrawal et al. [1] in 2004 to "encrypt" numerical values into ciphertexts without losing their order, i.e., for any plaintext $a < b$, their ciphertexts preserve the original order $c_a < c_b$. To improve the security of OPE schemes to hide the plain order of ciphertexts, [34] proposed an order-revealing encryption scheme, in which the encrypted data have no particular order and it uses a delicate comparison function to compare two ciphertexts. Bogatov et al. [26] analyzed and compared several well-known ORE-based range query protocols in both theoretical and experimental ways. Another useful search functionality is to allow users to search documents *approximately* matching the keyword, i.e., fuzzy search, which was first studied under the encrypted search context by Li et al. [174]. Since then, several later constructions have been proposed [27, 97, 181, 274, 277, 279, 298], with efforts trying to improve accuracy and efficiency or combine with other functionalities (e.g., multiple keywords). Besides, ranked search and other functionalities [44, 126, 257, 272, 276] also attract extensive attention from researchers.

Chapter 5
Security Impact of Leakage Profiles: Threats and Countermeasures

In Chap. 3, we discussed the security definitions of searchable encryption. In short, an SE scheme is said to achieve adaptively semantic security with a leakage function $\mathcal{L}(\cdot)$ if the information revealed during its operation is bounded by $\mathcal{L}(\cdot)$. Typically, allowed leakages include the size of encrypted data collection, whether a search token (trapdoor) has been repeated, which encrypted documents have been accessed, etc. In the extreme case, we can claim that a trivial plaintext solution *is* secure with $\mathcal{L}(\text{DB}, w_1, \ldots, w_t) = (\text{DB}, w_1, \ldots, w_t)$, i.e., it leaks all plaintext data, though this leakage function is meaningless since it obviously reveals confidential data to the untrusted server. Indeed, it is up to the system administrator or users to determine whether information captured by the leakage function will compromise user privacy or not.

As we have mentioned in Chap. 3, at the time those basic SSE schemes were proposed, it seemed that revealing the individual size of encrypted files, which encrypted files match the queried token, and whether a token has ever been queried before, does not appear to be that much harmful. Meanwhile, under this assumption of "reasonable" information leakage, SSE constructions could perform pretty well even on large-scale datasets.

However, in this chapter, we will soon find that an adversary with reasonable background knowledge of the encrypted dataset can exploit the aforementioned common leakage patterns to *effectively* recover underlying documents or private queries. After becoming aware of potential risks existing in those leakages, researchers soon proposed many approaches trying to find the right balances among security, performance, and functionality. Since then, the arms race of searchable encryption between defense and offense has kicked off and is still in progress.

In this chapter, we will first introduce and define common leakage patterns and other background information in Sect. 5.1. Then, we introduce several early but important leakage-abuse attacks by assuming that an adversary will *passively* observe the system operation in Sect. 5.2. Then, we move on to attacks by *actively* injecting some specially designed files in Sect. 5.3, as well as attacks with respect

K. Ren, C. Wang, *Searchable Encryption*, Wireless Networks,
https://doi.org/10.1007/978-3-031-21377-9_5

to other dimensions in Sect. 5.4, and some effective and notable countermeasures in Sect. 5.5. Finally, we will also provide suggested further readings under this topic in Sect. 5.6.

5.1   Understanding Leakage Profiles

We first briefly recall the security definition here. In a searchable encryption scheme Π, the *leakage profile* captures the information an adversary may obtain. Π is said to be *secure* if for all adversary $\mathcal{A}$ with some constraints (e.g., probabilistic polynomial time—PPT), there exists a (PPT) simulator $\mathcal{S}$ which takes as input the leakage profile $\mathcal{L}(\cdot)$ and returns output in the same format of Π, $\mathcal{A}$ cannot distinguish $\mathcal{S}$ and Π with all but negligible probability.

The adversary plays the role of an untrusted server, and the simulator plays the role of the client, which means that no adversary can learn any information beyond the given leakage profile/function $\mathcal{L}(\cdot)$ from the outputs or during the operations of Π.

A leakage profile consists of multiple *leakage patterns*, which are (families of) functions over the diverse spaces associated with the underlying data collections. We first list several well-known leakage patterns concluded by Blackstone et al. [23] as follows:

Search pattern   (or query equality pattern) is the function family $\mathsf{qeq} = \{\mathsf{qeq}_{\lambda,t}\}_{\lambda,t\in\mathbb{N}}$, where $\mathsf{qeq}_{\lambda,t} : \mathcal{D}_\lambda \times \mathcal{W}_\lambda^t \mapsto \{0,1\}^{t\times t}$ reveals if and when queries are equal: $\mathsf{qeq}_{\lambda,t}(\mathrm{DB}, w_1, \ldots, w_t) = M$, where $M[i,j] = 1$ if $w_i = w_j$, otherwise 0.

Access pattern   (or response identity pattern) is the function family $\mathsf{rid} = \{\mathsf{rid}_{\lambda,t}\}_{\lambda,t\in\mathbb{N}}$ with $\mathsf{rid}_{\lambda,t} : \mathcal{D}_\lambda \times \mathcal{W}_\lambda^t \mapsto [2^{[D]}]^t$ which reveals the identifiers matching each query w_i: $\mathsf{rid}_{\lambda,t}(\mathrm{DB}, w_1, \ldots, w_t) = (\mathrm{DB}(w_1), \ldots, \mathrm{DB}(w_t))$.

Response length pattern   is the function family $\mathsf{rlen} = \{\mathsf{rlen}_{\lambda,t}\}_{\lambda,t\in\mathbb{N}}$ with $\mathsf{rlen}_{\lambda,t} : \mathcal{D}_\lambda \times \mathcal{W}_\lambda^t \mapsto \mathbb{N}$ leaking the number of matching entries: $\mathsf{rlen}_{\lambda,t}(\mathrm{DB}, w_1, \ldots, w_t) = (n_{w_1}, \ldots, n_{w_t})$.

Co-occurrence pattern   is the function family $\mathsf{co} = \{\mathsf{co}_{\lambda,t}\}_{\lambda,t\in\mathbb{N}}$ with $\mathsf{co}_{\lambda,t} : \mathcal{D}_\lambda \times \mathcal{W}_\lambda^t \mapsto [D]^{t\times t}$ such that $\mathsf{co}_{\lambda,t}(\mathrm{DB}, w_1, \ldots, w_t) = M$ where $M[i,j] = |\mathrm{DB}(w_i) \cap \mathrm{DB}(w_j)|$ leaks the number of documents w_i and w_j both occur. This information can be deduced from rid and implies rlen.

Volume pattern   is the function family $\mathsf{vol} = \{\mathsf{vol}_{\lambda,t}\}_{\lambda,t\in\mathbb{N}}$ with $\mathsf{vol}_{\lambda,t} : \mathcal{D}_\lambda \times \mathcal{W}_\lambda^t \mapsto \mathbb{N}^t$ such that $\mathsf{vol}_{\lambda,t}(\mathrm{DB}, w_1, \ldots, w_t) = ((|\mathrm{doc}|)_{\mathrm{doc}\in\mathrm{DB}(w_1)}, \ldots, (|\mathrm{doc}|)_{\mathrm{doc}\in\mathrm{DB}(w_t)})$ leaks the bit length of matching entries.

Total volume pattern   is the function family $\mathsf{tvol} = \{\mathsf{tvol}_{\lambda,t}\}_{\lambda,t\in\mathbb{N}}$ with $\mathsf{tvol}_{\lambda,t} : \mathcal{D}_\lambda \times \mathcal{W}_\lambda^t \mapsto \mathbb{N}^t$ leaking the total bit length of matching entries:

$$\mathsf{tvol}_{\lambda,t}(\mathrm{DB}, w_1, \ldots, w_t) = \left(\sum_{\mathrm{doc}\in\mathrm{DB}(w_1)} |\mathrm{doc}|, \ldots, \sum_{\mathrm{doc}\in\mathrm{DB}(w_t)} |\mathrm{doc}| \right).$$

Additional patterns include $\mathsf{order}_{\lambda,t}(\mathrm{DB})$, the order of matching elements, and $\mathsf{rank}_{\lambda,t}(\mathrm{DB})$, the number of entities that are no greater than a specific value in a numerical collection.

Adversarial Model We also recall two types of adversarial models introduced in Sect. 1.1 as follows:

Snapshot adversaries only have snapshot accesses to the encrypted database and any associated ciphertexts. This captures attackers who corrupt a server and read its memory, or steal and transfer the encrypted data collections.

Persistent adversaries have long-term accesses to the entire encrypted database, the historical records of query and update operations, or even observing the query execution process. This captures an attacker who resides on a cloud server and observes all of its activities.

Target A leakage-abuse attack may target different information. For instance, an adversary may try to (partially) reconstruct the original data in a *data-recovery* attack, whereas in a *query-recovery* attack, it may try to (partially) reconstruct information about queries (e.g., query type, keywords).

Auxiliary Data Auxiliary information or knowledge is necessary for an adversary to launch leakage-abuse attacks. To be specific, a *known-data* attack demands a subset of the underlying plaintext of the encrypted data collection. On the other hand, a *sampled-data* attack demands some samples from a distribution statistically close to that of the target data, and the success rate of the attack is usually positively correlated with the quality of the samples A *known-query* attack demands the corresponding keywords of some search tokens.

Passive or Active In a passive attack, the adversary only observes the query execution. On the contrary, an adversary may actively interact with the user, e.g., inject well-designed data to boost its power.

5.1.1 A Leakage Hierarchy for SE

As you may already be a little confused after initial contact with the above various leakage patterns, we introduce four well-defined leakage profiles from [49] to characterize leakage profiles to help understand them. Besides the definitions, we describe the schemes that implement them and instantiate them as well. The descriptions are presented in order from the greatest leakage (L4) to the least (L1). It should also be noted that two dissimilar schemes may exhibit the same leakage profile. To avoid going into too much detail, we will only mention parts of SE schemes informally.

In-Place SE Schemes

We call the SE constructions of the first leakage profile as *in-place* schemes as they directly replace the plaintext keywords with encrypted ones. The untrusted server searches by going through every keyword for each encrypted document with the encrypted keyword granted by the client. Their implementations are quite straightforward, and they are of distinct interest due to their compatibility with many existing search APIs. This facilitates their deployment but results in more leakage.

Full-Text Substitution Cipher   This is the simplest approach to achieve searchable encryption and was proposed by Song et al. [245]. The client first extracts keywords in the document collection into the keyword set. Then, it encrypts each keyword with a *deterministic* cipher E, substitutes corresponding words in each document, and uploads the collection of ciphertexts. To search for a keyword w, the client sends its encryption, and the server scans the entire encrypted document collection to find matching ciphertexts. This type of schemes supports not only single-keyword searches but also Boolean and phrase queries. Nonetheless, stemming, wildcard, or approximate queries are not supported, as the server can only observe ciphertexts, which have no relation to the plaintext. Among all the schemes we discuss, these simple in-place schemes have the largest amount of information leakage. We define the corresponding leakage profile as:

L4:   *Full plaintext under deterministic word-substitution cipher [49].* The server learns the positions in the text where each keyword appears and how many times it appears in the documents.

Companies including Skyhigh Networks [199] make use of schemes with L4 leakage profile.

Appended-Keywords SE   Another type of searchable encryption schemes encrypt each document id with classic *randomized/probabilistic* symmetric encryption, and appends the following values to the resulting ciphertext:

$$F_K(\mathcal{W}(\text{id})[1]), \ldots, F_K(\mathcal{W}(\text{id})[m_i])$$

where K is a secret key and F_K is a PRF. The encrypted documents as well as appended hashed keyword lists are uploaded to the server. It is easy to search for a keyword w by sending the server encryption of w which will find all matches by a linear or index scan.

As discussed in detail in [132, 168], appended-keyword schemes offer the advantage of being legacy-compatible, i.e., the server can perform indexing on the uploaded keyword hashes, and it is easy to add or delete documents, etc. Besides, the client can perform stemming before extracting keywords.

This class of schemes does not offer additional hiding of occurrence patterns prior to the search. The server, therefore, can immediately learn co-occurrence patterns, the number of unique keywords in each document, ciphertext lengths, and the order of keyword appearance upon receiving the encrypted data collection. More formally, we present the following leakage profiles:

L3: *Fully revealed occurrence pattern with keyword order [49].* Using the conventional notions and fixing the order of keywords as $w_1, \ldots, w_W$, the profile outputs the sequence of sets:

$$\{(i, j) : \mathrm{doc}_i[j] = w_1\}, \ldots, \{(i, j) : \mathrm{doc}_i[j] = w_W\}.$$

The k-th set includes all pairs (i, j) in which the keyword w_k is the j-th term in the extracted keyword list of document i.

We stress that if one additionally includes repeats (i.e., allowing frequency-informed search), then the scheme would have L4 leakage.

In some appended PRF schemes, the PRF values are sorted before uploading. It improves the security of underlying schemes, as the sorting process hides the order of the first appearances of keywords in each document. The leakage is captured as follows:

L2: *Fully revealed occurrence pattern [49].* This profile is the same as leakage profile L3 except for the order of first occurrences of keywords. Formally, the profile outputs the sequence of sets:

$$\{i : w_1 \in \mathrm{doc}_i\}, \ldots, \{i : w_W \in \mathrm{doc}_i\}.$$

Inverted-Index SE

Most searchable encryption schemes we have learned are based on the inverted index. The client will set up an *inverted index* **I** before uploading the database, in which **I** includes lists of matching document identifiers for each keyword w. To perform a search, the client generates a per-query *trapdoor* or *token* and sends to the server. The trapdoor allows the server to decrypt *only* document ids matching target keyword. Unlike in-place substitution schemes, index-based schemes hide the word order that occurs in documents inherently.

Unencrypted Inverted Index   In this type of schemes, the document identifiers matching each keyword are sent to the server in plaintext. Though the document IDs are possibly generated with PRF and randomly permuted before upload, the server is still able to learn the exact document-keyword matrix, and thus obtain the co-occurrence matrix for all keywords and the length of result sets prior to any queries. In fact, this class of schemes has a leakage profile L2 as defined before. The main advantage is on the performance side: it only requires sublinear search time.

Encrypted Inverted Index Without Result Length Hiding   The main difference that distinguishes this type of schemes and the previous one is that each id list is encrypted as a whole, such that the same id presents differently in a different list.

The length of each list, however, is not protected. The server can still learn the size of result sets prior to any queries.

The client generates and sends a trapdoor for searching for a keyword w, which helps the server decrypt only matching entries. The server thus gains extra information of *searched* keywords, such as matching document ids and co-occurrence matrix for queries. Cash et al. [49] did not provide a separate leakage profile for this type of schemes. Instead, they put it under profile L1 as defined below:

Fully Length-Hiding SE   It provides the strongest security guarantee among those schemes considered in [49]. It additionally hides the size of individual result sets, so that the server learns nothing except the total size of the index before performing any queries. A solution completely hides result lengths without padding was first given in [74] by using an interwoven linked list. We define the smallest leakage profile of fully length-hiding SE as L1:

L1:   *Query-revealed occurrence pattern [49].* The same information is revealed as in the L2 profile, but only for terms that have been searched for. On this profile, initially only basic size information is leaked. When the server receives a trapdoor, it learns the access pattern of the query. Formally, when a sequence of queries $q_1, q_2, \ldots, q_t$ is issued, then the leakage profile includes the sequence of sets:

$$\{i : q_1 \in \mathrm{doc}_i\}, \{i : q_2 \in doc_i\}, \ldots, \{i : q_t \in doc_i\}$$

Depending on the concrete designs, the leakage function may randomly permute the indexes in order to conceal the initial connections between the ciphertexts and plaintexts. For each queried keyword, it leaks the number of matching documents. For accumulative queries, the profile reveals co-occurrence patterns.

An intuitive illustration of what the server "sees" before and after searching for the keyword "cat" for schemes with leakage profiles L4, L2, and L1 can be found in Fig. 5.1.

5.2   Exploit Leakage Profiles Against SE Schemes

Our leakage definitions tell people that our schemes do not reveal more information than the painted portrait. However, those definitions do not tell us if the leakage profile is exploitable or deleterious. It is trivial that people can easily infer some keywords in SE schemes with L4 profile via some statistical analysis. For example, if we encrypt this book with the abovementioned scheme, then the encrypted version of keywords "searchable" "encryption" will be quite frequent. Therefore, it is necessary for us to investigate them by showing some well-known attacks.

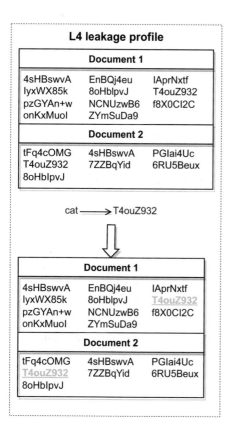

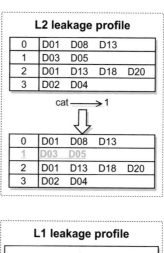

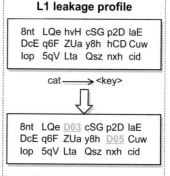

Fig. 5.1 Server's different views of searchable encryption schemes with L4, L2, and L1 leakage profiles before and after searching for the keyword "cat" [49]

5.2.1   Leveraging Co-Occurrence Pattern to Recover User Queries

Islam et al. [145] first studied the leakage-abuse attacks against searchable encryption schemes. They have shown that for an encrypted email repository, the adversary can exploit query co-occurrence patterns with few (5%) known queries to infer future queries. In particular, they exploit leakage patterns by solving an optimization problem that minimizes the distance between the estimated co-occurrence and the candidate. However, it is an NP-complete problem to find the optimal solution. The authors use a simulated annealing method to find an approximation.

To formulate their optimization problems, we first give some preliminary notions as follows. R_i is a vector of length D where $R_i[j] = 1$ if j-th document is in the result set for query q_i; otherwise, $R_i[j] = 0$. M is the co-occurrence frequency matrix estimated by the publicly available dataset. Besides, K_{a_i} is a unit vector with only i-th entry to be 1 and 0 elsewhere. a_i denotes the inferred keyword and w_i

denotes the actually searched keyword. Finally, a (small) subset $S \subset \mathcal{W}$ is known by the adversary. We then formulate the optimization problem as below:

$$\underset{a_1,\dots,a_t}{\arg\min} \sum_{q_i,q_j \in Q} \left(\frac{R_{q_i} \cdot R_{q_j}^T}{n} - \left(K_{a_i} \cdot M \cdot K_{a_j}^T \right) \right)^2 \tag{5.1}$$

$$\text{Constraints} : \forall j \text{ s.t. } q_j \in S, \ a_j = x_j$$

The constraint here guarantees that the correct keywords will be assigned to known queries, which helps check our solution. Their evaluations have demonstrated that only 5% of the keyword set is enough.

There are three major limitations in this work:

1. They evaluated only 2500 out of 77K+ keywords due to high time complexity to have a good recovery rate;
2. Auxiliary and test data are not independent; experiments in [49] show that it achieves 0% recovery rate with independent auxiliary data;
3. It is impractical to obtain 5% of the keyword set, which is about 4000 keywords in their entire email repository.

However, their seminal work did inspire many effective attacks we will discuss below.

5.2.2 The Count Attack

Cash et al. [49] proposed a simple COUNT attack that exploits the co-occurrence pattern to recover encrypted queries. There exist two versions of this attack. The first one is referred to as COUNT V.1 requiring partial plaintext and queries. Its original description was found to be buggy and was then fixed in an updated version, which leads to an improved variant, i.e., COUNT V.2 attack. Besides, the improved version only requires knowledge of partial data but no queries. COUNT V.2 builds a co-occurrence matrix based on the known data collection, and compares it with the observed co-occurrence matrix. The attack first identifies candidate matches via confidence intervals and then iteratively removes candidates who contradict previously confirmed matches.

If the number of documents matching each keyword is further known by adversaries, they can launch a more efficient and accurate query-recovery attack since expensive numerical optimization techniques are no longer necessary.

Attack Description

The adversarial server knows a keyword co-occurrence pattern co matrix C of size $t \times t$. Besides, we assume that the server knows the number of matching documents count(w)in the true document set for each keyword w. We will discuss how to launch an attack without the latter assumption as well.

We first observe that it is straightforward to associate a queried q with a keyword w if it has a unique result size count(q), by finding the keyword w s.t. count(w) = count(q). As indicated by Zipf's characterization of word distribution in natural language, the more frequently occurring keywords are more likely to have distinct result counts.

Of course, unique counts alone will not be able to recover many keywords that are singletons. Using this basic knowledge, the attack algorithm recovers queries that do not have unique results based on co-occurrence patterns. See Algorithm 6 for detailed description; some intuition and brief explanations are followed by a "▷" sign. We use a map $K = ((q_i, w_j), \dots)$ to store the association of query q_i to keyword w_j. When applying a set operator on K, we mean the set consists of q or w in K according to its context.

Algorithm 6 The COUNT attack algorithm [49]

Input: Plain-text keyword index Index, observed queries Q and results.

1: Compute co-occurrence counts C_q for observed queries and C_I for Index;
2: Initialize known-query map K with queries (q, w) having unique result counts;
3: **while** the size of the map K grows **do**
4:      **for** each unrecovered query $q \in Q - K$ **do**
5:          Set candidate keywords $S = \{w : \text{count}(w) = \text{count}(q)\}$;
                               ▷ The same count is necessary not sufficient
6:          **for** $w \in S$ **do**
7:              **for** known queries $(q', w') \in K$ **do**
8:                  **if** $C_q[q, q'] \neq C_I[w, w']$ **then**
                               ▷ The same co-occurrence count is also necessary
9:                      Remove w as $S \leftarrow S - \{w\}$;
10:      **if** $|S| = 1$ **then**   ▷ If $S := \{w\}$, otherwise break.
11:          Add (q, w) to K;

Since the co-occurrence matrix is hundreds or thousands of dimensions (i.e., t), it is extremely unlikely to have a false positive (namely, an incorrectly recovered query matches every entry in the true co-occurrence matrix). However, this informal argument does not hold for rarely occurring keywords. This reveals the drawback of COUNT attack: it only works for highly selective keyword searches, where the selectivity of a keyword w is simply the number n_w of matching documents. The experiments conducted by Kamara et al. [155] showed that for high selectivity setting, COUNT attack can recover 64% queries with 30% of the dataset. However, the success rate dramatically drops to 8% even with almost entire (90%) plaintext data in the low selectivity setting.

An effective and efficient countermeasure is to pad each inverted index list to the nearest multiple of an integer n with dummy values or fake IDs. The variation of n allows the user to adjust the security-space trade-off.

This simple countermeasure affects the attack in two aspects:

1. It reduces the number of unique results by expanding the candidate set for a given query;
2. It blocks the attack from being launched accurately, since the number of padded co-occurrences may exceed the number from the true document set.

At the extreme of setting n to be large enough such that no unique result count exists, then the count attack will fail completely. However, [49] modified the algorithm to allow an adversary to carry attacks out with less information. The generalization consists of the following two updates:

1. Instead of finding an exact match, it only requires the count falls within a window of the co-occurrences for the true documents;
2. The algorithm does not depend on initially finding queries with unique result counts, but on making an initial guess as to which candidate will match the query.

Practically, the generalized attack still works effectively with $3\times$ padding overhead, but completely fails with padding more than $7\times$ space overhead. Meanwhile, the COUNT attack demands the vast majority of queried keywords to be highly selective; otherwise, it will fail either.

5.2.3   *The* SUBGRAPH *Attack*

Due to the strong (impractical) assumptions on adversaries in the above attacks, [23] then proposed attacks relying on much weaker leakage profiles. The attacks rely on rid or vol leakage patterns, and the latter one even works against ORAM-based solutions.

Volume Analysis   It exploits the total volume pattern tvol, which is similar to the aforementioned frequency analysis. We map each unknown query to the keyword in the known keyword dataset having the *closet* total volume. This is based on the premise that keywords usually belong to documents with different volumes and the sum of volumes can thus be considered a feature of a keyword.

Specifically, the volume analysis takes a known dataset $\widetilde{DB}$ as auxiliary information and as leakage tvol $=$ $(DB, q_1, \ldots, q_t)$ $=$ $(v_1, \ldots, v_t)$, where $v_i =$ $\sum_{doc \in DB(q_i)} |doc|$. Then, it maps query q_i to the keyword $w \in \mathcal{W}$ having the closet *known* volume in $\widetilde{DB}$ to v_i, i.e., mapping q_i to

$$\arg\max_{w \in \mathcal{W}} \{\tilde{v}(w) : \tilde{v}(w) \le v_i\},$$

where $\tilde{v} = \sum_{\text{doc} \in \widetilde{\text{DB}}(q_i)} |\text{doc}|$.

Subgraph Attacks   We then describe the subgraph attack framework. In opposition to previous attacks, this framework exploits leakage patterns revealing information about *individual* matching record, including the response identity pattern (i.e., access pattern) and the (individual) volume pattern. For convenience, we refer to them as the *handle* of each matching document.

Setup   A high-level view of the attack treats the leakage pattern and the known dataset as two bipartite graphs. The vertices of a bipartite graph are split into two disjoint sets X and Y such that every edge connects a vertex in X and a vertex in Y. For the *leakage* bipartite graph, one part of the vertices are queries and the other part are handles (e.g., rid, vol). There is an edge connecting a query and a handle if and only if the handle is embodied in the query's leakage. For the *know-data* graph, the first (or left) vertex set consists of keywords, and the other (or right) set consists of handles again. Similarly, an edge connects a handle and a keyword if and only if the handle corresponds to the keyword in the known dataset. Note that the right vertices are identical in both graphs. The above operations correspond to the steps 2 and 3 in Algorithm 7.

Candidate Selection   The intuition behind the attacks is to find a subgraph mapping such that the *edge* distribution of both graphs is close. For instance, if there is a unique left vertex next to the same group of right vertices in each graph, then it is quite likely that the two vertices represent the same keyword. In particular, as the known data are a subset of the entire database, matching documents of any keyword w have to be a subset of q_i's matching documents, and equally for their handles. This is reflected in the step 6 in Algorithm 7. We use $N_G(v)$ to denote the neighboring vertices of the node v in the graph G.

After that, we observe that with high probability, the number of matching documents of keyword w in the known dataset divided by that of the corresponding query q_i in the entire dataset should be close to the known data rate δ. We also allow a reductive error ϵ, which corresponds to the step 8 in Algorithm 7.

Cross-Filtering   This step (9 and 10 in Algorithm 7) is optional and can be applied only if the handle function $h : \mathcal{D} \mapsto Y$ is a bijection and the known-data rate δ is large enough. It follows from the correctness of a searchable encryption scheme that the correct inferred keyword must be contained in all the documents in the set $h^{-1}(L_i)$. Take $h = \text{rid}$ as an example; the above statement translates to the fact that a potentially correct keyword has to be contained in all the documents $\{\text{doc}_{\text{id}}\}_{\text{id} \in L_i}$. However, we do not have the complete dataset, and we cannot invert h to all the documents but only in the known dataset. Therefore, we only use known documents in the set $\tilde{L} \cap L_i$.

If the size of the filtered set becomes 1, then we obtain the result keyword for the query q_i. And thus update the map accordingly.

Iterative Elimination Finally, with the observation that one keyword w cannot simultaneously be the correct match for two different queries q_i and q_j if the query equality pattern $\mathsf{qeq}[i, j] = 0$. And we thus can utilize the fixed candidate set with only one element to iteratively reduce the size of the others. It processes until the potential sets become stable, and then terminates.

Algorithm 7 The SUBGRAPH attack algorithm [23]

Let $\varepsilon \in \mathbb{N}$ be a public error parameter and δ be the known-data rate; $h : \mathcal{D} \mapsto Y$ be the function associated with specific leakage patterns.

SUBGRAPH$(\widetilde{\mathsf{DB}}, Q := (q_1, \ldots, q_t), \mathcal{L} := (L_1, \ldots, L_t), \varepsilon, \delta)$: $\triangleright \mathcal{L}$ is the leakage set

1: Initialize t empty sets $S_1, \ldots, S_t$ and a map $\alpha : [t] \to \mathcal{W}$;
2: Create a bipartite graph $\tilde{G} = \left(\left(\tilde{L}, \mathcal{W}\right), \tilde{E}\right)$ where

$$\tilde{L} = \{h\,(\mathrm{doc})\}_{\mathrm{doc} \in \widetilde{\mathsf{DB}}} \quad \text{and} \quad \tilde{E} = \left\{(w, h\,(\mathrm{doc})) : \forall w \in \mathcal{W}, \forall \mathrm{doc} \in \widetilde{\mathsf{DB}}, w \in \mathrm{doc}\right\};$$

3: Create a bipartite graph $G = ((L, Q), E)$ where

$$L = \{h\,(\mathrm{doc})\}_{\mathrm{doc} \in \bigcup_{i=1}^{t} \mathsf{DB}(q_i)} \quad \text{and} \quad Q = (q_1, \ldots, q_t) \quad \text{and}$$

$$E = \left\{(q_j, h\,(\mathrm{doc})) : \forall j \in [t], \forall \mathrm{doc} \in \bigcup_{i=1}^{t} \mathsf{DB}\,(q_i), h\,(\mathrm{doc}) \in L_j\right\};$$

4: **for** all $i \in [t]$ **do**
5:   **for** all $w \in \mathcal{W}$ **do**
6:     **if** $N_{\tilde{G}}(w) \subseteq N_G(q_i)$ **then** set $S_i^{(1)} = S_i^{(1)} \bigcup \{w\}$;
7:   **for** all $w \in S_i^{(1)}$ **do**
8:     **if** $|N_{\tilde{G}}(w)| \geq \delta \cdot |N_G(q_i)| - \varepsilon$ **then** set $S_i^{(2)} = S_i^{(2)} \bigcup \{w\}$;
9:   Compute

$$S_i^{(3)} = S_i^{(2)} \bigcap \left(\bigcap_{\mathrm{id} \in \tilde{L} \cap L_i} \mathrm{doc}_{\mathrm{id}}\right);$$

10:   **if** $|S_i^{(3)}| = 1$ **then** set $\alpha(i) = w$ where $S_i^{(3)} = \{w\}$;
11: Let $A \subseteq [t]$ be the set of all indexes for which $|S_i^{(3)}| = 1$;
12: **while** $|A|$ is increasing **do**
13:   **for** all $S_i^{(l)}$ with $|S_i^{(l)}| > 1$ **do**

$$S_i^{(l+1)} = S_i^{(l)} \setminus \left(\bigcap_{j \in A} \alpha\,(j)\right);$$

14:   **if** $|S_i^{(l+1)}| = 1$ **then** set $\alpha(i) = w$ where $S_i^{(l+1)} = \{w\}$;
15:   Update A and $l = l + 1$;
16: **return** α.

Efficiency The bipartite graph construction step is $O(\delta \cdot W \cdot D + \sum_{q_i \in Q} |\mathsf{DB}(q_i)|)$. The candidate selection step is $O(t \cdot W)$, and the cross-filtering step is

$$O\left(\sum_{i=1}^{t} \sum_{doc \in DB(q_i)} |doc|\right),$$

and the iterative elimination is $O(t^2)$. Therefore, the total time complexity is

$$O\left((\delta \cdot D + t) \cdot W + \sum_{i=1}^{t} \sum_{doc \in DB(q_i)} |doc|\right).$$

Practical Performance According to the evaluations in [23, 155], SUBGRAPH attacks with volume pattern and response identity patterns perform quite well with high selective queries, which can achieve a $70\% - 100\%$ recovery rate even with only $5\% - 10\%$ partial knowledge of the database. Meanwhile, aforementioned two attacks [49, 145] almost failed when the queried keywords are not selective, but SUBGRAPH attacks can still recover about $30\% - 40\%$ queries in this case. Besides, volume patterns seem to be more devastating in some datasets according to the evaluations in [155]; SUBGRAPH-VL attacks even achieve almost 100% recovery rate for highly selective keywords with little knowledge of the database.

5.3 File-Injection Attacks

The above attacks are executed by passively observing the information leakage combined with some auxiliary knowledge. Cash et al. [49] first considered file-injection attacks in which the adversarial server actively "plants" documents encrypted by the client and uploaded to the encrypted dataset. This attack is analogous to the chosen-plaintext attack in encryption. We can also find real-world situations in which an adversary can carry it out. For example, a malicious server can send emails to the client, who will process and upload the indexes and ciphertexts.

L3 Leakage with Known Hash Recall that the keywords are deterministically encrypted and stored in the order of their appearance in searchable encryption schemes with L3 (or L4) leakage profile. The malicious server can thus simply inject a document with any desired keywords, and the encrypted document will tell him the hashes/ciphertexts of those keywords. This attack is simplistic but extremely devastating, as it will reveal injected keywords in all documents.

L2 Leakage Without Known Hash and Order In this scenario, the server can learn the document identifiers corresponding to each keyword hash. Therefore, the adversarial server can take a straightforward strategy that it uploads W documents and each contains only one keyword. Then, it will be able to map each ciphertext to the underlying keyword. If we take a step further by utilizing a known *related* corpus, an adversary can inject fewer documents but with potentially small errors. The adversary first ranks keywords according to their frequency in the known corpus. Then, it fixes a document size k, and then divides the keyword list into k blocks with equal size k. After that, the server selects the top word from each block and thus generates a k-word document. The frequency distance between keywords is thus maximized. Finally, the adversary computes the frequency distribution of keyword hashes uploaded by the client, from which it can also find hashes of the words in the injected document. Then, the malicious server can make guesses according to their frequency ranks in the encrypted dataset. It makes successful guesses as long as there are no rank reversals between the known dataset and the encrypted one. The adversary may repeat this process until satisfied.

With large document sizes, the probability of a fail (i.e., observing reversed ranks) will be greater. Cash et al. [49] have shown that at around $k = 19$ keywords per document, the failing chance will become larger than the successful chance. Besides, this also offers the server trade-offs between the size/number of injected documents and error probability, yielding an efficient and flexible attack strategy.

5.3.1 Binary-Search Attack

To recover W keywords, the above attack requires the server to plant at least W/k documents, which is an improvement but still unsatisfactory. Zhang et al. [299] thoroughly investigated file-injection attacks under the searchable encryption context, which promoted the development of forward privacy in dynamic searchable encryption schemes. We first introduce a basic query-recovery attack that does not require any knowledge of the client's document collection. And it can recover all the searched keywords with perfect accuracy.

The basic idea behind the attack is that if the server injects a document doc consisting of half the keywords from $\mathcal{W}$, then it can learn one bit of information about the searched token t by observing whether the injected doc is contained in the result set. Since there are W distinct keywords, we can use $\lceil \log W \rceil$ injected files to learn comprehensive information about the search token. We give an example in Fig. 5.2.

The attack is formally described in Algorithm 8. For simplicity, we assume that W is a power of 2; otherwise, we add some dummy values. The attack begins by generating $\log W$ documents where i-th document contains exactly keywords with i-th bit of index equal to 1. After that, the server observes the response identity patterns to determine whether each injected file is returned. We denote that as $R = r_1 r_2 \cdots r_{\log W}$, where $r_i = 1$ if and only if i-th injected file is returned in response to the query. Then, the keyword w_R is the queried keyword.

We point out that files are generated non-adaptively and independent of the search token t in this attack. Once the files are injected, the malicious server can recover all the keywords corresponding to tokens issued by the client. Besides, the number of necessary files to be injected is quite reasonable. Concretely, a space of

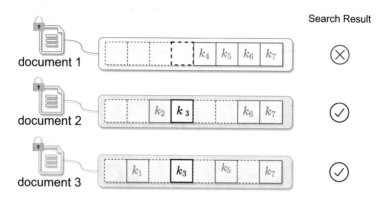

Fig. 5.2 An example of the binary-search attack with $W = 8$ keywords proposed by Zhang et al. [299]. Each document contains exactly four out of eight keywords in the figure. If both documents 2 and 3 are returned, then we can infer that the corresponding keyword is k_3

Algorithm 8 The binary-search attack

InjectFiles($\mathcal{W}$):
1: **for** $i = 1, \ldots, \lceil \log W \rceil$ **do**
2:      $\text{doc}_i \leftarrow \emptyset$;
3:      **for** $j = 0, \ldots, W - 1$ **do**
4:          **if** $j \,\&\, 2^{i-1} \neq 0$ **then** $\text{doc}_i \leftarrow \text{doc}_i \bigcup w_j$;   ▷ "&" is bitwise AND operation
5: **return** $\mathcal{D}_{\text{inject}} = (\text{doc}_1, \ldots, \text{doc}_{\lceil \log W \rceil})$.

Recover(rid, $\mathcal{W}$):
1: $R = 0$;
2: **for** id $\in$ rid **do**
3:      **if** doc_{id} corresponds to $\text{doc}_i \in \mathcal{D}_{\text{inject}}$ **then**
4:          $R = R \,|\, 2^{i-1}$;   ▷ "|" is bitwise OR operation
5: **return** w_R.

16,000 keywords only needs 14 malicious files and can be done within 2 weeks if the server injects one document per day. We also note that it is also applicable to a subset of the universal keyword space that the adversary is interested in.

Threshold Countermeasure

The binary-search attack is notable for requiring a large number of keywords (i.e., $W/2$) in each of the files to be injected to carry out the attack. A possible and simple countermeasure is to limit the number of keywords per document to a threshold of $T \ll W/2$. This could be done either by indexing only at most T keywords or simply not indexing the file.

We can set the threshold to a reasonably small value which seldom impacts the utility of the scheme. As an example, the Enron email dataset [68] has roughly 5000

Algorithm 9 Hierarchical-Search Attack

InjectFilesHierarchical($\mathcal{W}$):

1: Partition the universe into $p = \lceil W/T \rceil$ subsets $\mathcal{W}_1, \ldots, \mathcal{W}_p$ of T keywords each;

2: **for** $i = 1, \ldots, p$ **do**

3:     Generate a document doc_i containing every keyword $w \in \mathcal{W}_i$;

4: **for** $i = 1, \ldots, \frac{p}{2}$ **do**

5:     $\mathcal{D}_i \leftarrow$InjectFiles($\mathcal{W}_{2i-1} \bigcup \mathcal{W}_{2i}$);

6: **return** $\mathcal{D}_{\text{inject}} = \left\{ doc_1, \ldots, doc_p, \mathcal{D}_1, \ldots, \mathcal{D}_{\frac{p}{2}} \right\}$.

RecoverHierarchical($R, \mathcal{W}$):

1: Parse the search result R as

$$R = \left\{ r_1, \ldots, r_p, R_1, \ldots, R_{\frac{p}{2}} \right\},$$

corresponding to the results on the files in $\mathcal{D}_{\text{inject}}$ described above;

2: Set $x = \lceil \frac{i}{2} \rceil$, in which $r_i = 1$ and $r_j = 0$ for $j \neq i$;   ▷ Identify the target subset

3: **return** $k \leftarrow$ Recover($R_x, K_{2x-1} \cup K_{2x}$).

---

keywords, among which only 3% of the emails contain more than 200 keywords and the average number of keywords per email is 90. Therefore, it is obvious for the adversary to inject emails containing about 2500 distinct keywords, and they can be easily distinguished by the client.

Note that the above threshold countermeasure is not bulletproof. For example, the server could still launch an attack by planting much more documents as follows. Specifically, it splits each document doc_i in Algorithm 8 into $\lceil W/2T \rceil$ files $doc_{i,1}, \ldots, doc_{i,\lceil W/2T \rceil}$ each containing (at most) T words. Then, it is equivalent to the original document doc_i being returned if any one of them is returned. However, it results in at least $\lceil W/2T \rceil \cdot \log W$-injected documents. In the above Enron example, it requires the server to inject about 150 emails with a threshold of $T = 200$, which is perceptible to the client as well.

5.3.2   Hierarchical-Search Attack

We then present more sophisticated attacks which can defeat the threshold countermeasure above. We first show an attack using fewer documents than the modified binary-search attack without any knowledge of the client's document collection.

Firstly, we notice that the threshold countermeasure will not work if the adversary is interested in a small subset of keywords $\mathcal{W}' \subset \mathcal{W}$ with $W' = |\mathcal{W}'| \leq 2T$. We then leverage this property to learn the entire keyword set using the following *hierarchical-search attack* Algorithm 9. This attack starts with splitting the keyword universe into $\lceil W/T \rceil$ disjoint subsets each containing T keywords. Then, the server can learn which subset the keyword lies in based on the resulting set. In addition, the server also performs binary search attacks on two adjacent keyword sets to further identify the keyword exactly.

We then calculate the necessary number of documents to be injected. In steps 2–3, it injects $\lceil W/T \rceil$ documents. In steps 4–5, it injects $\lceil \log 2T \rceil$ documents for each binary search, and totally $\lceil W/2T \rceil \cdot \lceil \log 2T \rceil$ files. Therefore, the total number of injected documents is at most

$$\lceil W/2T \rceil \cdot (\lceil \log 2T \rceil + 2).$$

If we observe carefully, we can find that $\mathcal{D}_i$ generated by InjectFiles$(\cdot)$ contains the document doc_{2i-1}, which can thus be omitted. So the total file number can be improved to

$$\lceil W/2T \rceil \cdot (\lceil \log 2T \rceil + 1).$$

Taking the Enron email as an example again, it reduces the necessary number of injected documents to about 130 files. However, it still requires a multiplicative number of injections. We remark that with an *adaptive* version of the above attack, the number could be further reduced to $\lceil W/T \rceil + \lceil \log T \rceil$ files. Here, the adversary executes steps 2–3, as usual, to learn which subset the target keyword lies in. After that, the adversary carries out the binary-search attack on a subset of T keywords. It thus totally requires only $\lceil W/T \rceil + \lceil \log T \rceil$ files, or 33 documents in the Enron email dataset. But this version of the attack requires that the targeting SE scheme does not satisfy forward privacy, and the injected documents are only available to recover the keywords contained.

5.4   More Threats from Leakage Profiles

We then focus on attacks against encrypted search algorithms (ESAs). ESAs are a special form of searchable encryption schemes, where a client asks the server for a range (by specifying encrypted endpoints in usual) and the server returns a set of records matching the query. Most range query protocols make use of order-revealing encryption or order-preserving encryption schemes we have learned in Chap. 2. There are three variants of attacks in this setting:

Reconstruction attacks: recover the exact values in a numerical collection;
Approximate reconstruction attacks: recover an approximation of the values;
Count reconstruction attacks: recover the number of times values occur.

We first introduce some notations under the encrypted range schemes. Assume that the data collection consists of n records and $sk_1, \ldots, sk_n$ are their encrypted search keys. The domain of numerical values is $\mathcal{X} = \{1, \ldots, N\}$. Range attacks usually work "up to reflection," namely, the adversary recovers either the original numerical values $(v_1, \ldots, v_n)$ or its reflection $(N - v_1 + 1, \ldots, N - v_n + 1)$, which can be viewed as losing 1 bit of information.

5.4.1 Attacks Against Encrypted Range Queries

Kellaris et al. proposed the first two attacks against encrypted range schemes.

KKNO-1 The first attack assumes that the client issues queries uniformly at random and exploits the response identity pattern rid. It first accumulates sufficient queries to make sure that all subsets of identifiers matching a query are obtained. The attacker then determines the smallest (or largest) one by finding the symmetric difference between the largest proper subset of $[n]$ and $[n]$, since only the endpoints could be excluded in the vast majority of all result sets. It proceeds to find the second smallest one by searching for the smallest proper super-set containing the smallest element, and so on for the remaining elements until no smallest proper super-set can be found.

We obtain the order of all records in the database after the above operations. If we have $n = N$ (i.e, one record for each position in the domain X), then the recovery terminates as every possible value has been found. Otherwise, the attacker continues to determine the position of each record in the domain X. By the assumption of uniformly distributed queries, the number of queries (i.e., intervals) containing only records from the smallest value to the i-th value can be uniquely identified (as we will describe in KKNO-2).

Theoretical Bounds

Kellaris et al. have shown that it suffices to recover the order of records in the numeric data collection with only $O(N^2 \log N)$ queries. However, it requires $O(N^4 \log N)$ more queries to identify the position of each record. In addition, they also provide the lower bound of $\Omega(N^4)$ for the exact recovery attacks.

KKNO-2 Access pattern leakage can be suppressed by using cryptographic tools such as fully homomorphic encryption schemes and oblivious RAM, thus hiding the response identities. However, even with the above two powerful cryptographic primitives, response volume pattern vol will still be revealed.

We label n records as $1, 2, \ldots, n$ according to their order in the domain X and their positions as $1 \le sk_1 \le sk_2, \ldots, sk_n \le N$. Define

$$d_i = \begin{cases} sk_1 & i = 0, \\ sk_{i+1} - sk_i & 1 \le i \le n - 1, \\ N - sk_n + 1 & i = n. \end{cases}$$

Fig. 5.3 shows an example for $N = 16$ and $n = 4$ in which dots represent the domain positions and boxes represent records. The positions are $sk_1 = 3$, $sk_2 = 7$, $sk_3 = 13$, and $sk_4 = 16$, and thus we can compute $d_0 = sk_1 = 3$, $d_1 = sk_2 - sk_1 = 4$, $d_2 = sk_3 - sk_2 = 6$, $d_3 = sk_4 - sk_3 = 3$, and $d_4 = 16 - sk_4 + 1 = 1$.

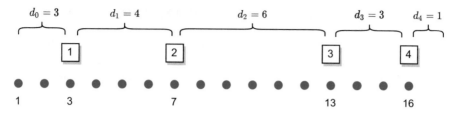

Fig. 5.3 Dataset example

It is easy to show that there are $\binom{N}{2} + N = \frac{N(N+1)}{2}$ distinct interval queries $[a, b]$, $1 \le a \le b \le N$. We then define u_i as the number of distinct queries (out of $\binom{N}{2} + N$) returning i records, and $\hat{u}_0$ as the number of distinct queries returning no records.

After that, we are able to verify the correctness of the following equation:

$$d_0 \cdot d_n = u_n.$$

In the above example, we have $u_4 = d_0 \cdot d_4 = 3$ queries (i.e., [1, 16], [2, 16], [3, 16]) including all records. In general, we have

$$u_m = \sum_{i=0}^{n-m} d_i \cdot d_{m+i}, \ 1 \le m \le n. \tag{5.2}$$

The number of queries $\hat{u}_0$ returning no records is a special case; we have the equation:

$$d_0^2 + d_1^2 + \cdots + d_n^2 = 2 \cdot \hat{u}_0 + N + 1$$

For simplicity, we define $u_0 = 2 \cdot \hat{u}_0 + N + 1$ as it also satisfies Eq. (5.2).

We now illustrate how to solve the system of quadratic Eq. (5.2). Consider two polynomials:

$$d(x) = d_0 + d_1 x + d_2 x^2 + \ldots d_n x^n,$$
$$d^R(x) = d_n + d_{n-1} x + d_{n-2} x^2 + \ldots d_0 x^n.$$

And define

$$F(x) = d(x) \cdot d^R(x).$$

It is crucial to observe that the coefficients of $F(x)$ are $u_0, \ldots, u_n$ as follows:

$$F(x) = u_n x^{2n} + u_{n-1} x^{2n-1} + \cdots + u_0 x^n + \cdots + u_{n-1} x + u_n.$$

Given values u_i on the result set volumes, we are able to construct $F(x)$ as well as factoring $F(x)$ into two polynomials to provide a solution to Eq. (5.2).

If $F(x)$ uniquely factors into two polynomials with natural number coefficients, then these would be $d(x)$ and $d^R(x)$. We hence obtain $u_0, \ldots, u_n$ for exact data reconstruction. In practice, we can use the LLL algorithm [169] to efficiently factor polynomials with integer coefficients.

5.4.2 Approximate Reconstruction Attacks

Grubbs et al. [124] attempted to weaken the assumptions of data density as well as a huge number of queries needed by KKNO attacks, and proposed three recovery attacks at the expense of accuracy. In particular, let $\varepsilon > 0$ be the desired precision parameter, and est-val(r) denote the predicted value of record r. Then Grubbs et al. defined so-called *sacrificial ε-Approximate Database Reconstruction* (ε-ADR) as follows. For every record r with $\varepsilon N \leq$ val$(r) \leq N + 1 - \varepsilon N$, either $|$est-val$(r) -$ val$(r)|$ or $|$est-val$(r) - (N + 1 - val(r))|$ is smaller than εN (i.e., up to reflection).

The boundary records (val$(r) < \varepsilon N$ or val$(r) > N + 1 - \varepsilon N$) are sacrificed as it is more difficult to recover them from the intuition that much fewer range queries touch them.

Generalized Range-Query Attack

The first one generalizes the KKNO attack to a sacrificial ε-ADR. For convenience, we also define symmetric value as symval$(r) := \min($val$(r), N + 1 - val(r))$. The attack proceeds in two steps. The first one is to recover the approximate value of each record up to reflection *individually*. And then it determines which values are on the same side of $N/2$.

The intuition starts with a natural observation: the probability that each record is touched by a range query is induced by a given query distribution. By empirically measuring that probability, we are able to infer the value of a record. More precisely, let A_k be the set of ranges in $[1, N]$ that contain $k \in [1, N]$, It is easy to verify that there are $|[1, k] \times [k, N]| = k(N + 1 - k)$ such ranges.

As there are in total $N(N + 1)/2$ possible ranges, we have the probability of

$$p(k) := \frac{2}{N(N + 1)} k(N + 1 - k),$$

where a uniform range falls within A_k, or contains the value k.

Algorithm 10 empirically measures $p(x)$ for each record and hence infers the record value (up to reflection) by choosing k such that the empirical probability is as close as possible to the theoretical $p(k)$.

To determine which records are on the same side of $N/2$, we need the help of an "anchor" record, which is set to be the one with **est-symval** closest to $N/4$. Another observation is that for any two records falling in different sides of $N/2$, there will be fewer records covering them simultaneously. We utilize this property to distinguish two (estimated) symmetric values as described in Algorithm 10.

Algorithm 10 Generalized KKNO Attack [124]

GETESTSYMVAL(Q):

1: **for** each record r **do**
2:     $c(r) \leftarrow \frac{|p(r)|}{|Q|}$;   ▷ $p(r)$ is the number of queries containing r
3:     est-symval$(r) \leftarrow \arg\min_{k \in [N/2]} |p(k) - c(r)|$;

4: **return** est-symval;

GETESTVAL(Q, est-symval):

1: $Q \leftarrow |Q|$;
2: $r_A \leftarrow \arg\min_r |\text{est-symval}(r) - N/4|$;   ▷ Select Anchor record
3: est-val$(r_A) \leftarrow$ est-symval(r_A);
4: **for** each record $r \neq r_A$ **do**
5:     $c'(r) \leftarrow \frac{|p(r) \cap p(r_A)|}{|Q|}$;
6:     **if** $c'(r) > \min\{\text{est-val}(r_A), \text{est-symval}(r)\}/N$ **then**
7:        est-val$(r) \leftarrow$ est-symval(r);
8:     **else**
9:        est-val$(r) \leftarrow N + 1 -$ est-symval(r);
10: **return** est-val;

In particular, the generalized KKNO attack suffices with $O(\varepsilon^{-4} \log \varepsilon^{-1})$ queries to achieve ε-sacrificial ADR. By setting $\varepsilon = 1/N$, we will have exact full database reconstruction with $O(N^4 \log N)$ queries, which is almost equivalent to the KKNO attack. A slight difference is that we sharply weaken the assumption from dense data collection to the existence of an anchor record in $[0.2N, 0.3N] \bigcup [0.7N, 0.8N]$.

By slightly modifying the above attack flow, we could further reduce the necessary number of queries to $O(\varepsilon^2 \log \varepsilon^{-1})$, saving roughly a square root factor over the previous one. The detailed analysis involves knowledge of probably approximately correct learning theory; we recommend referring to their paper [124]. However, the high-level idea here is to reduce the quadratic function $x \mapsto p(x)$ to a piecewise linear function in determining the side of each record.

The third attack uses a special data structure called PQ-tree to approximate the order of records on the basis of the response identity pattern rid.

5.4.3   Other Attacks Against ESAs

The (G)LMP Attacks Lacharité et al. proposed three attacks directly improving KKNO-1, which we refer to LMP-RK, LMP-ID, and LMP-APP. All of them in the persistent model exploit the response identity patterns rid, with LMP-RK using the rank pattern additionally. The last one only recovers an approximation of the values on small intervals, but all of them assume dense data distribution. At a high level, the attacks first identify the left endpoints of the records and then assign values to entries by excluding entries that differ in the response identities.

With an additional assumption of the dense database, we are able to fully recover records with only $N \log N + O(N)$ queries, or approximately recover with $\frac{5}{4} N \log \varepsilon^{-1} + O(N)$ queries, where ε is the approximation ratio—the recovered values have up to an additive error of εN rather than exactly.

Grubbs et al. [123] also proposed a new attack on the basis of the KKNO-2 attack, which only requires the response volume pattern vol. However, instead of recovering the values themselves, it only recovers the counts of value occurrences. In general, the attack first converts observed volume patterns to "elementary" queries and uses techniques in graph theory to reconstruct the data collection.

The KPT Attacks Kornaropoulos et al. [164] built another approximate value reconstruction attack agnostic to the query distribution. They reduced the query recovery problem to the problem of support size estimation, where we estimate the counts of outcomes not observed from the counts of observed outcomes. Subsequently, with the help of rid and qeq, we can recover the *order* of records.

5.5 Countermeasures and Future Directions

After understanding the hazards of leakage-abuse attacks, we then continue to discuss general approaches to *suppress* the leakage of searchable encryption schemes.

We first highlight again two generic tools to suppress most leakage patterns. Fully homomorphic encryption (FHE) supports arbitrary operations on the specially encrypted data and thus also equality searches. However, the search operation in SEs based on FHE requires time linear in the number of documents and has become quite impractical nowadays. Oblivious RAM-based searchable encryption requires a multiplicative overhead of $\log^{O(1)}(n)$, which is still unaffordable for large-scale data. In addition, both of them cannot suppress volume patterns, which have been shown to be harmful in many settings as well.

5.5.1 An Almost Zero-Leakage Searchable Encryption Scheme

We then introduce an almost zero-leakage (AZL) SE scheme [154], which first converts a dynamic SE scheme to a *rebuildable* one, and then transforms a rebuildable scheme leaking search pattern into a new one that does not leak. The latter phase borrows the high-level idea of [111]'s square-root ORAM solution but results in an asymptotically better complexity. We will describe the latter one first and then elaborate on how to rebuild an SE scheme in the following parts.

The Cache-Based Compiler

Goldreich et al. [111] proposed the first oblivious RAM design consisting of two components: a main memory storing the encrypted data together with dummy values and a cache in which data items are moved after being accessed. Every access to the ORAM structure first linearly scans the cache to look for the desired item, and retrieves either a real item (target not found in the cache) or a dummy item (target found in the cache) from the main memory.

It has been proved in [111] that the optimal size of the cache is $\sqrt{N}$, in which N is the main memory size. And after $\sqrt{N}$ accesses, we have to rebuild the entire data structure, since (in the worst case) we will access all dummy values and upcoming operations will access data items that have been accessed before. It then induces the necessity of a rebuildable SE scheme.

Similarly, given a data structure DS, a structured encryption scheme Π_{STE}, and an encrypted dictionary EDX, we first add $\sqrt{N}$ dummy items to DS and then encrypt DS with Π_{STE} as EDS (with $N + \sqrt{N}$ items), and an encrypted dictionary EDX with queries as keys and encrypted data items as values.

To perform a query q, the client executes EDX.Get on the cache. If it results in $\perp$ (i.e., has not been moved into the cache), then it issues a query to the server for data item r and updates EDX with (q, r). Otherwise, it obtains the result r and simply queries the server with an unused dummy value. Intuitively, we can see that EDS will not leak the search pattern as every item will be accessed at most once.

To rebuild the encrypted data structure, the client and server permute data elements obviously at random. To accomplish the goal, the client samples a random permutation, and the server runs a sorting network for all data items. For each gate of the network, the server asks the client to return the correct order of a pair, which thus results in a $O(N \log N) \sim O(N \log^2 N)$ round complexity. It is fortunate that the rebuild operation is periodic and thus could be amortized to each query.

Kamara and Moataz [150] proved that the amortized complexity of the above design is asymptotic better than directly applying each read/write operation in an ORAM system. Nonetheless, the malicious server could still observe the response length for each query and infer the keyword corresponding to each query. We then thus illustrate how to suppress volume patterns as well.

The Piggyback Scheme The high-level idea behind the volume pattern hiding scheme is quite simple. It divides the response set of a query q into blocks of equal size α, and pads the last block with $\perp$ to α. The client actively sends query tokens to retrieve each batch until it finds the empty symbol $\perp$ in the returned batch. The piggyback scheme protects the volume pattern of each query at the cost of latency. It has its application scenarios in practice as the client may only be interested in parts of the matching records.

5.5.2   Volume-Hiding Encryption Schemes

As it is quite hard to hide volume patterns in practice (even complicated FHE and ORAM solutions leak this type of pattern), we pay special attention to the volume-hiding encryption schemes in this section.

Naive Padding   One of the simplest ways to suppress volume patterns in searchable encryptions is naive padding. Given a multi-map MM, there are m keys and the i-th key has l_i values. We also denote $n := \sum_{i \in [m]} l_i$ as the total number of values and $l := \max_{i=[m]} l_i$ as the maximum number of values of a key. Then, the naive padding method simply adds dummy values to keys with less than l values until there are l values. We note that the resulting storage space is $m \cdot l$, which is usually much greater than the plaintext one n.

As an example, assume keys are sampled from a Zipf distribution $\mathcal{Z}_m$ with probability mass function

$$ f_m : [m] \mapsto [0, 1], \quad f_m(r) := \frac{r^{-1}}{\sum_{i=1}^m i^{-1}} \approx \frac{r^{-1}}{\ln m}, $$

where r is the rank of a key. Then, the most frequent one will have about $l = f(1) \cdot n \approx n/\ln m$ values. If we pad every key to that length, then there will be totally $m \cdot f(1) \cdot n \approx \frac{m}{\ln m} n$ values. With only $m = 500$ keys, the storage will explode $550\times$ to the original one, which seriously hinders its deployment in real-world applications. Therefore, we want to have a more practical scheme that can (partially) hide volume patterns and have storage close to n.

Pseudorandom Transform [151]   We then describe another simple method to hide volume patterns. Instead of padding tuples of each key to the maximum, we pad it to a number that is controlled by a public parameter λ and a PRF F. λ is the possible smallest number of values in a tuple, and we add it by $F(\cdot)$ to hide its true volume. Then, the transformed volume will be $\lambda + F(\cdot)$. If it the sum is smaller than the original volume, the extra values will be truncated. Fortunately, [151] have proved that under Zipf distribution, the number of truncation is small, or at most $m/\log m$ in particular. Unfortunately, it is only able to reduce the storage to *half* of the naive padding scheme, which is still not practical and the client has to bear the cost of losing data.

Dense Subgraph Transform [151]   The same authors in [151] also proposed non-lossy schemes to suppress volume pattern leakage as follows. It treats the multi-map as a bipartite graph where one vertex part consists of m keys and the other part consists of b empty bins. For the i-th key, we assign corresponding values into l_i bins such that at most one value appears in each bin. After assigning all keys, we then pad bins to the size of the maximum one.

By their analysis, the size of bins has to be $\Omega(\log n)$, which results in $\Omega(l \cdot \log n)$ search complexity as it must fetch all bins containing corresponding values. On the other hand, it achieves asymptotically better storage space $\Theta(n)$.

The highlight of this design is that for multi-maps where a large part of keys share numerous same values, it can concentrate those values such that duplicates only appear once in a set of bins. By doing so, we can achieve the storage space of $\Theta\left(n - \sqrt{m} \cdot \mathsf{polylog}(m)\right)$. The main flaw of this optimization is that the concentration is based on the hardness of the planted densest graph problem, which has not been heavily studied yet. Meanwhile, the analysis given in their research work [151] does not point out the choice of cryptographic parameters used in practice. Finally, the resulting search complexity is increased to $\Theta\left(l \cdot \frac{n}{\mathsf{polylog}(m)}\right)$ which is quite large indeed.

5.5.3 More Practical Volume-Hiding Multi-Maps

Before presenting the volume-hiding multi-maps, we will briefly introduce a special and famous hash function called *cuckoo hashing* firstly proposed in [208] and improved in [163].

From a high-level point of view, cuckoo hashing is composed of two hash tables of size $(1+\alpha)n$ with a small constant $0 < \alpha < 1$ stored in the server, and a stash with small size stored in the client. In particular, for a value v_i associated with a key k, it will be placed into one of three locations $F_K(k\|i\|0)$ in the first table, $F_K(k\|i\|1)$ in the other table, or in the stash. The empty locations in the two tables will be filled with dummy values and encrypted together.

Let's now consider how to search for a key k associated with l_k values. Then, it suffices for the client to send possible two locations for each value as $\{F_K(k\|i\|0), F_K(k\|i\|1)\}_{i\in[l]}$. The server simply fetches and returns corresponding values in the hash tables according to received location values. Patel et al. [217] proved that in this construction, the server will not be aware of whether a location is filled with a dummy or a real element; therefore, the scheme is volume-hiding.

Additionally, we observe that the messages sent by the client have a certain pattern—all of $2l$ PRF have the same prefix k. With the help of delegatable PRFs [111], the server will be able to derive $2l$ encrypted values based on one encrypted value $F_K(k)$. This optimization reduces the communication overhead from $2l$ PRF outputs to just one PRF output from the client to the server.

In the above solution, the query complexity is $2l$ for the server as it only needs to fetch $2l$ values. And it requires only $(2 + \alpha)n$ storage space on the server side and a very small stash on the client side (several KB in practice). Evaluations in [217] show that it is $10 \sim 16\times$ faster than the previous dense subgraph transform solution.

5.5.4 Differentially Private Volume-Hiding Scheme

In all the previous leakage suppressing schemes, our goal is to make the server not able to distinguish between a real value and a (pseudo-)random value. However, this security guarantee is too strong in some cases and becomes impractical as the amount of data grows. Due to the above requirements, people bring the notion of *differential privacy* into leakage suppression to offer a tunable balance between privacy and efficiency.

To define differential privacy, we first need to define two neighboring leakage profiles as follows.

Definition 1 Signatures $S_0 = (k, l_k)_{k \in \mathcal{K}}$ and $S_1 = (k, l'_k)_{k \in \mathcal{K}}$ are neighbors if there are two $k_0, k_1 \in \mathcal{K}$ such that

- for all $k \notin \{k_0, k_1\}$, $l_k = l'_k$;
- $l_{k_0} = l'_{k_1} + 1$ and $l_{k_1} = l'_{k_0} - 1$.

We then say that the volume leakage function is (ε, δ)-differentially private if for two neighboring signatures, the probability for all polynomial adversaries $\mathcal{A}$ to output 0, 1 is mutually bounded by e^ε and a failing chance δ.

Recall the pseudorandom transform approach we have learned; we use a PRF to generate corresponding volumes such that they are distorted to be "random" numbers. However, randomness introduces a small but non-negligible loss when returning the resulting set. Instead of using a PRF, we use a number sampled from Laplace distribution to mask the original volume. Specifically, $\tilde{l}_k := l_k + \mathsf{noise}(k)$, where the value noise is drawn according to Laplace distribution with parameter $2/\varepsilon$. To avoid data loss, we need to avoid truncation in the value tuples, i.e., to guarantee that $\tilde{l}_k \geq l_k$. We thus add one more element l_k^* into $\tilde{l}_k$ (i.e., $\tilde{l}_k := l_k + l_k^* + \mathsf{noise}(k)$) such that $\Pr\left[l_k^* < -\mathsf{noise}(k)\right]$ is negligible in λ. According to the property of Laplace distribution, $l_k^* = \omega(\log \lambda)$. As a result, all values associated with the key will be returned except with negligible probability.

With the relaxation of security notion, we are above to improve the average query overhead over the previous one by a factor of $150 \sim 240\times$ when encrypting $2^{16} \sim 2^{22}$ total values [217].

5.5.5 Frequency Smoothing

The key insight behind leakage-abuse attacks is that data accesses chosen from a certain distribution do provide some extra information that can be leveraged by passive and persistent adversaries. For instance, text documents have some frequent keywords tending to be queried more often. Or in a hospital database, some common chronic diseases or flues might be regularly queried and accessed. Thus, it is essential to smooth the access frequency in a key-value data store such that an adversary cannot gain useful information anymore.

Let's take the accesses distribution in Fig. 5.4 as an example. There are four different items in which 'KV1' has the highest frequency and "KV4" is the least frequent one. Combining some prior knowledge (e.g., public health information from the local government), an adversary will be able to associate each item with its plaintext value.

The first trivial approach is to replicate popular items such that transformed access distribution becomes uniform, as illustrated in Fig. 5.5. Another simple way to achieve uniform distribution is adding fake accesses to unpopular items to the most popular one (i.e., another form of padding) as Fig. 5.5. However, the former suffers from a lot of server-side storage overhead, and the latter may increase too much bandwidth pressure.

Grubbs et al. [125] therefore neatly combined two approaches to balance the storage and bandwidth costs as shown in Fig. 5.6. It firstly creates "just enough" replicas to *partially* smooth the frequency distribution with at most $2\times$ storage. After that, it adds fake accesses to completely smooth out the distribution. With rigorous analysis, one can show that the bandwidth overhead is at most $3\times$ of the original one.

Though it requires the client to set up a proxy locally (or in a trusted party) to issue fake accesses, experiments have shown that the proxy storage is only about 1% of the server storage, which is double of the insecure data store and a quarter of the PathORAM approach. Besides, it achieves about $230\times$ better throughput than PathORAM and within $3 \sim 6\times$ of the insecure implementation.

5.6 Further Reading

The real-ideal paradigm was first applied in the setting of searchable symmetric encryption by Broder and Mitzenmacher [41], for the special case of searchable encryption. Shortly thereafter, this definition and another game-based security definition, IND2-CKA [108], were improved to stronger *non-adaptive* and *adaptive*

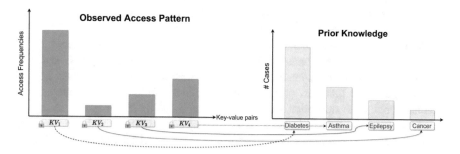

Fig. 5.4 Without smoothing access frequency, an adversary may recover the encrypted databases with some prior knowledge

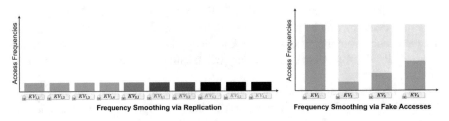

Fig. 5.5 Two simple frequency-smoothing approaches. Blocks of the same color in the left figure denote the replicas of the original items; light-colored blocks in the right figure denote fake accesses to the corresponding items

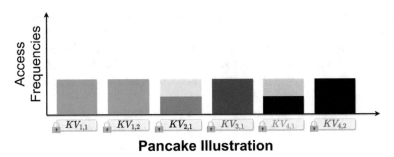

Fig. 5.6 Pancake illustration

definitions by Curtmola et al. [74]. With the evolution of searchable encryption, [38] have proposed formal forward and backward security definitions with different security levels. In particular, [26] comparatively studied the security and performance trade-offs of some popular order-revealing/order-preserving encryption schemes. To help inform better-informed decisions, they also evaluated the practical performance of each approach to determine whether the improved performance of some schemes is worth the uncertainty about their security.

Groot Roessink [118] introduced deterministic techniques from the COUNT attacks [49] to improve the IKK attack [145] by reducing the search space for the annealing process, and removing the assumption of prior query knowledge. Other well-designed leakage-abuse attacks include [200, 206, 207].

Cash et al. [49] systematically studied and classified the leakage profiles of SE designs in order to understand their practical security guarantees. Besides, they also designed and summarized some leakage-abuse attacks which exploit the leakage rather than any particular construction. After that, numerous attacks against searchable encryption emerged. Kamara et al. [155] proposed an open-source framework, called LEAKER, to enable the community to easily implement, evaluate, verify, and compare current and future leakage-abuse attacks. Their work has shown that the SUBGRAPH attack [23] consistently perform well on the real-world query logs and data under the single-keyword search setting.

Kamara and Moataz [150] considered a new approach, which utilizes the computational impossibility of some conjectures, to hide the volume leakage. Patel et al. [217] brought the first formal definition of *volume-hiding leakage functions*, as well as practically efficient volume-hiding schemes. Besides, they also introduced the notion of *differentially private volume-hiding leakage functions* and respective differentially private volume-hiding encrypted multi-map. Kamara et al. [154] built a framework consisting of two compilers to *rebuild* some structured encryption schemes to a newly "almost" zero-leakage SE scheme. George et al. [106] then introduced a similar framework that creates *fully dynamic* SSEs that conceals the query equality from semi-dynamic or mutable STE schemes. Note that the previous countermeasures all add dummy values to confuse the malicious server. Xu et al. [289] proposed an algorithm to introduce pseudorandom perturbations on the index matrix, such that we are able to obscure the invariant features of the database without much extra storage. Besides, [290] investigated a simple but overlooked leakage mitigation approach from another perspective that the client stashes a (small and efficient) index locally and offers rich search functionalities as well as good security guarantees.

Chapter 6
Toward Fully Functional Encrypted Databases

After acquiring sufficient knowledge about searchable encryption, we are now able to delve into the world of fully functional encrypted databases. First of all, as a real-world application, there are many other dimensions beyond the key functionality "search" that we have to pay attention to. For instance, how to support concurrent queries (i.e., handling multiple queries at the same time), how to deal with the failure caused by various accidental reasons (e.g., power interruptions, unstable network, I/O failures), and how to enforce constraints to guarantee data comply with certain rules, etc.

Fortunately, we have a proven set of tools as discussed in Sect. 6.1 to help us do these tasks. On the one hand, they are not directly related to the search tasks, which hence enable us to design these sub-modules separately. On the other hand, we cannot totally ignore the other modules when we implement an encrypted database, since there are also security issues among them as well. Furthermore, a *fully functional* encrypted database also has to support other types of workloads, including but not limited to data sorting, arithmetic operations over ciphertexts (e.g., addition, multiplication, averaging), and table joins (i.e., concatenating records from different tables with some constraints).

The above demands require us to pay much more attention to the overall or fully functional encrypted database designs from a systematic point of view. We stress that developing and deploying an encrypted database in the real world needs very careful consideration and large team support; otherwise, an oversight in a small detail could leak sensitive information.

From a realistic point of view, many companies have moved their enterprise data from their own data centers to third-party cloud infrastructures, such as Microsoft Azure, Alibaba Cloud, and Google Cloud over the last decade. There is also a trend for individuals including mobile users to outsource their private data to cloud providers, such as Huawei Cloud, iCloud, and OneDrive. These infrastructures are under the control and maintenance of potentially untrustworthy operators, who also have incentives to snoop on user data for commercial or other purposes, e.g.,

K. Ren, C. Wang, *Searchable Encryption*, Wireless Networks,
https://doi.org/10.1007/978-3-031-21377-9_6

accurate advertising delivery and data analysis. Meanwhile, the cloud server is shared among numerous clients. For instance, there are probably several virtual client instances co-locating a single AWS physical instance, some of those clients may be malicious. Therefore, it is of great importance to protect the confidentiality and integrity of user data from server owners, co-tenants, and other adversaries.

In this chapter, we will first have an overview of database systems in Sect. 6.1, and then describe two major approaches to design an encrypted database system in Sects. 6.2 and 6.3, respectively. After that, we will take *Enclage* as an example to show a practical encrypted database and other design choices in Sect. 6.4. Finally, we will discuss the future trend of encrypted databases in Sect. 6.5.

6.1   Overview of Database Systems

We provide background information on the database systems in this section for references. Essentially, a database is a searchable and dynamic collection of data that is designed and optimized for targeted queries (e.g., efficiently search for data records satisfying several conditions). Databases generally perform a search in time sublinearly in its scale by utilizing data structures such as binary search trees and B+-trees and parallel architectures.

After several decades of evolving, there have been several styles of database engines on the market. Relational (or SQL-style) databases have once dominated the market from the 1970s to the 1990s. Recently, NoSQL and NewSQL as new database paradigms have gained more popularity [133].

SQL   stands for "Structured Query Language," also known as relational databases, which offers a well-established interface and strong transaction guarantees in handling structured data. SQL databases are vertically scalable, i.e., we can enhance their performance with more computing resources. Another important feature of SQL databases is their compliance of ACID requirements [135]:

- Atomicity: A transaction is treated as a single "unit" which either *completely* succeeds or fails.
- Consistency (or Correctness): It guarantees that any data written to the database must be consistent with all predefined rules.
- Isolation: When multiple transactions are read or written concurrently, it ensures one can obtain the same database state if the transactions are executed in sequence.
- Durability: A committed transaction is guaranteed to remain committed even if failures happen (e.g., system crash or power cut).

NoSQL   (short for "not only SQL") databases came up in the mid-2000s. Due to growing amounts of unstructured data, the architecture of NoSQL is optimized for flexible data structures, fast data ingest, and relaxed transactional guarantees

[53]. Most NoSQL databases show excellent performance when future computations closely align with data models.

NewSQL   combines the transactional guarantees of SQL databases and scalability of NoSQL databases [219]. People have developed several NewSQL variants such as array data stores optimized for numerical data analysis and in-memory databases with high performance.

Future systems   are expected to efficiently run a small group of basic operations and behave differently. Several polystore or federated systems are being developed [101, 186].

After understanding the basic types of databases, we then move to the query bases which jointly offer complex search functionalities. We stress that it is necessary for the protected search community to keep in step with newly emerging database systems by taking a good grip on the underlying query bases. We will briefly describe three bases in database systems concluded by Fuller et al. [99] as follows:

Relational algebra,   proposed in 1970 by Codd [67], is composed of the following primitives: set difference, set union, joins (Cartesian product), selection, projection, and rename. More complex queries can be fulfilled by composing these operations. In addition, the query planner on the server side can optimize query execution processes based on the composability of operations.

Associative arrays   are the mathematical foundations of several database engines [161], such as key-value stores. It consists of the following basic operations: construction, find, associative array addition, array element-wise multiplication, and array multiplication [161]. The underlying algebraic concept of associative arrays is semi-ring, i.e., a ring without an additive inverse.

Linear algebra   consisting of matrix addition, multiplication, and element-wise operations is currently developed mainly for graph algorithms. Examples of how this type of newer algebra could be applied for solving popular graph problems can be found in [100, 137].

There are three important roles in a database system:

A data provider   provides and updates the data.

A querier   queries a subset of data with proper authentication. In many scenarios, a querier is the same as the data provider.

A server   manages the database system, as well as handles queries, data storage, and logs.

Besides, numerous operations supported by the vast majority of databases could be categorized into four types:

Initialization   is the process where the server obtains a processed collection of data from the data provider.

Query   protocol occurs when the querier wants to learn some information about the database, and issues a query to the server (and potentially the provider), who will perform computations on the database and return query results.

Update   happens when the data provider wants to modify the data collection, including insertions, deletions, and record modifications. An honest server should modify the database accordingly.

Refresh   occurs when sufficient data is accumulated on the server side, and the server may interact with the data provider to obtain a new database containing the exact same data but supporting more efficient or secure operations.

Informally, an encrypted database involves the above roles, and supports these operations as well. But each participant only learns intended results together with a well-defined leakage profile and nothing else. In particular, the server should learn nothing about the data collection nor the queries, and the querier (if not identical to the provider) should learn nothing more than the returned results. Many research works offered formal security proofs for their proposed designs; however, some of the commercial systems lacked formal security analysis. We emphasize that it is necessary to provide formal proof and analysis for users to understand the security guarantees of their products.

In general, there are two lines of work to construct an encrypted database which will be discussed in detail in the next two sections:

1. The traditional class of protected search systems with cryptographic primitives support direct operations over ciphertexts but at the cost of significant performance overheads, limited query types, or a large amount of information leakage.
2. Encrypted databases take advantage of trusted execution environments (TEE), which perform confidential operations in an isolated enclave to provide data security. However, the performance is still limited to the features of trusted hardware, and it requires one to trust the hardware manufacturer (e.g., Intel).

6.2   Using Cryptographic Primitives

In this section, we will introduce encrypted databases using cryptographic primitives, including fully homomorphic encryption, secure multi-party computation, functional encryption, private information retrieval, and oblivious random-access memory.

There have been several prototype systems for subsets of SQL but without confidentiality guarantees, which requires significant overhead on the server and computational efforts on the client side since 2002 [66, 75, 127]. For instance, [127] empirically divide the column domain into several partitions, storing which partition each record belongs to in plaintext, and demands the client to filter out query results. However, it still leaks the range within which a record falls and could be extremely harmful in many scenarios, e.g., income level of an individual and various health indicators (blood pressure, diabetes). Other tools such as disk encryption, static analysis, and language runtimes detect software vulnerabilities to help mitigate security risks in practice, but none of them provide data confidentiality when there is an adversary with high privileges residing in the database server.

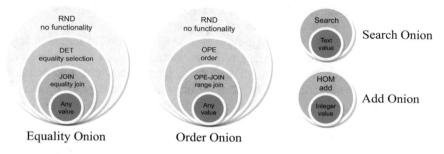

Fig. 6.1 An overview of onion encryption layers and the types of operations they allow. The names of onions represent the allowed operations at the corresponding layers (Order, Equality, Search, and Addition resp.) [224]

6.2.1 A Confidential Database System Over Efficient SQL-Aware Encryption Schemes

CryptDB proposed by Popa et al. [224] provides practical queries over encrypted databases and provable security against strong adversaries who have access to the server. Specifically, it prevents a curious database administrator (DBA) from snooping on the database server or learning private data. In addition, it protects private data of *logged-out* users against the adversary who has complete control of the database management system (DBMS) server, but it cannot ensure the confidentiality of logged-in users' data.

CryptDB adopts a layered encryption architecture, or *adjustable query-based encryption*. As we have learned in previous chapters, some encryption schemes leak more than others. For instance, OPE reveals the order of ciphertext, while ORE does not reveal ciphertext orders directly. Deterministic encryption schemes do not reveal plaintext order, but the same plaintext will be mapped to the same ciphertext, which is then fixed in a random encryption scheme. This architecture is called *onions* of encryption since each encryption layer is wrapped in another layer as shown in Fig. 6.1, which looks like an onion.

SQL-Aware Encryption

This section elaborates on how queries are executed over encrypted data in CryptDB. It does not modify the query planner in a DBMS except for the operators compromising the query, such as ordering, aggregation, and projection, which are executed on ciphertexts. For each cryptographic primitive, we will discuss its functionality and why CryptDB adopts it:

Random (RND) offers the highest security level—indistinguishability under chosen-plaintext attack (aka IND-CPA). The encryption is randomized; thus, even the same value will be encrypted as different ciphertexts by different encryption operations. The drawback of RND is obvious. The server cannot perform any efficient computation on the ciphertext.

Deterministic (DET)   has a slightly weaker security guarantee that only leaks which ciphertexts have the same plaintext value. Based on this property, the server can check the equality of underlying data values, which is useful in performing selects with equality joins, equality checks, count, group by, etc.

Order-preserving encryption (OPE)   provides weaker security than DET as it additionally reveals the order of ciphertext. If $a < b$, then $\text{OPE}_K(a) < \text{OPE}_K(b)$ for any secret key K. Therefore, the server can perform range queries on a column encrypted with OPE when given the encrypted endpoints $\text{OPE}_K(c_1)$ and $\text{OPE}_K(c_2)$, and returns records within the range $[c_1, c_2]$. Besides, it allows the server to perform operations such as min/max, order by, sort, etc.

Homomorphic encryption (HOM)   is a probabilistic encryption scheme that allows the server to perform (specific) computations over the ciphertexts. Though fully homomorphic encryption, which supports arbitrary computations, is prohibitively slow, the efficiency of HOM for specific operations is acceptable in practice. For instance, Paillier cryptosystem [209] allows the server to calculate the sum of two values as $\text{HOM}_K(a) \cdot \text{HOM}_K(b) = \text{HOM}_K(a + b)$, in which the result is a modulo of some public-key value. We thus can perform SUM aggregation in CryptDB.

Join (Equi-JOIN and Range-JOIN)   is supported in CryptDB when the predicate is based on equality and order respectively. To provide better privacy, we should not encrypt columns with the same key; otherwise, matching values between the two columns will be learned by the server. Therefore, we need different keys to encrypt the columns that will be joined.

If the client knows on which columns it will perform Equi-JOIN operations, we could use the same key to encrypt those columns only. However, sometimes we cannot determine targeted columns when initializing the database; therefore, we introduce a new crypto primitive called *adjustable join* (JOIN-ADJ) to allow runtime adjustment of the key for each column by the DBMS server. In particular, JOIN-ADJ should be deterministic such that the same input produces the same output, collision-resistant and non-invertible as required by many encryption schemes. Popa et al. proposed their own construction based on elliptic-curve cryptography in their research work.

For range joins, it is much harder to construct a similar dynamic adjustment algorithm; therefore, it requires the client to declare on which columns it will perform range-join operations, and choose the same key to encrypt those columns. Fortunately, such columns are rare in practice as shown in [224]: only 50 out of 128, 840 columns are used for range joins in a large SQL database.

Word Search (SEARCH)   is used to support operations such as the LIKE operator in MySQL by performing searches on encrypted text data. We could use many SSE schemes described in previous chapters to fulfill this requirement. Particularly, CryptDB uses the protocol of [245] with slightly better security guarantees by randomly permuting the ciphertext and padding each keyword to the same size. To perform a search query, the client sends a token that enables the server to find matching records. Note that only exactly match keyword searches are allowed in CryptDB due to the property of the underlying SE scheme.

Though we mentioned many different encryption schemes and different keys for columns, CryptDB chains encryption keys to user passwords, such that the password of the user is sufficient to decrypt a data record.

Improving Security and Performance

As discussed by Popa et al., it is also to improve the security and performance of CryptDB by applying several optional optimization techniques as described below. We first introduce four possible approaches to improve its practical security as follows:

Minimum onion layers. The user can specify the lowest (i.e., least secure) encryption layer in each onion revealed to the server for each column. By doing so, the user can prevent the server from analyzing some sensitive encrypted columns. For instance, the ID of individuals should always remain encrypted no more than RND or DET.

In-proxy processing. Though CrytDB supports rich functionalities on the server side, one can hand over some lightweight tasks to the proxy or the client self to hide additional information against the server. For example, the user wants to select the top *ten* data records from the server, which involves select, sort, and limit operations. Instead of returning ten records only, the server selects and returns all qualified data to the proxy, who will then sort and obtain *ten* desired records. In this way, we could reduce the vulnerable surface to the server by avoiding an OPE layer.

Training mode. Users can submit a set of queries to CryptDB and obtain the resulting onion encryptions, together with a warning of the unsupported set of queries. It provides the user to flexibly and intuitively select encryption levels for different columns.

Onion re-encryption. In some cases where the user issues infrequent queries requiring a low onion layer (less secure) such as OPE, CrytDB offers the option to re-encrypt the corresponding column back to a higher and more secure layer after the query has been finished. It will not introduce too much performance overhead since queries are infrequent. It also reduces the potential attack surface exposed to the server since some attackers may miss this time window.

After that, we then proceed to some performance optimizations:

Developer annotations. To reduce encryption overhead, CryptDB allows the user to explicitly annotate sensitive data fields if the majority of a table can be stored and processed in plaintext.

Known query set. For some cases such as many web applications, some queries are known in advance by the developer, who can then adjust onions to the correct layer and discard unnecessary layers to save both storage and computation costs accordingly.

Ciphertext pre-computing and caching.   By naturally assuming that the proxy is not always busy, we can ask the proxy to pre-compute or cache some randomness values required by HOM or OPE encryption schemes. Or it could reserve some frequently used constants under different keys. Experiments in [224] have shown a significant improvement in latency with the help of this optimization.

Popa et al. also provided public implementations of CryptDB for both Postgres 9.0 and MySQL 5.1 in https://github.com/CryptDB/cryptdb, consisting of a C++ library and a Lua module. Though CryptDB has been found to be vulnerable to many types of attacks, we emphasize its creativity and success, which has been inspired or directly adopted by a few well-known companies and organizations, including Microsoft's Always Encrypted SQL Server (the prior version), Google's Encrypted BigQuery, Skyhigh Networks, etc.

6.2.2   A More Secure Encrypted Database Using Semantically Secure Encryption

CryptDB took an important step in achieving a both confidential and functionally rich database system. However, it still faces a challenging security-performance trade-off, and there are two types of leakage in CryptDB:

- Leakage from data could be observed by an offline/snapshot adversary. To efficiently execute some types of queries such as equal-join, and range searches, CryptDB adopts a set of property-preserving encryption schemes, e.g., deterministic encryption and order-preserving encryption. However, a sequence of attacks (including what we have learned in the previous chapter) have demonstrated the potential detriment of those information leakages.
- Leakage from queries could be observed by persistent adversaries during query processing, such as access patterns and volume patterns, which could be exploited by the adversary in certain scenarios. It requires the adversaries to be more powerful than in the previous setting, and one needs to pay much more overheads to hide those leakages. Effective countermeasures include oblivious protocols (e.g., ORAM) and padding.

To protect a database against snapshot adversaries as well as take steps against persistent attackers, Poddar et al. proposed Arx, an encrypted database that remains practical and functionally rich by *always* encrypting data with probabilistic (i.e., semantically secure) cryptosystems. In semantic security, no information except for its size and layout about the plaintext will be revealed. Compared to CryptDB, Arx only reveals the order relations or frequency involved in the queried data items rather than every item in the database. Though after a sufficiently large number of queries, it exposes the same information as CryptDB, we argue that the security of Arx is significantly improved against short-lived adversaries, and it is difficult for an attacker to collect enough leakages in practice.

In particular, Arx introduces two new query types—ArxEq for equality queries and ArxRange for range queries. We point out that range queries can be used for finding equalities, but ArxEq is substantially faster. ArxRange builds a search tree on the data and utilizes a *garbled circuit* to compare the searched value with the node value. To further reduce structural leakage, the tree is history-independent. In addition, Arx brings the concept to Garbled RAM such that while performing a traversal on the tree, the input labels for the child circuit to be accessed will be produced by the garbled circuit of the current node. Arx thus is able to find all results in a single round. To reduce leakage, every accessed node will be destroyed and later repaired as new nodes. Fortunately, we only need to repair a logarithmic number of nodes, and the repairing process is thus efficient.

ArxEq, similar to the approach adopted in the inverted index of searchable encryption, builds a regular index array over encrypted data collection via integrating a counter into duplicate values, which guarantees that the ciphertexts of two equal values will be different and prevents the server from learning frequency information. To perform a search, the server will expand the token provided by the client to many search tokens for all matching results. Besides, ArxEq is also forward private and thus prevents the adversary from using invalid tokens to search for new data. Based on the above two indexes, Arx transforms aggregations into three lookups and speeds up the process via ArxAgg, and introduces foreign-key joins with ArxJoin.

Architecture Overview

As shown in Fig. 6.2, the application and the database systems in Arx remain the same. As an alternative, two components are introduced between the original database server and the application server:

1. A trusted client proxy provides the same API to the application as the DB server, such that the developer does not need to modify the application;
2. An untrusted server proxy invokes unmodified APIs to interact with the database server like a normal client.

The *lightweight* client proxy takes the responsibility of managing the master key, rewriting queries, encrypting data, and forwarding processed queries to the server proxy. It stores some metadata such as schema information, some states, and possibly a cache to speed up the query process. The database server stores a huge amount of the data and executes the computationally expensive part of queries. Typically, the client proxy will process the query results (e.g., decryption) only; however, it may perform some post-processing in some corner cases to enhance the security guarantees.

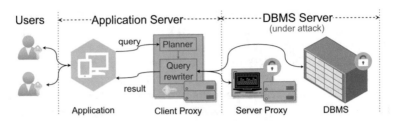

Fig. 6.2 The architecture of Arx [221]. Locks denote that private data will be encrypted at that component. Shaded boxes are new components introduced by the Arx design

Functionalities Supported by Arx

Next, we describe the types of queries Arx can handle. It allows the majority of query types which is sufficient for practical applications.

Read Queries Arx support read queries in the following form:

```
SELECT [AGG doc] attributes FROM collection
WHERE clause [ORDERBY attributes] [LIMIT l];
```

where AGG denotes the aggregate function in the form of $\sum f(\text{doc})$, $\sum$ could be any associative operator and f is an arbitrarily efficient function, such as MIN, SUM, COUNT, and MAX. The predict is a Boolean combination of $op(f_i)$, in which $op(f_i)$ is equality/inequality operations over an attribute f_i such as $\leq$, $>$, and $=$. A common form of join operation, i.e., foreign-key joins, is also supported by Arx as we will describe soon.

Write Queries Standard write queries such as inserts, updates, and deletes are supported by Arx.

Constraints Arx allows only limited range/order queries:

- Range queries across multiple encrypted attributes are not allowed, i.e., Arx supports $f_1 \leq 1 \wedge f_2 > 10$ only if one of them is in plaintext.
- The query may contain an ORDERBY operation over an encrypted field *alone* if it includes a LIMIT and range operation over the target field.

Building Blocks

Arx depends on three semantically secure encryption schemes as follows:

Base is a probabilistic encryption algorithm such as AES-CTR.

Eq utilizes an efficient and dynamic searchable encryption scheme (refer to the examples in the previous chapter) to enable equality checking. In particular,

$EQEnc_k(v) = (IV, AES_{KGen_k(v)}(IV))$, in which IV is an initialization vector (typically random/pseudorandom) and KGen is a key generation function. To perform a search on the keyword w, $EQToken_k(w)$ outputs the token as tok $= KGen_k(w)$. After that, the server proxy combines the token with IV to find matches over the ciphertext collection: $EQMatch((IV, c), tok) \rightarrow$ $(AES_{tok}(IV) \overset{?}{=} c)$. We point out that one cannot directly construct the *index* based on the above scheme due to its random component IV. Therefore, it is only applicable to non-indexed attributes. Arx uses ArxEq to build an index on this attribute.

To enable more efficient searches over attributes having unique values (e.g., ID, ISBN), Arx introduces EQunique which uses deterministic encryption. It does not weaken the security level since values are unique, and it is faster than the randomized one. In addition, Arx also applies this optimization for ArxEq as well.

AGG   uses the Paillier scheme [209] to enable additions.

ArxEq and Equality Queries

As discussed above, when the attributes are unique (e.g., ID, ISBN, primary key), it suffices for ArxEq to encrypt it with EQunique (i.e., deterministic encryption) and the regular index. We then discuss nonunique attributes in detail.

We note that there is a dictionary ctr in the client proxy to keep track of the counter/number of each distinct value v in the database. To encrypt or insert a document with the attribute value equal to v, the client proxy will retrieve and increment $ctr[v]$, and then encrypt v as

$$Enc(v) := H(EQunique(v), ctr[v]),$$

where H is a hash function. It provides both semantic security and forward privacy since we add randomness via $ctr[v]$ and the server cannot learn newly inserted values according to the old tokens. As you have noticed, we cannot decrypt the value from $Enc(v)$ as it is hashed by a one-way function, but we also encrypt v with **Base** as well, from which we can then recover the plaintext value.

When the client issues a query for searching v, the client proxy derives the search tokens for every counter from 1 to $ctr[v]$ as

$$H(EQunique(v), 1), \ldots, H(EQunique(v), ctr[v]). \tag{6.1}$$

After receiving the token list, the server proxy performs search by substituting WHERE clause in Sect. 6.2.2 with attributes equal to the disjunction of tokens in Eq. (6.1), i.e., att $= H(EQunique(v), 1) \vee \cdots \vee H(EQunique(v), ctr[v])$.

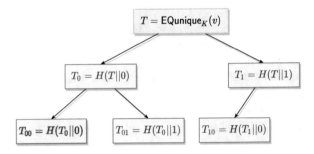

Fig. 6.3 Search token tree in Arx

Optimization We note that in the above construction, the client proxy has to compute and send $ctr[v]$ tokens, which might be expensive in some large-scale databases. We then show how to reduce the work from $ctr[v]$ to $\log ctr[v]$.

The brief idea is shown in Fig. 6.3. Instead of computing tokens for every counter from 1 to $ctr[v]$, the client proxy first computes as the search token tree root $EQunique(v)$. Non-root nodes will be obtained by hashing the concatenation of its parent's label and 0 if it's a left child or 1 if it is a right child. It stops generating children when the number of leaves in the tree becomes $ctr[v]$.

The client proxy no longer needs to generate every leaf node. Instead, it finds the exact *covering set* for leaf nodes, which are the minimum set of internal and leaf nodes whose subtrees (if exist) *exactly* cover the leaf nodes $1, \ldots, ctr[v]$. For example, the covering set of the instance in Fig. 6.3 is $\{T_0, T_{10}\}$. One can easily derive the covering set from the binary representation of $ctr[v]$, and the server proxy will expand the received covering set into the token list and proceed as before.

Arx does not provide backward privacy since it simply deletes the documents but not the indexes. It does not affect the accuracy but affects its performance due to the growing missing counters. Besides, it also leaks the number of deleted records to the server. Therefore, Arx adopts a simple cleanup process after one or more deletions as follows. The client proxy updates $ctr[v]$ by reducing the number of deletions, generates a new key k', and updates search tokens accordingly.

ArxRange and Order-Based Queries

We first present a straightforward but inefficient design as a starting point. For simplicity, the index is assumed to be a binary tree rather than a traditional B-tree. To ensure the target security level, each node in the index tree will be encrypted by a probabilistic symmetric cipher (*i.e.*, semantically secure), and thus could not be directly used by the server to traverse the tree. To find a value a in the tree, the server proxy interacts with the client proxy by providing the current encrypted node (starting from the root) to the client, who will then decrypt it into plaintext, compare it to the target value a, and tell the server where the next node is. The procedure proceeds until it reaches a leaf, which results in a logarithmic number of round trips, making it inefficient.

Noninteractive Traversal To enable the server to traverse the index tree on its own, Arx plants at each node a *garbled circuit* to perform the comparison without revealing a and v to the server.

Specifically, a garbling circuit scheme consists of three algorithms (Garble, Encode, Eval) [111, 293] as follows.

$(F, e) \leftarrow \text{Garble}(f)$ run by the client takes as input a Boolean circuit f and outputs a garbled version F of the circuit, together with some secret information e;

$e_a \leftarrow \text{Encode}(e, a)$ run by the client takes as input his secret information e together with the input a of the function f, and outputs an encoding e_a;

$y \leftarrow \text{Eval}(F, e_a)$ run by the server takes as inputs a garbled function F and an encoded input e_a, and returns the output $y \leftarrow f(a)$.

The security of garbled circuits ensures that the server will not learn anything about a or the data hard-coded in f but the output $f(a)$ (as well as the volume of a and f), *if* the garbled circuit is used *only once*. Or in other words, if the client provides another message e_b encoded with e as well, the server will break the security guarantees.

To avoid interactions, it is necessary for each node to *re-encode* the input for its child, since each encoding e_a differs from the other. We thus chain the garbled circuits such that the output of the current node is compatible with the consequent child node. Figure 6.4 presents how the server traverses the index tree avoiding interactions with the client proxy. The number presents the value v hard-coded in the garbled circuit.

Repairing the Index The garbled circuits along the search path are destroyed during the search as it could be used at most once. Therefore, we ask the client to provide new circuits to substitute consumed ones. It is trivial that only a logarithmic number of them are accessed during each search process. To further reduce the communication bandwidth, the server only sends IDs of consumed circuits to the client since every ID is unique for each circuit. Indeed, the encoding message contained in the circuit is not small—1 KB for a 32-bit numeric value comparison— which is dozens of times of original communication costs.

Performance of Arx

Queries supported by Arx are fewer than queries than CryptDB; however, their functionalities are comparable in the real-world dataset, and Arx covers the vast majority of common queries. At the expense of significantly stronger security guarantees, range and equality queries in Arx cost a few milliseconds, which are several times more expensive than CryptDB but still practical. The repairing process

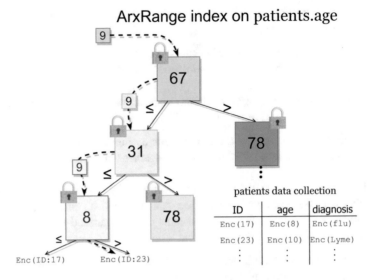

Fig. 6.4 ArxRange example from [221], where Enc is **Base** encryption

accounts for the main part of the whole search query. By utilizing more efficient AES-based functions, aggregation over a range in Arx is considerably (orders of magnitude) faster than CryptDB with the same security level due to the expensive homomorphic operations in the latter one.

6.2.3 Interoperable Encrypted Database

Another drawback of CryptDB is the inability to process complex queries which pipe the output of one operation to another, i.e., lack of *data interoperability*. For instance, the selection operation "unit-price×quantity>\$8000" requires the server to compare the multiplication results at the same time and thus is not supported by CryptDB. Wong et al. proposed an encrypted database named SDB to achieve data interoperability by utilizing a special type of multiplicatively homomorphic encryption scheme. It generates a new key to multiply ciphertexts encrypted by different keys as

$$E(k_3, v_1 \times v_2) \leftarrow E(k_1, v_1) \times E(k_2, v_2)$$

In addition, it is additively homomorphic only for ciphertexts encrypted by the same key:

$$E(k, v_1 + v_2) \leftarrow E(k, v_1) + E(k, v_2)$$

All data items in a database are initially encrypted under different keys. When the client wants to add two columns, it helps the server to update respective items in two columns to be under the same key, such that the server can perform an addition operation. The key updating also helps the server and data owner decrypt an entire column with constant communication overhead.

To compare two values, e.g., $v_1 < v_2$, the server first updates $E(k_1, v_1)$ and $E(k_2, v_2)$ to be encrypted by the same key k_3 with the assistance of the data owner, and computes $E(k_3, v_1 - v_2) \leftarrow E(k_3, v_1) - E(k_3, v_2)$. Then it computes

$$E(k_5, u(v_1 - v_2)) \leftarrow E(k_3, v_1 - v_2) \times E(k_4, u),$$

where $E(k_4, u)$ was supplied by the data owner previously and u is a small random number that will not change the sign of $v_1 - v_2$ but hide the value of $v_1 - v_2$. Finally, the server decrypts $u(v_1 - v_2)$ and selects the rows satisfying $u(v_1 - v_2) < 0$.

To sum a column of n encrypted items $E(k_1, v_1), \ldots, E(k_n, v_n)$, the server updates those items to $m^{-1}v_1, \ldots, m^{-1}v_n$ with the assistance of the data owner, where m is a random number. Then, it returns $m^{-1} \sum_{i=1}^{n} v_i$ to the data owner. Other operations such as equi-join and group-by can be realized in the same approach.

However, this encrypted database is vulnerable to co-prime attacks as described in [45]. The first insight behind their attacks is that for α randomly picked integers from $\mathbb{Z}_M$, the probability that they are co-prime is $\frac{1}{\zeta(\alpha)} + O(\frac{1}{|M|})$, where ζ is the Riemann ζ-function and $\zeta(\alpha) = \sum_{i=1}^{+\infty} \frac{1}{i^\alpha}$. For example, the probability for 4 randomly picked 32-bit integers being co-prime is about 93%.

We then observe that the additively homomorphic encryption is deterministic, which implies that

- $E(k, v) = E(k, v')$ if and only if $v = v'$;
- $\gamma E(k, v) = E(k, \gamma v)$ can be viewed as adding γ ciphertexts together.

Consider the scenario where the server sums α ciphertexts up as $E(k, \sum_{i=1}^{\alpha} v_i) \leftarrow \sum_{i=1}^{\alpha} E(k, v_i)$, and the adversary wants to recover all these α plaintexts. With the above two properties, the adversary can compute the ratio between v_1 and v_i, by finding γ_1^i and γ_i such that

$$\gamma_i E(k, v_1) = \gamma_1^{(i)} E(k, v_i).$$

Then $\frac{v_1}{v_j} = \frac{\gamma_1^{(j)}}{\gamma_i}$. The adversary can find all $\left(\gamma_1^{(i)}, \gamma_i\right)$ by enumerating all possible pairs in $\mathbb{Z}_M^2$ and introduces $O(M^2)$ computational costs. After that, the adversary obtains all ratios $\left(\gamma_1^{(2)}, \gamma_2\right), \ldots, \left(\gamma_1^{(\alpha)}, \gamma_\alpha\right)$ and computes $\gamma_1 \leftarrow$ LCM$(\gamma_1^{(2)}, \ldots, \gamma_1^{(\alpha)})$, where LCM denotes the least common multiple of the given numbers. Then the ratio among $v_1, \ldots, v_\alpha$ is

$$\gamma_1 : \frac{\gamma_1 \gamma_2}{\gamma_1^{(2)}} : \cdots : \frac{\gamma_1 \gamma_\alpha}{\gamma_1^{(\alpha)}}$$

Since $v_1, \ldots, v_\alpha$ are extremely likely to be co-prime, their values correspond to their ratios.

We note that the above attack succeeds only if the domain of plaintext values $\mathbb{Z}_M$ is relatively small, since the computational efforts grow linearly with the size of the domain size. Their experiments showed that it takes about half an hour to recover ciphertexts if the domain size is 2^{20}. And for a common unsigned integer domain (i.e., 2^{32}), it will take decades to recover the desired ciphertexts. Therefore, one efficient and effective countermeasure is to enlarge the plaintext space by each item by multiplying a random value. It does not suffice to protect those values since it will not change their ratios. Therefore, a small random noise will be added to the new plaintext values. This countermeasure requires little extra effort but will dramatically enlarge the plaintext domain and nullify the co-prime attacks.

6.3   Using Hardware-Assisted Secure Enclave

After learning encrypted databases based on special-purpose cryptographic primitives, we will then move to some encrypted databases leveraging trusted computing processors. The former usually requires high-performance overheads to guarantee strong security levels, or results in large leakage profiles such as order-preserving encryption. Some encrypted databases, e.g., Cipherbase [10] and TrustedDB [17], utilize non-standard trusted computing platforms (e.g., FPGAs) and are limited to the architecture of the devices used. Therefore, we will focus on some encrypted database systems leveraging a standard CPU with Intel Software Guard Extensions (SGX) instruction set [71]. Intel SGX only allows a predefined trusted code to create and access an encrypted memory container (i.e., *encalve*), which is protected against untrusted parties, including the administrators, the operating system, and the hypervisor. The performance restrictions of Intel SGX mainly come from frequent context switching, i.e., in to/out of the enclave, and the limited capacity of the enclave, which results in frequent data encryption/decryption for loading required data. Though there do exist some attacks on Intel SGX, we will not take vulnerabilities of SGX itself into account since most of them are impractical and will soon be fixed by Intel. However, we will consider the remaining potential attack surface, such as how the enclave interacts with the main memory, and the volume of data loaded into or flushed out to the external storage.

The maximum Enclave Page Cache (EPC) size for Intel SGX was originally limited to 128 MB (and 256 MB for a few newer personal processors), of which only about 93 MB could be used by applications. With the development of technology, the third-generation Intel Xeon (Server) Processor now supports large enclave capacities from 8 GB to 512 GB, which may accommodate the entire database or index structures. Therefore, one of the main restrictions of Intel SGX will be greatly alleviated in the short future.

In addition to three essential aspects to evaluate a conventional encrypted database, i.e., security, functionality, and performance, a practical one leveraging on trusted hardware also pays attention to another critical dimension "intrusiveness level," which is the number of changes made to the underlying DBMS. It requires developers to rewrite and partition code into trusted and untrusted segments. The developers have to consider many different implementation details, and a deep or highly intrusive transformation to the Intel SGX version will occur many engineering problems. Though there are some recent works such as Scone [11], Haven [19], and Graphene [262] to load unmodified executable programs into enclaves, it still suffers from the limited working memory size as well as serious penalties that occurred when going beyond that limit [204]. Moreover, even with larger enclave sizes, the integrity protection (e.g., Merkle tree) for memory pages performs unsatisfactorily with larger enclaves. Therefore, one cannot naively try to "run a DBMS system in an enclave," just like one cannot naively try to encrypt everything in a database in the previous section. It is of great importance for the designer to achieve desirable security, performance, and functionality goals with delicate changes. Besides, due to the distinct set of security and usability requirements of each trusted hardware platform, the end-to-end security guarantees may not be preserved when we simply port the design from another platform such as FPGAs.

In this section, we will first describe a scalable encrypted database supporting full SQL query types called *StealthDB*. After that, we will introduce *ObliDB*, an efficient and oblivious database engine based on the enclave for general-purpose SQL databases and stronger security. The formal one focuses more on functionality and performance, while the latter concentrates on obliviousness and security guarantees. We will then explore different design choices from five aspects and their trade-offs to assist database practitioners in finding their own design "equilibrium." Finally, we will present an encrypted database design called *Enclage* as a practical engineering design.

6.3.1   A Scalable Encrypted Database Supporting Full SQL Query Types with Intel SGX

Firstly, let's briefly review the concept of trusted execution environment (TEE) and Intel Software Guard Extensions (SGX). A TEE is a secure area that offers confidentiality and integrity of data and computation. By employing TEEs, secure applications can be built in untrusted environments where a malicious host may operate (e.g., on a third-party server). Intel SGX is a popular and well-designed implementation among many TEE designs, attracting attention from both academia and industry. Protection of SGX is provided by a concept called *enclave*, whose features include sealing, isolation, and attestation.

An enclave represents a virtual address space within a process. Enclave page caches (EPC) are protected memory pages where both code and data reside whose contents are inaccessible by the host, that is, by the rest of the process or by the other processes outside the enclave. The data in EPC is in ciphertext as well. There is a memory encryption engine (MEE), which will automatically decrypt the page from the EPC and handle it to the CPU, or encrypt or encrypt data from the CPU cache to the EPC, sitting *transparently* between the CPU and the EPC. Therefore, data in EPC is "unencrypted" from the CPU standpoint. In addition, clients can verify an enclave's authenticity from a remote host with SGX's *remote attestation* service, through which the client and the enclave can establish a secure channel (e.g., for exchanging secret keys). The reasons the most encrypted database designs do not use another promising alternative called AMD SEV [156, 210] to guarantee the data confidentiality are lacking integrity protection [210] and security-proven remote attestation [42]. However, the latter is one of the fundamental modules for secure key provision in encrypted database designs. The absence of integrity assurance also compromises their security on the cloud.

We present the architecture of SteathDB in Fig. 6.5. As discussed above, most of the components in StealthDB are built on top of unmodified DBMSs, with few changes being made to the underlying DBMS. Next, we'll proceed to the entire process of database creation and query execution in StealthDB, explaining every component as necessary.

Database Creation

Upon creating a database, the data owner provides a schema to define the database structure. StealthDB allows the owner to specify which columns are sensitive and should be protected by the *encrypted datatypes*, i.e., encrypted versions of their underlying plaintext datatypes. For example, encrypted 4-byte floats are represented by the encrypted datatype *enc_float4*, encrypted strings are represented by *enc_text*. And the user can therefore create a table *item* with three columns, including a unique id, encrypted name, and its price, as follows:

```
CREATE TABLE item (
id int NOT NULL,
name enc_text NOT NULL,
price enc_float4 NOT NULL,
PRIMARY KEY (id)
);
```

StealthDB will encrypt the corresponding data types with a semantically secure scheme (i.e, AES-CTR) to offer data confidentiality.

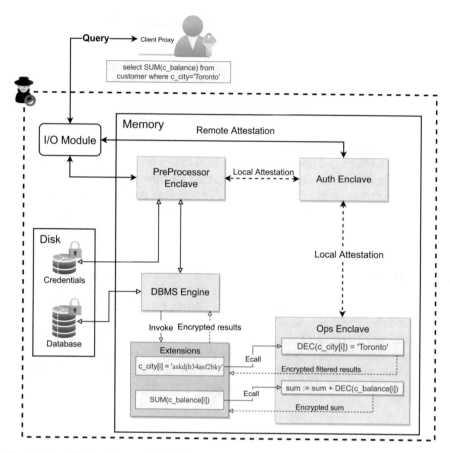

Fig. 6.5 StealthDB architecture [269]. The shaded-arrow lines represent protected communication between those entities

DBMS Initialization

During the startup of a DBMS, the following additional steps need to be taken in StealthDB.

Enclave Creation Three enclaves on the database server are created: Auth enclave for client authentication, PreProcessor enclave for query preprocessing, and Ops for actual data operations. It is the *untrusted* DBMS runtime that loads these enclaves; however, the client can later *attest* (i.e., verify) whether the enclaves load the code correctly or not. The following section will provide a detailed explanation of this step and the functionalities of these enclaves.

StealthDB introduces an I/O layer on the cloud server to facilitate the user-enclave communication, which is responsible for redirecting requests between the

DBMS and the appropriate enclaves and outside the SGX trusted computing base. It hence is untrusted and may be controlled by the adversary.

Key Generation It is the duty of the Auth enclave to generate a random 128-bit secret key K for the AES encryption and decryption. For simplicity, this master key K is designed for encrypting all the sensitive data in the databases. One can easily extend this design to enable different keys for different columns in the databases by integrating a key management service.

After being generated, the master key K is transferred to the other two enclaves as follows. The Auth enclave performs a local attestation with each of the PreProcessor and the Ops enclaves individually, and then establish a secure channel between them. After successfully setting up the secure channels, Auth then sends the master key K to the other two enclaves via the secure channels. Upon receiving the key K, they will use the SGX seal operation to encrypt and store K on the external storage for future uses.

Credentials Transfer The last step of the initialization is to transfer the client credentials (e.g., its password or its SSH key) and access policies to the Auth enclave, which will be authenticated by a client proxy. From then on, Auth and PreProcessor will be viewed by the DBMS as a client that has full access to the database. To accomplish this, the client remotely attests Auth and establishes a secure channel. Afterward, it transfers the master credentials as well as client credentials, and access policies to Auth via the secure channel. Upon receiving these materials, Auth uses SGX's sealing functionality to encrypt and store them.

Client Authentication

Another challenge that the designer needs to address is to guarantee that the encrypted database system is only accessible to authorized entities. To this end, StealthDB uses an authentication mode based on an existing DBMS. The following instructions should be followed by a client who wishes to authenticate to the Auth enclave.

First, the client proxy uses remote attestation to verify that the *correct* code has been loaded into Auth in the DBMS and establish a secure channel, through which the client will authenticate with its credentials (e.g., its SSH key or password) to the Auth enclave. On the server side, the I/O layer will lead the client authentication requests to Auth enclave, which will unseal the credential database to verify newly received credentials.

Once the authentication step completes successfully, PreProcessor enclave will begin to interact with the client. For this purpose, the I/O layer will transfer the session key of the secure channel from Auth enclave to PreProcessor via a token transfer function through another secure channel built between two enclaves.

Fig. 6.6 Operator "=" for
*enc_int*4

```
CREATE OPERATOR = (
    LEFTARG = enc_int4,
    RIGHTARG = enc_int4,
    PROCEDURE = enc_int4_eq,
    COMMUTATOR = '=',
    NEGATOR = '<>',
    RESTRICT = eqsel,
    JOIN = eqjoinsel,
    HASHES, MERGES
);
```

Query Execution

Now that a client has been authenticated, we will proceed to process and execute queries in StealthDB. The client proxy will encrypt the *entire* query string with an authentication session key and other authentication data when a client issues a query. On the server-side, **PreProcessor** enclave first decrypts the query ciphertext and checks whether the client has the privilege to execute this query. After passing the checks, **PreProcessor** identifies and encrypts the data values in the query which correspond to the columns in the database. The output `encquery` will be given to the DBMS for execution.

Since the *structure* of `encquery` is identical to that of the plaintext query issued by the client, the DBMS is oblivious to the modifications made by the encryption. Hence, the DBMS will be able to parse this query as usual and obtain a query plan. However, we need to enhance the DBMS to enable encryption datatype operations as follows.

Firstly, a set of *primitive* operators, which are indivisible operators, used by the underlying DBMS are identified:

Logical operators   such as AND, OR, NOT, etc.
Arithmetic operators   such as $+, -, *, /$, etc.
Hash functions   used to build indexes.
Relational operators   such as $<=, >=, <, >, <>$, etc.
Advanced math functions   such as trigonometric functions (e.g., sin, cos, tan), logarithmic functions etc.

StealthDB defines a function inside the **Ops** enclave for every possible input datatype tuple. For instance, StealthDB implements the relational operator "=" on Postgres as shown in Fig. 6.6. Given two encrypted data values (e_1, e_2) and a binary operator $\oplus$, the corresponding function inside **Ops** will perform:

1. *Decrypt* the inputs e_1, e_2 to get plaintext values p_1, p_2;
2. *Execute the operator function* to get $p_{out} = p_1 \oplus p_2$;
3. *Encrypt* the result p_{out} to get a cihpertext e_{out}.

It depends on the operator function and how many inputs and outputs it has. Once the final result of the query is obtained, **PreProcessor** re-encrypts the resulting ciphertexts using the session key and sends them back to the client proxy.

Standard SGX *ocall/ecall* interactions with enclaves cost a lot of computation resources, especially when there are many calls. For example, if the client issues a query requiring sorting a numeric column, then there will be $O(n \cdot \log n)$ ecall to compare n encrypted data in that column and thus result in frequent context switching. To mitigate this, StealthDB adopts an *exitless* mechanism [204] for Ops, which greatly enhances performance by avoiding context switching between trusted and untrusted zones for each call to the operator.

In addition, there are also other inherent advantages of its design:

- There are no overheads associated with queries involving only plaintext data types since the query processing and execution are carried out in a *native* way.
- It allows computations between encrypted and unencrypted datatypes, and the client could specify whether the output should be encrypted to further protect the user privacy.

Security Analysis

We first analyze the security guarantees of StealthDB against passive and semi-honest adversaries. And we further distinguish the adversaries into snapshots, who get some snapshots of the memory and external storage, and persistent adversaries, who can observe the memory of the system during its entire execution life cycle.

After initialization, StealthDB leaks the database schema, the shape of the tables, and views (i.e., the number of rows and columns). If the indexes are built on a specific column, the snapshot adversaries will observe the shape of the indexes, including the number of index keys in each internal node of a B-tree. However, a persistent adversary will observe the order of each encrypted key in the index, which will *degrade* the security level of that column to an order-revealing level, which has shown to be *catastrophic* when the range of that column is not large (e.g., age, salary, birthday).

To alleviate this problem, StealthDB uses re-encryption to detach the relationship between the values in the table and the index, which is effective against adversaries who do not observe the index creation process. Otherwise, the adversary is still able to link the re-encrypted ciphertext with the original one.

During the query phase, a snapshot adversary learns at most the shape information and other leakages due to the miscellaneous information maintained by the underlying DBMS, e.g., log information, and auxiliary information in the query plan. For a persistent adversary, it will learn the access patterns and the order patterns of involved encrypted data, as well as some possible plaintext outputs of the Ops enclave. Therefore, StealthDB has a relatively large attack surface and many LAA attacks we have introduced in Chap. 5 could be deployed to usurp user's sensitive data.

Performance Evaluation

Vinayagamurthy et al. [269] share their implementation of StealthDB on https://github.com/cryptograph/stealthdb. In addition to offering relatively strong end-to-end security guarantees, it provides a scalable encrypted cloud database supporting full SQL query types with a modest 30% drop in throughput and a slight latency increase of approximately one millisecond.

However, without building an index on the encrypted column, the sorting or some aggregation functions (e.g., max, $\sum$) overhead could be magnified dozens of times due to frequent encryption and decryption operations, while the index could sometimes be disastrous in an encrypted database.

6.3.2 Oblivious Query Processing for Secure Databases

We will then have a deep look at an encrypted database supporting a diverse array of oblivious operators leveraging trusted hardware, including insertions, deletions, aggregation, joins, and point queries. In comparison with other approaches, ObliDB gives speedups of an order of magnitude over general-purpose ORAM approaches, $1.1 - 19\times$ faster than Opaque [301] over range queries, an oblivious system *only* for analysis based on secure enclaves, $7\times$ faster than HIRB [230] over point queries, an oblivious index based on crypto primitives.

In addition to the assumptions of Intel SGX we have made in the previous section (e.g., security of the enclave and no one can subvert the remote attestation process), we assume a small amount of oblivious buffer (i.e., memory) inside the enclave which is free of access pattern leaks. In other words, the adversary cannot observe any useful memory access inside the enclave. Though SGX does not inherently offer this feature, other similar TEE implementations such as RISC-V's Keystone or Sanctum do offer it at reasonable performance costs. Besides, many ObliDB oblivious operators remain oblivious even without any oblivious buffer. ORAM can be reduced to as little as a few megabytes at the expense of performance.

Security Guarantees

Since all operators are oblivious, only the input, intermediate, and result table sizes and the chosen query plans will be leaked. One of SELECT algorithms additionally leaks if the resulting rows are from a continuous part of the queried table. Furthermore, if it is unacceptable to leak the intermediate table volumes, ObliDB could be combined with other padding algorithms, including full padding or more advanced padding techniques such as [18], to provide full obliviousness or differential privacy.

Generally, it depends on the actual circumstances whether intermediate table volumes are sensitive. For instance, when only one row from each table is selected in

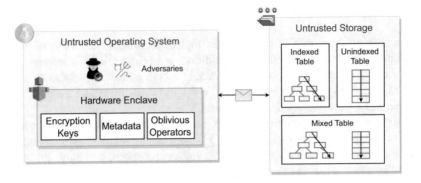

Fig. 6.7 The architecture overview of ObliDB [87]

a join of two tables (e.g., the lasted order from the order table and the corresponding customer record from the customer table), the sizes of those intermediate results (i.e., 1 row for each) are normally not considered to be sensitive. However, a query that requires all orders of a specific custom (perhaps followed by an aggregation function, like $\sum$) will let an adversary learn the number of orders the anonymous customer has made, and thus infers who or a set the anonymous customer belongs to. To avoid leaking such sensitive information, ObliDB introduces a fused select, project, and aggregate operator.

Similarly, a query plan may leak information about the query structure, e.g., whether the executor uses an index, or whether an INSERT or DELETE query was executed. ObliDB only protects query parameters such as the target value to be deleted or the key in an index to be requested, or whether the current key was ever repeated. In practice, it suffices to hide which data were accessed during query execution and thwarts many leakage-abuse attacks.

Finally, ObliDB does not hide which tables are accessed during query execution (and hence the number of tables accessed) for performance reasons. But it offers integrity guarantees against malicious OS from tampering with data, such as addition/deletion of rows, rollbacks to a previous state, or shuffling of contents.

Architecture and Data Structures

We demonstrate an overview of ObliDB architecture in Fig. 6.7, which is composed of a trusted code base within a secure enclave and tables queried by oblivious operators which we will elaborate on very soon.

It stores encrypted and authenticated tables in untrusted rich memory and obliviously accesses them if needed. The encryption key for those tables always resides inside the enclave and will be sealed into the external storage as described in StealthDB. ObliDB stores data in two approaches: indexed, flat, or both. The flat approach demands going through the entire table on each incoming query multiple times to offer obliviousness, whereas the indexed method uses B$^+$-tree stored in oblivious memory.

Since integrity protection is not the focus of our book, we will briefly introduce the idea here. The data are divided into blocks of configurable size; then the MAC of each block is attached to every block and encrypted as a whole. Each block of MACed data keeps a record of which rows the block contains and a "revision number" of that block, i.e., a copy of which block is cached inside the enclave. We will increment the revision numbers of those blocks after any legitimate modification. It will be discovered whenever a row is duplicated, shuffled, or removed if the row number of requested data does not match the data received or does not exist. When the revision numbers of stored blocks differ from the latest revision number stored inside the enclave, rollbacks will be detected.

Flat Storage Method   simply keeps rows in adjacent blocks without any built-in mechanism to guarantee obliviousness; therefore, any access to the table requires scan every block to hide access patterns. Therefore, there are multiple scans involved in the execution of operators on those tables. Small tables, operations returning large portions of tables, and analytics involving a large portion of tables are better suited for this method. It is a major challenge for designing algorithms for flat storage to reduce the number of scans and data processing operations with a limited enclave space to improve the performance.

Insertions, deletions, and updates on a flat table require one scan over it, where unaffected or undesired blocks will receive a dummy write (i.e., write with the original data but with re-randomized and re-encryption). For insertions, a real write is performed on the first free or available block encountered, i.e., write with the inserted data. For deletions (or updates), the target rows will be marked unused and overwritten by dummy values (or updated), respectively.

In tables with few deletions, we can also apply an efficient insertion algorithm that keeps track of the last inserted row's index, and inserts a newly incoming record directly into the next memory block. It hence skips expensive scanning and results in a constant time complexity. The insertion does not leak the access pattern since it is independent of the content of the data. As every entry in a table is encrypted, it is impossible for an adversary to tell whether the inserted data has been modified or removed by later operations. It will not cause a notable performance overhead as there are few deletions and the overall space utilization will be high.

Indexed storage method   involves more beyond a trivial combination with ORAM since a standard insertion or deletion operation leak information about the internal structure of the B$^+$-tree by observing splitting or merging nodes. To ensure obliviousness, we pad additional dummy accesses in both insertion and deletion operations to the worst possible number of the respective accesses. In other words, every update on the index should access h blocks, where h denotes the height of the B$^+$-tree. However, B$^+$-trees guarantee the same number of node accesses due to the fact that all data is stored in the leaves, so no padding is required in this case. In cases where operations result in the same number of accesses, we can adopt ORAM techniques to ensure obliviousness. Note that we use a separate RAM for each table since it is more computationally efficient to use multiple smaller ORAMs rather than a single large one, in the case that we already leak which table will be accessed.

In addition, another two optimization techniques are applied to significantly speed oblivious B^+-trees up. First, it uses a "lazy write back" strategy, i.e., the ORAM will be written back only when necessary, otherwise keeping them in the enclave. Second, it removes all parent pointers in the standard B^+-tree, since every operation will start from the root to ensure obliviousness, then there is no need to update the parent pointers in the siblings of the target node and thus save some ORAM writes.

Oblivious Query Processing

In ObliDB, we facilitate the query execution with a group of customized oblivious algorithms. They can execute queries over flat or indexed storage efficiently. We will elaborate those algorithms for a large portion of query types, and also a query planner to select the algorithm that maximizes performance. We will discuss the algorithms in the flat storage context, and then describe how to extend to index storage if necessary. We denote the input of a query as table T and the result as table R, whose sizes will be leaked as we discussed above. The enclave obtains the size of result table R from the query planner prior to the query execution, and hence improves the performance by allocating appropriate memory space to fill the output data structures.

Oblivious Selection   It selects eligible rows (i.e., records) from a table matching a given predicate clause (e.g., age >= 18). One natural way would be sequentially scanning the entire table and writing out the row if it satisfies the given predicate. Although every row of the table is touched once, this approach does not offer obliviousness, since an adversary could observe the access patterns to the output table to learn whether a row is written out and thus learn exactly which groups of rows match (or do not match) the predicate.

To protect against this and other subtle attacks, ObliDB offers the following oblivious SELECT algorithms as illustrated in Fig. 6.8. As mentioned above, we know the output table size $|R|$ before the execution phase:

Naive.   The naive oblivious algorithm simply transfers a non-oblivious SELECT to an oblivious one via general-purpose ORAM. It executes an ORAM operation after examining each row, i.e., either makes a real write if the row should be included in the output, or makes a dummy read to an arbitrary block. After finishing the scan of the input table, the server converts the ORAM data to the flat storage format and returns it to the client. The naive approach demands $4|R|$ bytes of ORAM to construct the output.

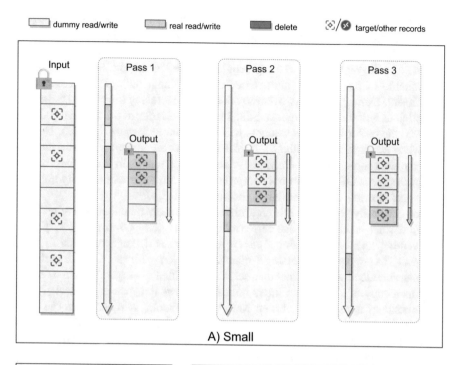

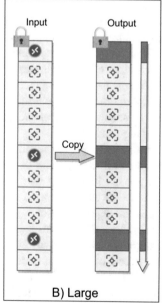

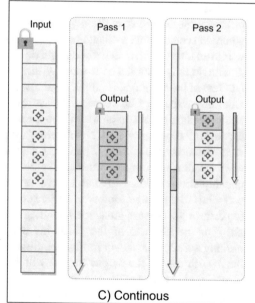

Fig. 6.8 Small, large, and continuous SELECT algorithms in [87]

In the following improvements, we explore the balances between removing ORAM from the enclave by using appropriate data structures, and making multiple oblivious and fast passes over data.

Small.   If the result table R only requires several times the amount of space available in the enclave, multipasses over the input table T are sufficiently efficient. During each scan over the table T, we store any selected rows into an oblivious buffer inside the enclave and maintain the index of the last checked row. Once the buffer is full, its contents will be written to R *after* that pass. Despite several scans in linear with $|R|$, it does not suffer significant performance loss. It requires some oblivious memory to store selected rows in the enclave buffer; however, less ORAM does not compromise the correctness or security but only its performance. This algorithm is shown in Fig. 6.8.

One can easily verify that this algorithm leaks no more than the sizes of tables T and R since an adversary can derive the number of passes over the input table T given $|R|$, and each "oblivious" pass reveals only the size of input table T.

Large.   If a large portion of table T matches the given predicate, ObliDB performs a *reverse* selection, i.e., rather than selecting qualified rows from T, it first creates R as a copy of T and then filters unqualified rows out, where unselected rows are marked unused and selected rows receive dummy writes. Since the copy operation is independent of the input data, every row receives a read followed by either a real or a dummy write. The algorithm remains oblivious without any oblivious memory as shown in Fig. 6.8.

Continuous.   If selected rows from a continuous section of the table T, ObliDB produces the output R with only *one* pass over T as shown in Fig. 6.8. It is a common scenario that a client queries for data such as salary, dates, names, etc., within an interval. To deal with such queries, ObliDB first creates the output table R with dummy values. The i mod $|R|$-th row of the output table R will receive i-th row of the input table T if the input row is qualified; otherwise, it will receive a dummy write for obliviousness. Since rows are continuous in the input table, this procedure results in an identical appearance of the selected segment except for shifting those rows a bit. No oblivious memory is required either.

Apart from the table sizes $|T|$ and $|R|$, this algorithm reveals that the resulting rows are drawn from a continuous segment in the input table. Knowing that a client queries for data within an interval is normally not sensitive as we hide the endpoints of the range. However, a client concerned with this leakage can choose to perform the other approaches, including a more general approach below.

Hash.   In the absence of the preceding special scenarios, ObliDB utilizes a hashing solution as shown in Fig. 6.9. Similar to the previous continuous case, the $h(i)$-th row of the output table R will receive i-th row of the input table T if the input row meets the conditions, where $h : [\![1, |T|]\!] \mapsto [\![1, |R|]\!]$ is a hash function. Otherwise, it will receive a dummy write for obliviousness. Since the hash function depends on the index rather than the actual content of a row, the access patterns will not leak any information about the data contents, and the algorithm uses no oblivious memory either.

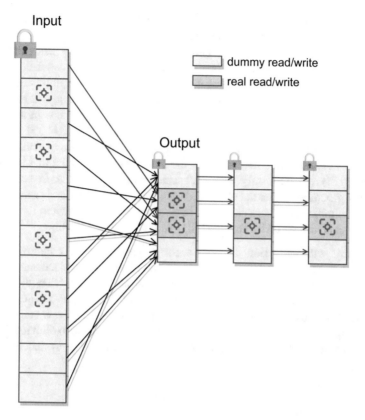

Fig. 6.9 Hash SELECT algorithm of [87]

One important topic in designing a hash function is how to handle collisions. In addition to other properties, we need to ensure that the collision resolution must not break obliviousness, which further requires that every row of T must result in the same number of accesses to memory no matter whether it is selected or not. It is handled by having every write make the worst expected number of memory accesses. Under the guidance of research [15], it suffices to use double hashing and a fixed-length list of $five$ slots for each row in R to guarantee negligible failure probability. The overall operation results in 10 accesses to R for each row in T, and 5 for each hash function.

Oblivious Aggregate and Group-By Queries

Since any aggregate function over the whole of a subset of a table will go through it, we aggregate each row of the input table inside the enclave in $O(|T|)$ time.

The aggregate operations are inherently oblivious with no oblivious memory, and nothing beyond the size of the input table will be leaked.

Grouped aggregation is handled similarly with an extra array inside the enclave to keep track of aggregates for each group. Because we do not want to show how each row affects the group's aggregation, extra 4 bytes of the oblivious buffer is necessary to store the corresponding aggregations. ObliDB deploys a hash bucket to load the hashed value of each group. While processing each row in the table T, we will compute the row hash and compare it with the hash table, if a match is found, then the current row will be referred to as a known group; otherwise, the current row is added as a new group to the hash table. It is trivial that the running time is $O(|T|)$ due to the only sequential scan over the input table. In case there are too many groups such that the oblivious memory inside the enclave cannot hold the entire hash table (quite rare situations in practice), we could switch to a sort-and-filter approach discussed by Opaque [301] with $O(|T| \log^2 |T|)$ time.

Combining with Selection For the above aggregate query counting the total number of orders after a specific date, it will be completely unnecessary to run an oblivious SELECT algorithm to produce the intermediate table/view that contains all the order records after "2022-04-01." Instead, ObliDB computes aggregates (i.e., count here) directly over the input table T while examining each row before feeding it to the aggregate functions. It reduces time and memory space to obliviously create the table to store selected rows, since they will be discarded immediately after the aggregate.

```
SELECT count(*) FROM Orders WHERE order_date >=
    '2022-04-01';
```

Oblivious Join Queries

JOIN is another important operator in relational databases used to combine rows from two or more tables based on a related column between them. For simplicity, we denote the two tables to be joined as T_1 and T_2. We introduce two simple join approaches: an oblivious hash join requires a small amount of ORAM, and an oblivious sort-merge join requires null *oblivious* memory.

Oblivious Hash Join We join two tables by checking their hash equality. First, we use as much oblivious memory as possible in the enclave to construct a hash table containing records from T_1. Then, we fetch one row from T_2 each time (until processing the entire table T_2) to compute its hash value to check for equality. The next block of the output R will receive a write regardless of the check results. If two rows from each table indeed match, then the joined row is written to R; otherwise, a dummy row will be written to that slot of the output table. We repeat this process until checking every row in T_1.

Since the output table always receives a write for each comparison between T_1 and T_2, the memory access pattern is oblivious to any adversary. The complexity is asymptotically same as the traditional join algorithm, i.e., $O(|T_1| \cdot |T_2|)$. Similar to the small selection case, this algorithm does need some oblivious memory; however, the amount of ORAM only affects the performance but not correctness nor security. With more ORAM available, we can load more rows from T_1 into the enclave and thus speed up the whole process.

Another deficiency of this algorithm is that it always outputs a table of size $|T_1| \cdot |T_2|$ containing some dummy rows. Therefore, we bring the following two join algorithms with special attention to foreign key joins, in which the result table size is no greater than the larger one of T_1 and T_2, i.e., $|R| \leq \max(|T_1|, |T_2|)$.

Oblivious Sort-Merge Join We first introduce a basic scheme requiring some oblivious memory and then describe how to enhance it to better one without ORAM. The base algorithm first puts the contents of two tables together into a new one, which will be then divided into chunks of data that could fit into the enclave's ORAM. We then use ORAM inside the enclave to *sort* those chunks separately and *merge* these sorted chunks with a bitonic sorting network. The final step left is to get rid of rows without any match, and merge matching rows into the output table R by linearly scanning the sorted table since all matched values are consecutive after sorting. Aside from requiring oblivious memory, an adversary may exploit timing side channels if we use quick-sort to speed the join up as well, which should be overlooked for a real-scenario application.

We then elaborate on how to further remove the need for oblivious memory in the above mechanism. The algorithm first uses bitonic sort on both rows based on the join conditions rather than sorting chunks inside the enclave's ORAM. It takes advantage of the bitonic sort that the set of comparisons for a bitonic sorting network is independent of the input data; therefore, we can claim that the sorting process is oblivious. We also apply a trick to accelerate it by performing the sort inside the enclave as long as the size of the recursive sort could fit into the enclave. It reduces the extensive enclave and untrusted memory communication costs and whence optimizes the whole process.

Query Planner

In a traditional database, the DBMS will help optimize the query process by collecting statistics about a database, such as the most common values in each column or a histogram representing the approximate data distribution, to generate a more efficient query plan. However, that information could be catastrophic in an encrypted database and reveals vital information of the underlying data. Besides, it is not trivial to get those values as any qualified probabilistic encryption will inherently hide those values if only given the ciphertexts. However, ObliDB does utilize known information (i.e., sizes of the input and output tables) to somehow improve its performance. Generally speaking, the planner in ObliDB performs a fast scan over the table being queried that will give some useful information, such as the sizes of the input and output table and whether the selected rows are consecutive, to make an optimization decision without exposing any further information about

the data or query. Based on the preliminary information, the encrypted database
will then be able to determine which operator it will run according to some set
of thresholds (empirically, precomputed, or using a machine learning model to
predict). For maximum flexibility, users can manually force which operator to run
as well.

Performance and Security

The asymptotic time complexity for small select is $O(|T|^2/S)$ which requires S
bytes of ORAM, as we linearly scan the table T of size N for $\frac{|T|}{S}$ times. It is
easy to verify that the time complexity for large and continuous selections are both
$O(|T|)$ since they only involve several scans of the input and output tables. For
hash selection suffers the highest performance overhead $O(|T| \cdot C)$ where C is the
number of hash slots for each entry and is a general solution. All the above select
algorithms are better than directly combining an ORAM, which requires $O(|R|)$
bytes of ORAM and the running time is $O(|T| \cdot \log |T|)$.

The running time for both oblivious aggregate algorithms is the same $O(|T|)$,
while group aggregate requires additionally $O(|R|)$ bytes of ORAM. As for hash
join, since we need to check every row in T_2 with a hash table for $|T|/S$ times, where
S is the size of ORAM available, the total time complexity will hence be $O(|T_1| \cdot
|T_2|/S)$. For the base merge-sort join algorithm, the major time costs come from the
oblivious sorting which requires $O\left((|T_1| + |T_2|) \cdot \log^2\left(\frac{|T_1|+|T_2|}{S}\right)\right)$ and S bytes of
ORAM since we are obliviously merging $(|T_1|+|T_2|)/S$ chunks. To run without any
ORAM, the running time is slightly worse, i.e., $O\left((|T_1| + |T_2|) \cdot \log^2(|T_1| + |T_2|)\right)$
since we are sorting a merged table of size $|T_1| + |T_2|$ obliviously.

The experimental evaluations in their paper demonstrated that ObliDB is far more
efficient than the others: 19× faster than Opaque [301], and 7× faster than HIRB,
a previous oblivious index structure. Besides, the obliviousness can be offered by
ObliDB within 2.6× of the plaintext solution.

From the security point of view, ObliDB leaks the sizes of the input and
output tables without padding. Furthermore, performing the continuous select also
indicates that the eligible rows are from a continuous segment of the queried table.
But we can eliminate it by forcing the hash select operator.

6.4   Design Choices in Building Encrypted Databases

After learning about encrypted database designs with different focuses, we will
extensively explore and discuss possible design choices in building TEE-based
encrypted databases from the perspectives of security, performance, and functionality. One observation is that some of them are orthogonal and their combination will
determine the general tradeoffs for the encrypted database. Besides, we also present

an enclave-native storage design called *Enclage* proposed by Sun et al. [254] which makes practical trade-offs by adopting reasonable design choices and optimizations for the enclave. It reduces the aforementioned leakage patterns to page level while preserving high throughput and storage efficiency.

6.4.1 Exploration to a Broader Design Space

Instead of discussing any concrete construction directly, we explore the various design options for building TEE-based encrypted databases from the following five different dimensions:

Encryption Granularity. Sensitive data such as data records and indexes are encrypted to prevent the adversary from learning any plaintext value. One can encrypt data at the item level or page level.

In general, item-level (e.g., a column value or an index key) encryption is more flexible and portable, which allows various operations to go past the enclave, such as node splitting while updating a B+-tree index and row accesses. However, it suffers from heavy computation and storage overhead since many encryption schemes need extra metadata or padding. For instance, each ciphertext requires a metadata field of a fixed size (e.g., 32 bytes in *Enclage*) regardless of the ciphertext size. If we encrypt a column of 4-byte integers one by one, then the ciphertext will be amplified to $32 + 4 = 36$ bytes, and the entire encrypted database will be $9\times$ larger. Furthermore, it leaks the structural information of the encrypted data as described earlier. During a query execution process, the access patterns will make it vulnerable to most leakage-abuse attacks.

On the other hand, page-level encryption will notably reduce leakage patterns, and has much fewer ciphertext amplification, e.g., a 4 KB page encrypted with 32-byte metadata will be amplified by a factor less than 0.8%. It is particularly useful for accessing data with high locality since the costs of both encryption and decryption will be amortized across all data items. However, it requires the enclave to manipulate all data at once and is unfriendly to small data pieces.

Memory Access Granularity. In addition to encryption granularity, we also pay attention to the granularity of memory accesses from the enclave, which can be tracked by a persistent adversary. Similarly, item-level accesses only fetch or write requested data into the enclave. It is hence faster but leaks item-level access patterns. In contrast, the enclave will load the entire page if only one byte is needed in page-level access mode. It hides which item is actually accessed by the enclave to a certain extent at the expense of a page copy. We'd also like to point out that oblivious algorithms [70, 87, 111] hide access patterns by introducing additional fake accesses to unrelated data, which are hence independent of the access granularity and could also be adopted to further protect the database.

Execution Logic in Enclave. One could fully hide online status, such as execution flow and data operations against the adversary by putting the entire execution logic into the enclave. However, there is always a dilemma of determining an appropriate trusted computing base size, since designs with a smaller TCB size will be more robust and scalable; however, it makes more execution logic unprotected and suffers from leakage-abuse attacks, while a larger TCB size will lead to a burdensome patching process and could be incompatible with other platforms. Therefore, the choice of TCB size is of essential importance. In particular, the minimum TCB must cover key comparisons in indexes and basic data operators. The rest logic such as query planner and memory/storage management could be fully executed out of the TCB.

Enclave Memory Usage.   Recall that on the older SGX platforms, the EPC capacity is extremely limited to 128 MB. The performance of an SGX-based encrypted database depends heavily on both local and global EPC usage. It is necessary to cache frequently used data into unused EPC space to avoid encryption/decryption costs. We could also hide access patterns to some degree by doing so, since the adversary cannot observe frequently accessed items or pages.

Record Identity Protection.   First of all, it is necessary to encrypt the record identifiers to protect them against the adversary. However, by observing two identical ciphertexts, an adversary can also infer that the two are ciphertexts in fact equal. Therefore, we also need to deploy ciphertext re-encryption to solve this problem. And it is almost for free as we always encrypt data before writing them to the untrusted memory or storage. However, re-encryption alone may not be sufficient and requires assistance from other perspectives. For instance, key comparisons in the index lookup process will leak entry identity immediately and re-encryption alone is useless here.

Though each dimension has several different design choices, not all combinations among them are meaningful or valid in practice. For instance, it does not make sense to encrypt by page level when the table stores with none in an enclave. From a security point of view, the overall leakage of an encrypted database mainly depends on the weakest one among the five dimensions.

Rather than giving an exhaustive evaluation on all possible combinations, we will discuss an enclave-native storage engine called *Enclage* due to its practical feasibility.

6.4.2   An Enclave-Native Storage Design for Practical Encrypted Databases

Enclage is composed of two major components: a heap-file-like table store and a B^+-tree-like index. Design choices made in Enclage render reasonable tradeoffs among performance, security, and functionality. Basically, it applies page-level encryption for both table stores and indexes to take advantage of its stronger security and storage efficiency. However, we note that better performance requires meticulous tuning of the page size due to costly encryption/decryption operations and EPC capacity constraints; we will elaborate on how to select those parameters for data pages and index nodes, respectively.

On the contrary, Enclage Store and Index make different choices on other dimensions. Since index efficiency is predominant in the entire query execution process and heap-file-like table stores preserve low data locality in general, most of the EPC space will be allocated to cache index nodes with fixed EPC usage by Enclage. And we adopt index *node access* in the enclave to reduce ECalls costs as many as possible. In Enclage Store, we adopt data *page access* in the enclave to utilize data-page encryption, and we will not cache pages inside the enclave due to its low locality in practice. Besides, we always use record identifiers and ciphertext re-encryption in default. Therefore, data or record accesses inside a page are indistinguishable in the Enclage design.

Enclage Index

We present the overall design architecture of Enclage Index in Fig. 6.10. It consists of the following three tiers:

EBuffer   resides in the enclave and is responsible for managing page transfers between the protected EPC and untrusted host memory. Each page in **EBuffer** contains an index node in the *plaintext* form.

MBuffer   resides in the host memory and is responsible for managing encrypted page transfers between the untrusted memory and external storage (e.g., disk, SSD). In general, each **MBuffer** page contains multiple **EBuffer** pages.

External Storage   stores encrypted indexes for future uses.

We note that **EBuffer** and **MBuffer** differ in the encryption status and capacity, e.g., **EBuffer** processes plaintext nodes in limited enclave memory but **MBuffer** process encrypted pages in rich host memory. However, both buffers are composed of three parts, i.e., a hash map, a buffer descriptor, and a buffer pool.

The buffer pool carries an array of entry slots storing index nodes in **EBuffer** or pages in **MBuffer**, which can be directly located with its identifier. When given an identifier, we leverage a hash map to support a fast lookup of the node or the page in the buffer pool. And a buffer descriptor containing metadata of the pages in the buffer is built to help the fast lookup procedure. Furthermore, we also need to translate the addresses of different page representations between two adjacent tiers, e.g., converting a nodeID to a pageID with an offset, or a pageID to a physical address.

Optimizations We enhance the Enclage Index from the following three aspects. Firstly, to reduce EPC page swapping overhead, we allocate most of EPC capacity to **EBuffer** and adopt a faster EPC swapping protocol which will be discussed later. Secondly, due to expensive decryption costs, we will derive the optimal node size in **EBuffer** using a cost model. Lastly, since we can access a page in **MBuffer** in the

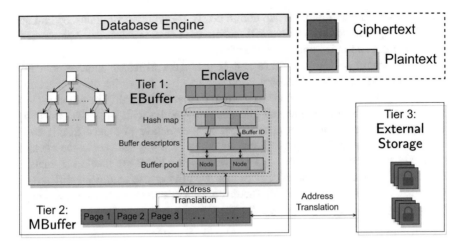

Fig. 6.10 Enclage Index with three tiers from [254]

enclave as long as it is in a known placement in the host memory, we will port part of **MBuffer**'s execution logic in the enclave to reduce unnecessary and expensive OCall operations.

Parameter Selection

As the index node size has a great deal of impact on Enclage Index, including node fanout, encryption/decryption cost, and buffer hit ratio, it is of great importance to choose an appropriate node size to improve the overall performance. We will therefore develop a cost model to determine the optimal node size. The following analysis shows that we will achieve optimal performance with a common node size in between 1 KB and 2 KB, which has been shown to be consistent with the experimental results in [253].

Assumptions We make the following reasonable assumptions to help simplify the cost model:

- A uniformly distributed query key.
- Only the bottom two levels (leaf nodes and their parents) of the B$^+$-tree need to be evicted to the **MBuffer**, since 10 MB is sufficient to store all the upper levels in practice.
- **MBuffer** can accommodate all index nodes, i.e., no I/O operations occur in the index lookup execution.
- A write-back probability r_{back} is fixed for each index node, which is dominated by the write ratio in a workload.

We denote h as the height of the B$^+$-tree, N as the number of indexed keys, n_e/n_m as then number of entries in EBuffer/MBuffer, f_o as the max fanout of index nodes, L_{meta} as the metadata size, L_{key} as the key size, L_{id} as the nodeID and rid size, and S_e as the EBuffer size.

We aim to derive the node size p (in bytes). All the notations in capital letters are constants determined by the environment. And we can derive the remaining accordingly. For instance, the total number of entries in EBuffer $n_e = \frac{S_e}{p}$. Since L_{meta} is generally much smaller than p (several bytes vs several kilobytes), we have

$$f_o = \frac{p - L_{meta}}{L_{key} + L_{id}} \approx \frac{p}{L_{key} + L_{id}}$$

Each node in a B$^+$-tree has $\left\lceil \frac{f_o}{2} \right\rceil$ to f_o entries. In the worst case, where each node contains $\left\lceil \frac{f_o}{2} \right\rceil$ keys and the tree height is h, we have the number num_i of nodes in i-th level as

$$num_i = \left\lceil \frac{f_o}{2} \right\rceil^{i-1}, \ 1 \le i \le h.$$

Therefore, the total number of nodes excluding the bottom two levels is

$$num_{[1,h-2]} = \sum_{i=1}^{h-3} \left\lceil \frac{f_o}{2} \right\rceil^{i-1} = \frac{\left\lceil \frac{f_o}{2} \right\rceil^{h-2} - 1}{\left\lceil \frac{f_o}{2} \right\rceil - 1},$$

which resides in the enclave all the time. And there are $num_{[h-1,h]} = \left\lceil \frac{f_o}{2} \right\rceil^{h-2} + \left\lceil \frac{f_o}{2} \right\rceil^{h-1}$ nodes in the last two levels. As there are $\left\lceil \frac{f_o}{2} \right\rceil$ entries in each leaf node, we have $\left\lceil \frac{f_o}{2} \right\rceil^{h} \ge N$, which implies $h = \left\lceil \log_{\lceil f_o/2 \rceil} N \right\rceil$.

Based on the above observations, we model the following costs accordingly.

EBuffer miss ratio. Since the remaining number of available entries in EBuffer for the last two levels is $n_e - num_{[1,h-2]}$ and the uniform access assumption, the probability of a miss in EBuffer is

$$r_{miss} \approx 1 - \frac{n_e - num_{[1,h-2]}}{num_{[h-1,h]}}$$

Since we need to access two nodes in the last two levels for each index lookup, the expected number of misses is $E_{miss} = 2 \cdot r_{miss}$.

EBuffer lookup cost consists of two parts: (1) computing a hash to locate the target node and (2) checking a list of nodes to find the target node which is proportional to n_e. Therefore, the total cost is $C_{\text{EBuffer}} = T_{Ehash} + T_{Elist} \cdot n_e$, where two T-factors are implementation-specific constants. In addition, there are h accesses to **EBuffer** for each query.

MBuffer lookup cost occurs when there is an **EBuffer** miss. Similarly, $C_{\text{MBuffer}} = T_{Mhash} + T_{Mlist} \cdot n_m$. And the expected number of accesses to **MBuffer** is E_{miss}.

Node decryption cost equals to the number of E_{miss} times the decryption cost for each node, which is further composed of preparation cost T_{dinit} and the formal decryption cost proportional to the node size. Therefore, the decryption cost for each node is $C_{dec} = T_{dinit} + T_{dec} \cdot p$, where two T-factors are implementation-specific constants.

Node encryption cost for each node is $C_{enc} = T_{einit} + T_{enc} \cdot p$, while the number of nodes to be encrypted is affected by the write-back probability, i.e., $E_{miss} \cdot r_{back}$.

Key comparison cost for each *key* is assumed to be T_{cm}. The cost of key comparisons for each *node* is $C_{cmp} = T_{cmp} \cdot \log \left\lceil \frac{f_o}{2} \right\rceil$ with binary search.

Therefore, the total cost for an index lookup can be calculated by accumulating the above costs as

$$C_{total} = (C_{EBuffer} + C_{cmp}) \cdot h + (C_{MBuffer} + r_{back} \cdot C_{enc} + C_{dec}) \cdot E_{miss}.$$

In a common setting where $S_e = 80\,\text{MB}$, $N = 10^7$, $L_{key} = 8B$, $L_{meta} = 24B$, and $L_{id} = 8B$, the total cost C_{total} first decreases and then increases when p shifts from $0.5\,\text{KB}$ to $16\,\text{KB}$ and achieves the minimum when $p \in [1\,\text{KB}, 2\,\text{KB}]$. Besides, the dominant factor in choosing an appropriate p is the key length L_{key}. For instance, the optimal interval changes to $[2\,\text{KB}, 4\,\text{KB}]$ when L_{key} changes to $4B$.

Enclage Store

Enclage store is a heap-file-like table store where incoming records are appended to a heap file with a unique id. Meanwhile, a key-id pair will be inserted into the Enclage Index if necessary. The record identifier contains its location used to retrieve or update it in the future. As opposed to a conventional heap file where we can simply append new records, Enclage Store needs to encrypt each page individually. Therefore, there is an active page maintained in the enclave for caching newly coming records, which will be encrypted and flushed to **MBuffer** once it's full.

As a result of the append-only mechanism, Enclage Store preserves poor data locality compared to Enclage Index. Therefore, it is reasonable to reserve most EPC capacity for Enclage Index to improve overall performance. On the other hand, we need to load and decrypt the entire page into the enclave to retrieve the target record. To speed this process up, we further utilize a delta decryption protocol that only decrypts the target record instead of the entire page. Consequently, Enclage

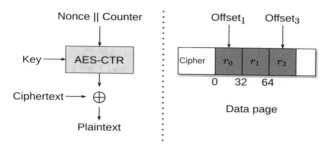

Fig. 6.11 The delta decryption protocol from [254]

Store could align its data page size with other choices (e.g., 4/8/16 KB) without compromising the performance.

Delta Decryption Protocol We adopt an AES-CTR-based decryption protocol, which allows a small portion of a large cipher to be decrypted alone. AES-CTR uses a monotonous counter for each block to initialize the decryption as shown in Fig. 6.11. Concatenating a page-wise nonce with a record-wise counter gives the IV of each individual record. The nonce is kept as the metadata for each page, while the counter could be computed as $\lceil offset_i/16 \rceil$ if the offsets are aligned to 16B.

Scalability and Integrity Protection

Multi-threading and thread synchronization primitives are provided by SGX. As for concurrency control algorithms, we can implement in-enclave data structures almost identically to their counterparts in the untrusted world with similar scalability. The scalability issue, therefore, is almost independent of Enclage construction. There are almost many scalable B-tree variants and lock-free data structures [21, 40, 84, 196] that could be further applied to the Enclage for better scalability.

In addition to protecting data confidentiality, we can also equip the Enclage with integrity protection if necessary. Merkle B-tree [171] could substitute the B^+-tree to offer integrity against data tempering and replay attacks [103, 250]. Each index node in a Merkle B-tree further contains the digest of the child nodes, and any update will trigger cascaded digest re-computation back to the root. Fortunately, we can delay the re-computation of a cached node inside the enclave until it is to be evicted, since the enclave inherently protects data integrity. Consequently, there is a substantial reduction in computation costs and an increase in concurrency. For table stores, we could adopt Merkle-tree to protect heap pages similarly and authenticated encryption schemes such as AES-GCM are more than enough.

6.5 Further Reading and Future Suggestions

There are thousands of data breaches happening every year, resulting in millions of records being exposed. Though parts of the data have been anonymized, most records are still in plaintext and thus compromise user privacy. In fact, storing records in ciphertext without taking side-channel leakage into account is sufficient to eliminate the vast majority of data breach hazards. CryptDB [224] is a seminal work in this area using numerous encryption schemes to execute different types of queries over encrypted data. It then spurred a rich line of work such as Cipherbase [10], which offers a scalable design for transactional workloads with a strong leakage profile and complete SQL support, and Monomi [263] for performing secure analytic workloads over sensitive data. Cash et al. [51] introduces a novel technique for indexing joins, called partially precomputed joins, in encrypted SQL databases achieving less information leakage and lower overheads.

Pappas et al. [215] designed and built scalable DBMS with an efficient sublinear search for arbitrary Boolean queries and provable security. Naveed [197] demonstrated that in some settings, it could be more efficient to stream the encrypted database back to the client who will work out query results locally than executing the encrypted database on a server. There are also numerous customized oblivious algorithms [87, 194, 301] for encrypted databases to fully eliminate access pattern during the query execution.

The main focus of research in database security over the past two decades has been on end-to-end encrypted database management systems (EDBs). In this period, a number of systems have been proposed with a variety of limitations, including poor performance, weak security, and a restricted amount of query expression. By properly leveraging techniques and ideas from both database and security communities, we believe we can make significant progress on this important problem. As we have discussed in Chap. 5, various leakage patterns are non-negligible factors while designing encrypted databases. Otherwise, a strong adversary may easily recover encrypted records and further compromise user privacy. On the other hand, the full protection mechanisms including (general-purpose and customized) oblivious algorithms and full padding approaches significantly downgrade the performance of an encrypted database. We also argue that the theoretical lower bound $\Omega(\log n)$ for oblivious algorithms makes them impractical for large-scale databases. From the adversarial point of view, a small amount of information leakage may not be sufficient to launch a leakage-abuse attack. Indeed, we have also covered some impossibilities on the power of adversaries in Chap. 5.

We hence believe that one future focus will be designing EDBs with small and controllable information leakage. Specifically, differential privacy as a hot topic at the moment could be a handy tool. We may treat various leakage patterns as statistics to be released. In addition, if we protect leakage patterns via DP approaches, then overall leakage and other disclosed statistics would jointly be differentially private as well (by applying standard DP composition theorems [83]), hence achieving an "end-to-end DP" goal.

Another worth trying direction is to systematically quantify information leakage and build a long-term monitoring system for encrypted database operations. Once the quantified leakage reaches a certain "red bar," the system will automatically reject future queries to prevent it against possible adversaries and wait for an oblivious reconstruction to fully empty the previous leakage.

Chapter 7
Conclusion

The demand for data ownership guarantees has been ever-increasing, and keeping data always encrypted in transit, at rest, and in use has become one of the widely agreed principles to safeguard private data in a worry-free manner. Searchable encryption, as a specific line of research along the direction of securing data in use, has made tremendous progress since its first construction was proposed in the early 2000s. The progress has significantly pushed forward the frontiers of functionality, performance, and security, transforming the area from early theoretical research proposals with slow performance to powerful cryptographic tools capable of working with real systems. This book provides a comprehensive introduction to the broadly defined notion of searchable encryption, and a systematic overview of the progress landscape spanning the past two decades.

Roadmaps Toward Modern Definitions Formulating the problem of searching over encrypted data has been a fine art among trade-offs between security and performance. Generic cryptographic tools like homomorphic encryption, multiparty computation, and even ORAM, which are surely capable of supporting encrypted searching, are unlikely to give practical performance. On the other hand, adopting property-preserving encryption (also known as property-revealing encryption) primitives like deterministic encryption makes the encrypted search problem easier to handle, but leaves undesirably extensive leakage profiles that could severely threaten the security. It has taken quite a long period of development for the community to largely agree upon the modern definition of searchable symmetric encryption (later known as structured encryption), with the allowed leakages on access pattern and search pattern, as a more balanced trade-off between security and performance.

Making the Constructions Scale On the performance aspect, the ongoing evolution has enabled today's mature searchable encryption constructions to support big datasets with practical performance. The first few encrypted data structures and algorithm designs for searchable encryption were very slow in the early stage. The encrypted search performance was comparable to a complete dataset scan

K. Ren, C. Wang, *Searchable Encryption*, Wireless Networks,
https://doi.org/10.1007/978-3-031-21377-9_7

in the encrypted settings. Subsequent constructions have achieved asymptotically sublinear performance in an almost theoretically optimal way, e.g., the search time cost majorly dominated by the number of documents that match the encrypted query. Today, mature constructions, primarily based on encrypted multi-map structures, can further pave away the obstacles toward practical performance, such as data locality and I/O efficiency, parallelism, space utilization, and more.

Enriching the Functionality with Complex Queries On functionality, searchable encryption has also made tremendous progress, from the early constructions focusing only on single-keyword queries to subsequent designs proposing new notions and constructions for encrypted fuzzy search, ranked search, multi-keyword conjunctive search. Modern constructions can support even more complex queries like Boolean conjunctive, substring, range, wildcard, and even phrase queries, with different trade-offs on the related leakage profiles. Besides, they can also handle dynamic data in realistic workloads, with cryptographically enforced forward and/or backward privacy, which are additional security requirements corresponding to adding new files and/or deleting old files, respectively. Another demonstration of the ongoing enrichment of functionality is the support of multiple users. While early constructions focused on managing the search rights of different users to "read" the encrypted database, more recent designs have investigated definitions and constructions to allow multiple writers to "update" the encrypted database.

Understanding Leakage Profiles and Leakage Suppression Modern constructions of searchable symmetric encryption have largely followed the well-established structured encryption framework, where there are well-defined leakage profiles, such as the access pattern and search pattern. Note that this is an intentional design choice to trade off security for better efficiency, as opposed to more hefty cryptographic primitives like oblivious RAM that, by design, are without such allowed leakages. At the early stage, these leakage profiles do not seem to attract too much attention from a security standpoint. But as the searchable encryption constructions are becoming more and more mature in performance and functionality, the community has started to focus on better understanding such leakage profiles with impact to security. Establishing such knowledge is especially important when deploying searchable encryption in real-world settings under different threat models and adversary assumptions.

Since then, there has been an ongoing arms race about the newly identified leakage-abuse attack vectors, the new attack models/tools that essentially speed up the attacks, and the various leakage suppression efforts to mitigate such threats. On the attack side, we have witnessed simple counting attacks, file injection attacks, generic volume-leakage attacks, file co-occurrence attacks, reconstruction attacks against range queries, etc., to name a few. On the defense side, we have seen proposals on space-efficient paddings, response-hiding and volume-hiding constructions, frequency-smoothing techniques, and adopting randomized perturbations (through differential privacy) on the document and/or matching result set. There are also generic leakage-suppression pipeline designs that are expected to automatically transform a given structured encryption into a new one with suppressed leakage profiles against known leakage-abuse attacks. The area has quickly turned into an active searchable encryption subfield, generating valuable insights, helpful techniques, and guidelines to better direct future searchable encryption constructions and the related real-world deployment.

Building Full-Fledged Encrypted Database Systems Research and development on searchable encryption constructions, which focus more on document search with keywords, have also motivated a series of latest efforts in building full-fledged encrypted database systems. Full-fledged database systems are pillar stones in modern computing infrastructure. Through several decades of advancements, these full-fledged database systems are not just providing indispensable means to organize, store, index, and retrieve data at different scales. They also meet stringent requirements to support various database applications, like enforcing data access policies, providing applications with transaction guarantees, supporting structured queries (e.g., SQL) with rich expressibility, performing sophisticated data analytics, and many more. As full-fledged databases are often highly optimized and complex in nature, building such an encrypted database system inevitably demands much more than encrypted indexing and searching. Simply integrating insights from modern searchable encryption constructions (and other cryptographic primitives) would be just a starting point and far from sufficient to meet all the demands of modern database systems on functionality, performance, usability, and security. Fortunately, the recently emerging proliferation of hardware-assisted secure enclaves has provided alternative technical and systemization options to complement where cryptographic primitives alone are lacking. In this regard, a handful of recent noteworthy proposals nicely integrate observations from searchable encryption and leakage suppression with database systems and hardware-assisted security primitives. The resulting designs have demonstrated outstanding potential, with which it's possible to support encrypted database applications in a transparent way.

The Pathway Ahead The rising demand for personal data assurance and rapidly expanding data protection regulations are jointly pushing forward a long-term vision, where data remains always encrypted in transit, at rest, and in use. Searchable encryption, as one of the critical enabling technologies, has demonstrated that such a vision is not just theoretically feasible, but practical enough for deployment and adoption in the real world. As search is ubiquitous, we expect future advancements in searchable encryption would provide organizations and individuals more options to develop privacy-preserving data applications with built-in encrypted search functionality. Encrypted search would also find great value in opening up new data marketplaces, where data can be searched, shared, and traded in an always-encrypted fashion. On the specific front of full-fledged encrypted database systems, we would like to call for closer collaborations among researchers and practitioners from searchable encryption (and secure computations in general), systems engineering, and database designs. Such synergies would more rapidly transform the latest advancements in encrypted search into highly optimized fully functional encrypted database systems. Indeed there are many challenges ahead, but there are also great opportunities in this exciting field. With this optimistic view, we would like to conclude this book.

References

1. Agrawal R, Kiernan J, Srikant R, Xu Y (2004) Order-preserving encryption for numeric data. In: Proceedings of the ACM SIGMOD International Conference on Management of Data, Paris, France, June 13–18, 2004, ACM, pp 563–574
2. Ahn JH, Boneh D, Camenisch J, Hohenberger S, Shelat A, Waters B (2015) Computing on authenticated data. Journal of Cryptology 28(2):351–395
3. Amazon (June, 2022) Encryption of Data at Rest. Online at https://docs.aws.amazon.com/whitepapers/latest/efs-encrypted-file-systems/encryption-of-data-at-rest.html
4. Amjad G, Kamara S, Moataz T (2019) Forward and backward private searchable encryption with SGX. In: Proceedings of the 12th European Workshop on Systems Security, EuroSec@EuroSys 2019, Dresden, Germany, March 25, 2019, ACM, pp 4:1–4:6
5. Andola N, Gahlot R, Yadav VK, Venkatesan S, Verma S (2022) Searchable encryption on the cloud: a survey. The Journal of Supercomputing 78(7):9952–9984
6. Angel S, Chen H, Laine K, Setty STV (2018) PIR with compressed queries and amortized query processing. In: 2018 IEEE Symposium on Security and Privacy, SP 2018, Proceedings, 21–23 May 2018, San Francisco, California, USA, IEEE Computer Society, pp 962–979
7. Antonopoulos P, Arasu A, Singh KD, Eguro K, Gupta N, Jain R, Kaushik R, Kodavalla H, Kossmann D, Ogg N, Ramamurthy R, Szymaszek J, Trimmer J, Vaswani K, Venkatesan R, Zwilling M (2020) Azure SQL database always encrypted. In: Proceedings of the 2020 International Conference on Management of Data, SIGMOD Conference 2020, online conference [Portland, OR, USA], June 14–19, 2020, ACM, pp 1511–1525
8. Araki T, Barak A, Furukawa J, Lichter T, Lindell Y, Nof A, Ohara K, Watzman A, Weinstein O (2017) Optimized honest-majority MPC for malicious adversaries—breaking the 1 billion-gate per second barrier. In: 2017 IEEE Symposium on Security and Privacy, SP 2017, San Jose, CA, USA, May 22–26, 2017, IEEE Computer Society, pp 843–862
9. Arasu A, Kaushik R (2014) Oblivious query processing. In: Proceedings of 17th International Conference on Database Theory (ICDT), Athens, Greece, March 24–28, 2014, OpenProceedings.org, pp 26–37
10. Arasu A, Blanas S, Eguro K, Kaushik R, Kossmann D, Ramamurthy R, Venkatesan R (2013) Orthogonal security with cipherbase. In: Sixth Biennial Conference on Innovative Data Systems Research, CIDR 2013, Asilomar, CA, USA, January 6–9, 2013, Online Proceedings, www.cidrdb.org
11. Arnautov S, Trach B, Gregor F, Knauth T, Martin A, Priebe C, Lind J, Muthukumaran D, O'Keeffe D, Stillwell M, Goltzsche D, Eyers DM, Kapitza R, Pietzuch PR, Fetzer C (2016) Scone: Secure Linux containers with intel SGX. In: 12th USENIX Symposium on Operating Systems Design and Implementation, OSDI 2016, Savannah, GA, USA, November 2–4, 2016, USENIX Association, pp 689–703

12. Aronesty E, Cash D, Dodis Y, Gallancy DH, Higley C, Karthikeyan H, Tysor O (2022) Encapsulated search index: Public-key, sub-linear, distributed, and delegatable. In: Public-Key Cryptography—PKC 2022—25th IACR International Conference on Practice and Theory of Public-Key Cryptography, Virtual Event, March 8–11, 2022, Proceedings, Part II, Springer, Lecture Notes in Computer Science, vol 13178, pp 256–285

13. Asharov G, Segev G, Shahaf I (2021) Tight tradeoffs in searchable symmetric encryption. Journal of Cryptology 34(2):9

14. Asharov G, Komargodski I, Lin WK, Peserico E, Shi E (2022) Optimal oblivious parallel ram. In: Proceedings of the 2022 ACM-SIAM Symposium on Discrete Algorithms, SODA 2022, Virtual Conference / Alexandria, VA, USA, January 9–12, 2022, SIAM, pp 2459–2521

15. Azar Y, Broder AZ, Karlin AR, Upfal E (1994) Balanced allocations (extended abstract). In: Proceedings of the Twenty-Sixth Annual ACM Symposium on Theory of Computing, 23–25 May 1994, Montréal, Québec, Canada, ACM, pp 593–602

16. Backes M, Barbosa M, Fiore D, Reischuk RM (2015) ADSNARK: Nearly practical and privacy-preserving proofs on authenticated data. In: 2015 IEEE Symposium on Security and Privacy, SP 2015, San Jose, CA, USA, May 17–21, 2015, IEEE Computer Society, pp 271–286

17. Bajaj S, Sion R (2014) TrustedDB: A trusted hardware-based database with privacy and data confidentiality. IEEE Transactions on Knowledge and Data Engineering 26(3):752–765

18. Bater J, He X, Ehrich W, Machanavajjhala A, Rogers J (2018) Shrinkwrap: Efficient SQL query processing in differentially private data federations. Proceedings of the International Conference on Very Large Databases 12(3):307–320

19. Baumann A, Peinado M, Hunt GC (2015) Shielding applications from an untrusted cloud with haven. ACM Transactions on Computer Systems 33(3):8:1–8:26

20. Bellare M, Boldyreva A, O'Neill A (2007) Deterministic and efficiently searchable encryption. In: Advances in Cryptology—CRYPTO 2007, 27th Annual International Cryptology Conference, Santa Barbara, CA, USA, August 19–23, 2007, Proceedings, Springer, Lecture Notes in Computer Science, vol 4622, pp 535–552

21. Bender MA, Fineman JT, Gilbert S, Kuszmaul BC (2005) Concurrent cache-oblivious b-trees. In: SPAA 2005: Proceedings of the 17th Annual ACM Symposium on Parallelism in Algorithms and Architectures, July 18–20, 2005, Las Vegas, Nevada, USA, ACM, pp 228–237

22. Bindschaedler V, Grubbs P, Cash D, Ristenpart T, Shmatikov V (2018) The Tao of inference in privacy-protected databases. Proceedings of the International Conference on Very Large Databases 11(11):1715–1728

23. Blackstone L, Kamara S, Moataz T (2020) Revisiting leakage abuse attacks. In: 27th Annual Network and Distributed System Security Symposium, NDSS 2020, San Diego, California, USA, February 23–26, 2020, The Internet Society

24. Bloom BH (1970) Space/time trade-offs in hash coding with allowable errors. Communications of the ACM 13(7):422–426

25. Boemer F, Lao Y, Cammarota R, Wierzynski C (2019) nGraph-HE: a graph compiler for deep learning on homomorphically encrypted data. In: Proceedings of the 16th ACM International Conference on Computing Frontiers, CF 2019, Alghero, Italy, April 30–May 2, 2019, ACM, pp 3–13

26. Bogatov D, Kollios G, Reyzin L (2019) A comparative evaluation of order-revealing encryption schemes and secure range-query protocols. Proceedings of the International Conference on Very Large Databases 12(8):933–947

27. Boldyreva A, Chenette N (2014) Efficient fuzzy search on encrypted data. In: Fast Software Encryption—21st International Workshop, FSE 2014, London, UK, March 3–5, 2014. Revised Selected Papers, Springer, Lecture Notes in Computer Science, vol 8540, pp 613–633

28. Boldyreva A, Chenette N, Lee Y, O'Neill A (2009) Order-preserving symmetric encryption. In: Advances in Cryptology—EUROCRYPT 2009, 28th Annual International Conference on the Theory and Applications of Cryptographic Techniques, Cologne, Germany, April 26–30, 2009. Proceedings, Springer, Lecture Notes in Computer Science, vol 5479, pp 224–241

29. Boldyreva A, Chenette N, O'Neill A (2011) Order-preserving encryption revisited: Improved security analysis and alternative solutions. In: Advances in Cryptology—CRYPTO 2011—31st Annual Cryptology Conference, Santa Barbara, CA, USA, August 14–18, 2011. Proceedings, Springer, Lecture Notes in Computer Science, vol 6841, pp 578–595

30. Boneh D, Franklin MK (2001) Identity-based encryption from the Weil pairing. In: Advances in Cryptology—CRYPTO 2001, 21st Annual International Cryptology Conference, Santa Barbara, California, USA, August 19–23, 2001, Proceedings, Springer, Lecture Notes in Computer Science, vol 2139, pp 213–229

31. Boneh D, Crescenzo GD, Ostrovsky R, Persiano G (2004) Public key encryption with keyword search. In: Advances in Cryptology—EUROCRYPT 2004, International Conference on the Theory and Applications of Cryptographic Techniques, Interlaken, Switzerland, May 2–6, 2004, Proceedings, Springer, Lecture Notes in Computer Science, vol 3027, pp 506–522

32. Boneh D, Goh EJ, Nissim K (2005) Evaluating 2-dnf formulas on ciphertexts. In: Theory of Cryptography, Second Theory of Cryptography Conference, TCC 2005, Cambridge, MA, USA, February 10–12, 2005, Proceedings, Springer, Lecture Notes in Computer Science, vol 3378, pp 325–341

33. Boneh D, Sahai A, Waters B (2011) Functional encryption: Definitions and challenges. In: Theory of Cryptography—8th Theory of Cryptography Conference, TCC 2011, Providence, RI, USA, March 28–30, 2011. Proceedings, Springer, Lecture Notes in Computer Science, vol 6597, pp 253–273

34. Boneh D, Lewi K, Raykova M, Sahai A, Zhandry M, Zimmerman J (2015) Semantically secure order-revealing encryption: Multi-input functional encryption without obfuscation. In: Advances in Cryptology—EUROCRYPT 2015—34th Annual International Conference on the Theory and Applications of Cryptographic Techniques, Sofia, Bulgaria, April 26–30, 2015, Proceedings, Part II, Springer, Lecture Notes in Computer Science, vol 9057, pp 563–594

35. Bossuat A, Bost R, Fouque PA, Minaud B, Reichle M (2021) SSE and SSD: Page-efficient searchable symmetric encryption. In: Advances in Cryptology—CRYPTO 2021—41st Annual International Cryptology Conference, CRYPTO 2021, Virtual Event, August 16–20, 2021, Proceedings, Part III, Springer, Lecture Notes in Computer Science, vol 12827, pp 157–184

36. Bost R (2016) Implementation of $\Sigma\_o\phi o\varsigma$. Online at https://gitlab.com/sse/sophos

37. Bost R (2016) $\sum o\varphi o\varsigma$: Forward secure searchable encryption. In: Proceedings of the 2016 ACM SIGSAC Conference on Computer and Communications Security, Vienna, Austria, October 24–28, 2016, ACM, pp 1143–1154

38. Bost R, Minaud B, Ohrimenko O (2017) Forward and backward private searchable encryption from constrained cryptographic primitives. In: Proceedings of the 2017 ACM SIGSAC Conference on Computer and Communications Security, CCS 2017, Dallas, TX, USA, October 30–November 03, 2017, ACM, pp 1465–1482

39. Boyle E, Couteau G, Gilboa N, Ishai Y, Kohl L, Scholl P (2019) Efficient pseudorandom correlation generators: Silent OT extension and more. In: Advances in Cryptology—CRYPTO 2019—39th Annual International Cryptology Conference, Santa Barbara, CA, USA, August 18–22, 2019, Proceedings, Part III, Springer, Lecture Notes in Computer Science, vol 11694, pp 489–518

40. Braginsky A, Petrank E (2012) A lock-free B+tree. In: 24th ACM Symposium on Parallelism in Algorithms and Architectures, SPAA '12, Pittsburgh, PA, USA, June 25–27, 2012, ACM, pp 58–67

41. Broder AZ, Mitzenmacher M (2003) Survey: Network applications of bloom filters: A survey. Internet Mathematics 1(4):485–509

42. Buhren R, Werling C, Seifert JP (2019) Insecure until proven updated: Analyzing AMD SEV's remote attestation. In: Proceedings of the 2019 ACM SIGSAC Conference on Computer and Communications Security, CCS 2019, London, UK, November 11–15, 2019, ACM, pp 1087–1099

43. Bulck JV, Moghimi D, Schwarz M, Lipp M, Minkin M, Genkin D, Yarom Y, Sunar B, Gruss D, Piessens F (2020) LVI: Hijacking transient execution through microarchitectural load value injection. In: 2020 IEEE Symposium on Security and Privacy, SP 2020, San Francisco, CA, USA, May 18–21, 2020, IEEE, pp 54–72

44. Cao N, Wang C, Li M, Ren K, Lou W (2014) Privacy-preserving multi-keyword ranked search over encrypted cloud data. IEEE Transactions on Parallel and Distributed Systems 25(1):222–233

45. Cao X, Liu J, Lu H, Ren K (2021) Cryptanalysis of an encrypted database in SIGMOD '14. Proceedings of the International Conference on Very Large Databases 14(10):1743–1755

46. Cash D, Tessaro S (2014) The locality of searchable symmetric encryption. In: Advances in Cryptology—EUROCRYPT 2014—33rd Annual International Conference on the Theory and Applications of Cryptographic Techniques, Copenhagen, Denmark, May 11–15, 2014. Proceedings, Springer, Lecture Notes in Computer Science, vol 8441, pp 351–368

47. Cash D, Jarecki S, Jutla CS, Krawczyk H, Rosu MC, Steiner M (2013) Highly-scalable searchable symmetric encryption with support for Boolean queries. In: Advances in Cryptology—CRYPTO 2013—33rd Annual Cryptology Conference, Santa Barbara, CA, USA, August 18–22, 2013. Proceedings, Part I, Springer, Lecture Notes in Computer Science, vol 8042, pp 353–373

48. Cash D, Jaeger J, Jarecki S, Jutla CS, Krawczyk H, Rosu MC, Steiner M (2014) Dynamic searchable encryption in very-large databases: Data structures and implementation. In: 21st Annual Network and Distributed System Security Symposium, NDSS 2014, San Diego, California, USA, February 23–26, 2014, The Internet Society

49. Cash D, Grubbs P, Perry J, Ristenpart T (2016) Leakage-abuse attacks against searchable encryption. IACR Cryptology ePrint Archive p 718

50. Cash D, Liu FH, O'Neill A, Zhandry M, Zhang C (2018) Parameter-hiding order revealing encryption. In: Advances in Cryptology—ASIACRYPT 2018—24th International Conference on the Theory and Application of Cryptology and Information Security, Brisbane, QLD, Australia, December 2–6, 2018, Proceedings, Part I, Springer, Lecture Notes in Computer Science, vol 11272, pp 181–210

51. Cash D, Ng R, Rivkin A (2021) Improved structured encryption for SQL databases via hybrid indexing. In: Applied Cryptography and Network Security—19th International Conference, ACNS 2021, Kamakura, Japan, June 21–24, 2021, Proceedings, Part II, Springer, Lecture Notes in Computer Science, vol 12727, pp 480–510

52. Chamani JG, Papadopoulos D, Papamanthou C, Jalili R (2018) New constructions for forward and backward private searchable encryption. In: Proceedings of the 2018 ACM SIGSAC Conference on Computer and Communications Security, CCS 2018, Toronto, ON, Canada, October 15–19, 2018, ACM, pp 1038–1055

53. Chang F, Dean J, Ghemawat S, Hsieh WC, Wallach DA, Burrows M, Chandra T, Fikes A, Gruber R (2006) Bigtable: A distributed storage system for structured data (awarded best paper!). In: 7th Symposium on Operating Systems Design and Implementation (OSDI '06), November 6–8, Seattle, WA, USA, USENIX Association, pp 205–218

54. Chang YC, Mitzenmacher M (2005) Privacy preserving keyword searches on remote encrypted data. In: Applied Cryptography and Network Security, Third International Conference, ACNS 2005, New York, NY, USA, June 7–10, 2005, Proceedings, Lecture Notes in Computer Science, vol 3531, pp 442–455

55. Chang Z, Xie D, Li F (2016) Oblivious ram: A dissection and experimental evaluation. Proceedings of the International Conference on Very Large Databases 9(12):1113–1124

56. Chase M, Kamara S (2010) Structured encryption and controlled disclosure. In: Advances in Cryptology—ASIACRYPT 2010—16th International Conference on the Theory and Application of Cryptology and Information Security, Singapore, December 5–9, 2010. Proceedings, Springer, Lecture Notes in Computer Science, vol 6477, pp 577–594

57. Chatterjee S, Das MPL (2015) Property preserving symmetric encryption revisited. In: Advances in Cryptology—ASIACRYPT 2015—21st International Conference on the Theory and Application of Cryptology and Information Security, Auckland, New Zealand, November 29–December 3, 2015, Proceedings, Part II, Springer, Lecture Notes in Computer Science, vol 9453, pp 658–682

58. Chen B, Lin H, Tessaro S (2016) Oblivious parallel ram: Improved efficiency and generic constructions. In: Theory of Cryptography—13th International Conference, TCC 2016-A, Tel Aviv, Israel, January 10–13, 2016, Proceedings, Part II, Springer, Lecture Notes in Computer Science, vol 9563, pp 205–234

59. Chen H, Huang Z, Laine K, Rindal P (2018) Labeled PSI from fully homomorphic encryption with malicious security. In: Proceedings of the 2018 ACM SIGSAC Conference on Computer and Communications Security, CCS 2018, Toronto, ON, Canada, October 15–19, 2018, ACM, pp 1223–1237

60. Chenette N, Lewi K, Weis SA, Wu DJ (2016) Practical order-revealing encryption with limited leakage. In: Fast Software Encryption—23rd International Conference, FSE 2016, Bochum, Germany, March 20–23, 2016, Revised Selected Papers, Springer, Lecture Notes in Computer Science, vol 9783, pp 474–493

61. Cheng R, Yan J, Guan C, Zhang F, Ren K (2015) Verifiable searchable symmetric encryption from indistinguishability obfuscation. In: Proceedings of the 10th ACM Symposium on Information, Computer and Communications Security, ASIA CCS '15, Singapore, April 14–17, 2015, ACM, pp 621–626

62. Cheon JH, Kim A, Kim M, Song YS (2017) Homomorphic encryption for arithmetic of approximate numbers. In: Advances in Cryptology—ASIACRYPT 2017—23rd International Conference on the Theory and Applications of Cryptology and Information Security, Hong Kong, China, December 3–7, 2017, Proceedings, Part I, Springer, Lecture Notes in Computer Science, vol 10624, pp 409–437

63. Choi SG, Dachman-Soled D, Gordon SD, Liu L, Yerukhimovich A (2021) Compressed oblivious encoding for homomorphically encrypted search. In: CCS '21: 2021 ACM SIGSAC Conference on Computer and Communications Security, Virtual Event, Republic of Korea, November 15–19, 2021, ACM, pp 2277–2291

64. Chu CK, Chow SSM, Tzeng WG, Zhou J, Deng RH (2014) Key-aggregate cryptosystem for scalable data sharing in cloud storage. IEEE Transactions on Parallel and Distributed Systems 25(2):468–477

65. Cimpanu C (April 2021) Phone numbers for 533 million Facebook users leaked on hacking forum. Online at https://therecord.media/phone-numbers-for-533-million-facebook-users-leaked-on-hacking-forum/

66. Ciriani V, di Vimercati SDC, Foresti S, Jajodia S, Paraboschi S, Samarati P (2009) Keep a few: Outsourcing data while maintaining confidentiality. In: Computer Security—ESORICS 2009, 14th European Symposium on Research in Computer Security, Saint-Malo, France, September 21–23, 2009. Proceedings, Springer, Lecture Notes in Computer Science, vol 5789, pp 440–455

67. Codd EF (1970) A relational model of data for large shared data banks. Communications of the ACM 13(6):377–387

68. Cohen WW (October, 2019) Enron email dataset. Online at https://www.cs.cmu.edu/~enron/

69. Corporation S (1999) SolarWinds backup. Online at https://www.solarwinds.com/

70. Costa M, Esswood L, Ohrimenko O, Schuster F, Wagh S (2017) The pyramid scheme: Oblivious ram for trusted processors. CoRR abs/1712.07882, 1712.07882

71. Costan V, Devadas S (2016) Intel SGX explained. IACR Cryptology ePrint Archive p 86

72. Cowan M, Dangwal D, Alaghi A, Trippel C, Lee VT, Reagen B (2021) Porcupine: a synthesizing compiler for vectorized homomorphic encryption. In: PLDI '21: 42nd ACM SIGPLAN International Conference on Programming Language Design and Implementation, Virtual Event, Canada, June 20–25, 2021, ACM, pp 375–389

73. Crockett E, Peikert C, Sharp C (2018) ALCHEMY: A language and compiler for homomorphic encryption made easy. In: Proceedings of the 2018 ACM SIGSAC Conference on Computer and Communications Security, CCS 2018, Toronto, ON, Canada, October 15–19, 2018, ACM, pp 1020–1037
74. Curtmola R, Garay JA, Kamara S, Ostrovsky R (2006) Searchable symmetric encryption: improved definitions and efficient constructions. In: Proceedings of the 13th ACM Conference on Computer and Communications Security, CCS 2006, Alexandria, VA, USA, October 30–November 3, 2006, ACM, pp 79–88
75. Damiani E, di Vimercati SDC, Jajodia S, Paraboschi S, Samarati P (2003) Balancing confidentiality and efficiency in untrusted relational DBMSs. In: Proceedings of the 10th ACM Conference on Computer and Communications Security, CCS 2003, Washington, DC, USA, October 27–30, 2003, ACM, pp 93–102
76. Dathathri R, Saarikivi O, Chen H, Laine K, Lauter KE, Maleki S, Musuvathi M, Mytkowicz T (2019) CHET: an optimizing compiler for fully-homomorphic neural-network inferencing. In: Proceedings of the 40th ACM SIGPLAN Conference on Programming Language Design and Implementation, PLDI 2019, Phoenix, AZ, USA, June 22–26, 2019, ACM, pp 142–156
77. Demertzis I, Papamanthou C (2017) Fast searchable encryption with tunable locality. In: Proceedings of the 2017 ACM International Conference on Management of Data, SIGMOD Conference 2017, Chicago, IL, USA, May 14–19, 2017, ACM, pp 1053–1067
78. Demertzis I, Chamani JG, Papadopoulos D, Papamanthou C (2020) Dynamic searchable encryption with small client storage. In: 27th Annual Network and Distributed System Security Symposium, NDSS 2020, San Diego, California, USA, February 23–26, 2020, The Internet Society
79. Demmler D, Schneider T, Zohner M (2015) ABY—A framework for efficient mixed-protocol secure two-party computation. In: 22nd Annual Network and Distributed System Security Symposium, NDSS 2015, San Diego, California, USA, February 8–11, 2015, The Internet Society
80. Devices AM (2022) AMD secure encrypted virtualization (SEV). Online at https://developer.amd.com/sev/, online
81. Dinov ID (2016) Volume and value of big healthcare data. Journal of medical statistics and informatics 4
82. Dobler P (April, 2013) Sybase adaptive server enterprise. Online at https://blogs.sap.com/2013/04/23/sap-sybase-ase-keeping-private-data-private/
83. Dwork C, Rothblum GN, Vadhan SP (2010) Boosting and differential privacy. In: 51th Annual IEEE Symposium on Foundations of Computer Science, FOCS 2010, October 23–26, 2010, Las Vegas, Nevada, USA, IEEE Computer Society, pp 51–60
84. Ellen F, Fatourou P, Ruppert E, van Breugel F (2010) Non-blocking binary search trees. In: Proceedings of the 29th Annual ACM Symposium on Principles of Distributed Computing, PODC 2010, Zurich, Switzerland, July 25–28, 2010, ACM, pp 131–140
85. Eskandarian S, Boneh D (2021) Clarion: Anonymous communication from multiparty shuffling protocols. IACR Cryptology ePrint Archive p 1514
86. Eskandarian S, Zaharia M (2017) An oblivious general-purpose SQL database for the cloud. CoRR abs/1710.00458, 1710.00458
87. Eskandarian S, Zaharia M (2019) ObliDB: Oblivious query processing for secure databases. Proceedings of the International Conference on Very Large Databases 13(2):169–183
88. Etemad M, Küpçü A (2013) Database outsourcing with hierarchical authenticated data structures. In: Information Security and Cryptology—ICISC 2013—16th International Conference, Seoul, Korea, November 27–29, 2013, Revised Selected Papers, Springer, Lecture Notes in Computer Science, vol 8565, pp 381–399
89. Evans D, Kolesnikov V, Rosulek M (2018) A pragmatic introduction to secure multi-party computation. Foundations and Trends in Privacy and Security 2(2-3):70–246
90. Fahmida Y Rashid (November, 2020) What Is Confidential Computing? Online at https://spectrum.ieee.org/computing/hardware/what-is-confidential-computing

91. Fellows M, Koblitz N (1994) Combinatorial cryptosystems galore! In: Finite fields: theory, applications, and algorithms (Las Vegas, NV, 1993), Contemp. Math., vol 168, American Mathematical Society, Providence, Rhode Island, pp 51–61

92. Fiat A, Naor M (1993) Broadcast encryption. In: Advances in Cryptology—CRYPTO '93, 13th Annual International Cryptology Conference, Santa Barbara, California, USA, August 22–26, 1993, Proceedings, Springer, Lecture Notes in Computer Science, vol 773, pp 480–491

93. Fisch B, Vinayagamurthy D, Boneh D, Gorbunov S (2017) Iron: Functional encryption using intel SGX. In: Proceedings of the 2017 ACM SIGSAC Conference on Computer and Communications Security, CCS 2017, Dallas, TX, USA, October 30–November 03, 2017, ACM, pp 765–782

94. Fletcher CW (2016) Oblivious ram: from theory to practice. PhD thesis, Massachusetts Institute of Technology, Cambridge, USA

95. Fowler J (February 2021) Report: American cable and internet giant comcast exposed development database online. Online at https://www.websiteplanet.com/blog/comcast-leak-report/

96. FreshMinds (2015 [Online]) Big & fast data: The rise of insight-driven business. Online at https://www.capgemini.com/wp-content/uploads/2017/07/big_fast_data_the_rise_of_insight-driven_business-report.pdf

97. Fu Z, Wu X, Guan C, Sun X, Ren K (2016) Toward efficient multi-keyword fuzzy search over encrypted outsourced data with accuracy improvement. IEEE Transactions on Information Forensics and Security 11(12):2706–2716

98. Fuhry B, A JJH, Kerschbaum F (2021) EncDBDB: Searchable encrypted, fast, compressed, in-memory database using enclaves. In: 51st Annual IEEE/IFIP International Conference on Dependable Systems and Networks, DSN 2021, Taipei, Taiwan, June 21–24, 2021, IEEE, pp 438–450

99. Fuller B, Varia M, Yerukhimovich A, Shen E, Hamlin A, Gadepally V, Shay R, Mitchell JD, Cunningham RK (2017) SoK: Cryptographically protected database search. In: 2017 IEEE Symposium on Security and Privacy, SP 2017, San Jose, CA, USA, May 22–26, 2017, IEEE Computer Society, pp 172–191

100. Gadepally V, Bolewski J, Hook D, Hutchison D, Miller BA, Kepner J (2015) Graphulo: Linear algebra graph kernels for NoSQL databases. In: 2015 IEEE International Parallel and Distributed Processing Symposium Workshop, IPDPS 2015, Hyderabad, India, May 25–29, 2015, IEEE Computer Society, pp 822–830

101. Gadepally V, Chen P, Duggan J, Elmore AJ, Haynes B, Kepner J, Madden S, Mattson T, Stonebraker M (2016) The BigDAWG polystore system and architecture. In: 2016 IEEE High Performance Extreme Computing Conference, HPEC 2016, Waltham, MA, USA, September 13–15, 2016, IEEE, pp 1–6

102. Gamal TE (1985) A public key cryptosystem and a signature scheme based on discrete logarithms. IEEE Transactions on Information Theory 31(4):469–472

103. Gassend B, Suh GE, Clarke DE, van Dijk M, Devadas S (2003) Caches and hash trees for efficient memory integrity verification. In: Proceedings of the Ninth International Symposium on High-Performance Computer Architecture (HPCA'03), Anaheim, California, USA, February 8–12, 2003, IEEE Computer Society, pp 295–306

104. Gentry C (2009) Fully homomorphic encryption using ideal lattices. In: Proceedings of the 41st Annual ACM Symposium on Theory of Computing, STOC 2009, Bethesda, MD, USA, May 31–June 2, 2009, ACM, pp 169–178

105. Gentry C, Goldman KA, Halevi S, Jutla CS, Raykova M, Wichs D (2013) Optimizing ORAM and using it efficiently for secure computation. In: Privacy Enhancing Technologies—13th International Symposium, PETS 2013, Bloomington, IN, USA, July 10–12, 2013. Proceedings, Springer, Lecture Notes in Computer Science, vol 7981, pp 1–18

106. George M, Kamara S, Moataz T (2021) Structured encryption and dynamic leakage suppression. In: Advances in Cryptology—EUROCRYPT 2021—40th Annual International Conference on the Theory and Applications of Cryptographic Techniques, Zagreb, Croatia, October 17–21, 2021, Proceedings, Part III, Springer, Lecture Notes in Computer Science, vol 12698, pp 370–396

107. Ghosh E, Ohrimenko O, Tamassia R (2015) Zero-knowledge authenticated order queries and order statistics on a list. In: Applied Cryptography and Network Security—13th International Conference, ACNS 2015, New York, NY, USA, June 2–5, 2015, Revised Selected Papers, Springer, Lecture Notes in Computer Science, vol 9092, pp 149–171

108. Goh EJ (2003) Secure indexes. IACR Cryptology ePrint Archive p 216

109. Goldreich O (2001) The Foundations of Cryptography—Volume 1: Basic Techniques. Cambridge University Press

110. Goldreich O, Ostrovsky R (1996) Software protection and simulation on oblivious rams. Journal of the ACM 43(3):431–473

111. Goldreich O, Goldwasser S, Micali S (2019) How to construct random functions. In: Providing Sound Foundations for Cryptography: On the Work of Shafi Goldwasser and Silvio Micali, ACM, pp 241–264

112. Goodrich MT, Mitzenmacher M (2010) MapReduce parallel cuckoo hashing and oblivious ram simulations. CoRR abs/1007.1259, 1007.1259

113. Goodrich MT, Mitzenmacher M (2011) Privacy-preserving access of outsourced data via oblivious ram simulation. In: Automata, Languages and Programming—38th International Colloquium, ICALP 2011, Zurich, Switzerland, July 4–8, 2011, Proceedings, Part II, Springer, Lecture Notes in Computer Science, vol 6756, pp 576–587

114. Goodrich MT, Tamassia R, Triandopoulos N, Cohen RF (2003) Authenticated data structures for graph and geometric searching. In: Topics in Cryptology—CT-RSA 2003, The Cryptographers' Track at the RSA Conference 2003, San Francisco, CA, USA, April 13–17, 2003, Proceedings, Springer, Lecture Notes in Computer Science, vol 2612, pp 295–313

115. Google (June, 2022) Encryption at rest in Google Cloud. Online at https://cloud.google.com/docs/security/encryption/default-encryption

116. Goyal V, Pandey O, Sahai A, Waters B (2006) Attribute-based encryption for fine-grained access control of encrypted data. In: Proceedings of the 13th ACM Conference on Computer and Communications Security, CCS 2006, Alexandria, VA, USA, October 30–November 3, 2006, ACM, pp 89–98

117. Green MD, Miers I (2015) Forward secure asynchronous messaging from puncturable encryption. In: 2015 IEEE Symposium on Security and Privacy, SP 2015, San Jose, CA, USA, May 17–21, 2015, IEEE Computer Society, pp 305–320

118. Groot Roessink R (2020) Experimental review of the IKK query recovery attack: Assumptions, recovery rate and improvements

119. Group A (2009) Alibaba cloud. Online at https://www.alibabacloud.com/

120. Grubbs P, McPherson R, Naveed M, Ristenpart T, Shmatikov V (2016) Breaking web applications built on top of encrypted data. In: Proceedings of the 2016 ACM SIGSAC Conference on Computer and Communications Security, Vienna, Austria, October 24–28, 2016, ACM, pp 1353–1364

121. Grubbs P, Ristenpart T, Shmatikov V (2017) Why your encrypted database is not secure. In: Proceedings of the 16th Workshop on Hot Topics in Operating Systems, HotOS 2017, Whistler, BC, Canada, May 8–10, 2017, ACM, pp 162–168

122. Grubbs P, Sekniqi K, Bindschaedler V, Naveed M, Ristenpart T (2017) Leakage-abuse attacks against order-revealing encryption. In: 2017 IEEE Symposium on Security and Privacy, SP 2017, San Jose, CA, USA, May 22–26, 2017, IEEE Computer Society, pp 655–672

123. Grubbs P, Lacharité M, Minaud B, Paterson KG (2018) Pump up the volume: Practical database reconstruction from volume leakage on range queries. In: Proceedings of the 2018 ACM SIGSAC Conference on Computer and Communications Security, CCS 2018, Toronto, ON, Canada, October 15–19, 2018, ACM, pp 315–331

124. Grubbs P, Lacharité MS, Minaud B, Paterson KG (2019) Learning to reconstruct: Statistical learning theory and encrypted database attacks. In: 2019 IEEE Symposium on Security and Privacy, SP 2019, San Francisco, CA, USA, May 19–23, 2019, IEEE, pp 1067–1083

125. Grubbs P, Khandelwal A, Lacharité MS, Brown L, Li L, Agarwal R, Ristenpart T (2020) Pancake: Frequency smoothing for encrypted data stores. In: 29th USENIX Security Symposium, USENIX Security 2020, August 12–14, 2020, USENIX Association, pp 2451–2468

126. Guo Y, Yuan X, Wang X, Wang C, Li B, Jia X (2019) Enabling encrypted rich queries in distributed key-value stores. IEEE Transactions on Parallel and Distributed Systems 30(6):1283–1297

127. Hacigümüs H, Iyer BR, Li C, Mehrotra S (2002) Executing SQL over encrypted data in the database-service-provider model. In: Proceedings of the 2002 ACM SIGMOD International Conference on Management of Data, Madison, Wisconsin, USA, June 3–6, 2002, ACM, pp 216–227

128. Hahn F, Kerschbaum F (2014) Searchable encryption with secure and efficient updates. In: Proceedings of the 2014 ACM SIGSAC Conference on Computer and Communications Security, Scottsdale, AZ, USA, November 3–7, 2014, ACM, pp 310–320

129. Halevi S (January 2020) Advanced cryptography: Promise, progress, and challenges. The Booz Allen Hamilton Distinguished Colloquium Series

130. Halevi S, Shoup V (2018) Faster homomorphic linear transformations in HElib. In: Advances in Cryptology—CRYPTO 2018—38th Annual International Cryptology Conference, Santa Barbara, CA, USA, August 19–23, 2018, Proceedings, Part I, Springer, Lecture Notes in Computer Science, vol 10991, pp 93–120

131. Hamlin A, Shelat A, Weiss M, Wichs D (2018) Multi-key searchable encryption, revisited. In: Public-Key Cryptography—PKC 2018—21st IACR International Conference on Practice and Theory of Public-Key Cryptography, Rio de Janeiro, Brazil, March 25–29, 2018, Proceedings, Part I, Springer, Lecture Notes in Computer Science, vol 10769, pp 95–124

132. He W, Akhawe D, Jain S, Shi E, Song DX (2014) ShadowCrypt: Encrypted web applications for everyone. In: Proceedings of the 2014 ACM SIGSAC Conference on Computer and Communications Security, Scottsdale, AZ, USA, November 3–7, 2014, ACM, pp 1028–1039

133. Hellerstein JM, Stonebraker M (2005) Readings in Database Systems: Fourth Edition. The MIT Press

134. Hoang T, Yavuz AA, Durak FB, Guajardo J (2019) A multi-server oblivious dynamic searchable encryption framework. Journal of Computer Security 27(6):649–676

135. Härder T, Reuter A (1983) Principles of transaction-oriented database recovery. ACM Computing Surveys 15(4):287–317

136. Hua Z, Gu J, Xia Y, Chen H, Zang B, Guan H (2017) vTZ: Virtualizing arm TrustZone. In: 26th USENIX Security Symposium, USENIX Security 2017, Vancouver, BC, Canada, August 16–18, 2017, USENIX Association, pp 541–556

137. Hutchison D, Kepner J, Gadepally V, Fuchs A (2015) Graphulo implementation of server-side sparse matrix multiply in the Accumulo database. In: 2015 IEEE High Performance Extreme Computing Conference, HPEC 2015, Waltham, MA, USA, September 15–17, 2015, IEEE, pp 1–7

138. IBM (June, 2022) Data At Rest Encryption. Online at https://www.ibm.com/docs/en/strategicsm/10.1.3?topic=security-data-rest-encryption

139. IETF RFC 8446 (June, 2022) The Transport Layer Security (TLS) Protocol Version 1.3. Online at https://datatracker.ietf.org/doc/html/rfc8446

140. Incorporation B (April 2007) Backblaze b2 cloud storage. Online at https://www.backblaze.com/

141. Incorporation D (March 2017) Dropbox. Online at https://www.dropbox.com/home

142. Incorporation I (1995) Idrive backup. Online at https://www.idrive.com/

143. Intel (2020) Intel/linux-sgx. Online at https://github.com/intel/linux-sgx

144. Ishai Y, Kushilevitz E, Lu S, Ostrovsky R (2016) Private large-scale databases with distributed searchable symmetric encryption. In: Topics in Cryptology—CT-RSA 2016—The Cryptographers' Track at the RSA Conference 2016, San Francisco, CA, USA, February 29–March 4, 2016, Proceedings, Springer, Lecture Notes in Computer Science, vol 9610, pp 90–107

145. Islam MS, Kuzu M, Kantarcioglu M (2012) Access pattern disclosure on searchable encryption: Ramification, attack and mitigation. In: 19th Annual Network and Distributed System Security Symposium, NDSS 2012, San Diego, California, USA, February 5–8, 2012, The Internet Society

146. James Rundle (June, 2022) Human Error Often the Culprit in Cloud Data Breaches. Online at https://www.wsj.com/articles/human-error-often-the-culprit-in-cloud-data-breaches-11566898203

147. Jarecki S, Jutla CS, Krawczyk H, Rosu MC, Steiner M (2013) Outsourced symmetric private information retrieval. In: 2013 ACM SIGSAC Conference on Computer and Communications Security, CCS'13, Berlin, Germany, November 4–8, 2013, ACM, pp 875–888

148. Johnson T (June, 2022) Software supply chain attacks: Who owns the risk and what can be done? Online at https://www.cloudbees.com/blog/software-supply-chain-attacks-who-owns-risk

149. Kamara S, Moataz T (2017) Boolean searchable symmetric encryption with worst-case sub-linear complexity. In: Advances in Cryptology—EUROCRYPT 2017—36th Annual International Conference on the Theory and Applications of Cryptographic Techniques, Paris, France, April 30–May 4, 2017, Proceedings, Part III, Lecture Notes in Computer Science, vol 10212, pp 94–124

150. Kamara S, Moataz T (2018) Encrypted multi-maps with computationally-secure leakage. IACR Cryptology ePrint Archive p 978

151. Kamara S, Moataz T (2019) Computationally volume-hiding structured encryption. In: Advances in Cryptology—EUROCRYPT 2019—38th Annual International Conference on the Theory and Applications of Cryptographic Techniques, Darmstadt, Germany, May 19–23, 2019, Proceedings, Part II, Springer, Lecture Notes in Computer Science, vol 11477, pp 183–213

152. Kamara S, Papamanthou C (2013) Parallel and dynamic searchable symmetric encryption. In: Financial Cryptography and Data Security—17th International Conference, FC 2013, Okinawa, Japan, April 1–5, 2013, Revised Selected Papers, Springer, Lecture Notes in Computer Science, vol 7859, pp 258–274

153. Kamara S, Papamanthou C, Roeder T (2012) Dynamic searchable symmetric encryption. In: the ACM Conference on Computer and Communications Security, CCS'12, Raleigh, NC, USA, October 16–18, 2012, ACM, pp 965–976

154. Kamara S, Moataz T, Ohrimenko O (2018) Structured encryption and leakage suppression. In: Advances in Cryptology—CRYPTO 2018—38th Annual International Cryptology Conference, Santa Barbara, CA, USA, August 19–23, 2018, Proceedings, Part I, Springer, Lecture Notes in Computer Science, vol 10991, pp 339–370

155. Kamara S, Kati A, Moataz T, Schneider T, Treiber A, Yonli M (2022) SoK: Cryptanalysis of encrypted search with leaker—a framework for leakage attack evaluation on real-world data. In: 7th IEEE European Symposium on Security and Privacy, EuroS&P 2022, Genoa, Italy, June 6–10, 2022, IEEE, pp 90–108

156. Kaplan D (2016) AMD x86 memory encryption technologies

157. Kaspersky (June, 2022) What is Social Engineering. Online at https://www.kaspersky.com/resource-center/definitions/what-is-social-engineering

158. Katz J, Sahai A, Waters B (2008) Predicate encryption supporting disjunctions, polynomial equations, and inner products. In: Advances in Cryptology—EUROCRYPT 2008, 27th Annual International Conference on the Theory and Applications of Cryptographic Techniques, Istanbul, Turkey, April 13–17, 2008. Proceedings, Springer, Lecture Notes in Computer Science, vol 4965, pp 146–162

159. Kellaris G, Kollios G, Nissim K, O'Neill A (2016) Generic attacks on secure outsourced databases. In: Proceedings of the 2016 ACM SIGSAC Conference on Computer and Communications Security, Vienna, Austria, October 24–28, 2016, ACM, pp 1329–1340

160. Keller M (2020) MP-SPDZ: A versatile framework for multi-party computation. In: CCS '20: 2020 ACM SIGSAC Conference on Computer and Communications Security, Virtual Event, USA, November 9–13, 2020, ACM, pp 1575–1590

161. Kepner J, Gadepally V, Hutchison D, Jananthan H, Mattson TG, Samsi S, Reuther A (2016) Associative array model of SQL, NoSQL, and NewSQL databases. In: 2016 IEEE High Performance Extreme Computing Conference, HPEC 2016, Waltham, MA, USA, September 13–15, 2016, IEEE, pp 1–9

162. Kerschbaum F (2015) Frequency-hiding order-preserving encryption. In: Proceedings of the 22nd ACM SIGSAC Conference on Computer and Communications Security, Denver, CO, USA, October 12–16, 2015, ACM, pp 656–667

163. Kirsch A, Mitzenmacher M, Wieder U (2009) More robust hashing: Cuckoo hashing with a stash. SIAM Journal on Computing 39(4):1543–1561

164. Kornaropoulos EM, Papamanthou C, Tamassia R (2020) The state of the uniform: Attacks on encrypted databases beyond the uniform query distribution. In: 2020 IEEE Symposium on Security and Privacy, SP 2020, San Francisco, CA, USA, May 18–21, 2020, IEEE, pp 1223–1240

165. Kushilevitz E, Lu S, Ostrovsky R (2012) On the (in)security of hash-based oblivious ram and a new balancing scheme. In: Proceedings of the Twenty-Third Annual ACM-SIAM Symposium on Discrete Algorithms, SODA 2012, Kyoto, Japan, January 17–19, 2012, SIAM, pp 143–156

166. Lacharité M, Minaud B, Paterson KG (2018) Improved reconstruction attacks on encrypted data using range query leakage. In: 2018 IEEE Symposium on Security and Privacy, SP 2018, Proceedings, 21–23 May 2018, San Francisco, California, USA, IEEE Computer Society, pp 297–314

167. Lai RWF, Chow SSM (2017) Forward-secure searchable encryption on labeled bipartite graphs. In: Applied Cryptography and Network Security—15th International Conference, ACNS 2017, Kanazawa, Japan, July 10–12, 2017, Proceedings, Springer, Lecture Notes in Computer Science, vol 10355, pp 478–497

168. Lau B, Chung SP, Song C, Jang Y, Lee W, Boldyreva A (2014) Mimesis aegis: A mimicry privacy shield-a system's approach to data privacy on public cloud. In: Proceedings of the 23rd USENIX Security Symposium, San Diego, CA, USA, August 20–22, 2014, USENIX Association, pp 33–48

169. Lenstra AK, Lenstra HW, Lovász L (1982) Factoring polynomials with rational coefficients. Mathematische annalen 261(ARTICLE):515–534

170. Lewi K, Wu DJ (2016) Order-revealing encryption: New constructions, applications, and lower bounds. In: Proceedings of the 2016 ACM SIGSAC Conference on Computer and Communications Security, Vienna, Austria, October 24–28, 2016, ACM, pp 1167–1178

171. Li F, Hadjieleftheriou M, Kollios G, Reyzin L (2006) Dynamic authenticated index structures for outsourced databases. In: Proceedings of the ACM SIGMOD International Conference on Management of Data, Chicago, Illinois, USA, June 27–29, 2006, ACM, pp 121–132

172. Li H, Liu D, Jia K, Lin X (2015) Achieving authorized and ranked multi-keyword search over encrypted cloud data. In: 2015 IEEE International Conference on Communications, ICC 2015, London, United Kingdom, June 8–12, 2015, IEEE, pp 7450–7455

173. Li H, Xu G, Tang Q, Lin X, Shen XS (2018) Enabling efficient and fine-grained DNA similarity search with access control over encrypted cloud data. In: Wireless Algorithms, Systems, and Applications—13th International Conference, WASA 2018, Tianjin, China, June 20–22, 2018, Proceedings, Springer, Lecture Notes in Computer Science, vol 10874, pp 236–248

174. Li J, Wang Q, Wang C, Cao N, Ren K, Lou W (2010) Fuzzy keyword search over encrypted data in cloud computing. In: INFOCOM 2010. 29th IEEE International Conference on Computer Communications, Joint Conference of the IEEE Computer and Communications Societies, 15–19 March 2010, San Diego, CA, USA, IEEE, pp 441–445

175. Li R, Liu AX (2017) Adaptively secure conjunctive query processing over encrypted data for cloud computing. In: 33rd IEEE International Conference on Data Engineering, ICDE 2017, San Diego, CA, USA, April 19–22, 2017, IEEE Computer Society, pp 697–708

176. Li Y, Xu W (2019) PrivPy: General and scalable privacy-preserving data mining. In: Proceedings of the 25th ACM SIGKDD International Conference on Knowledge Discovery & Data Mining, KDD 2019, Anchorage, AK, USA, August 4–8, 2019, ACM, pp 1299–1307

177. Liao J (2020) Liaojinghui/awesome-sgx: A curated list of SGX code and resources. Online at https://github.com/Liaojinghui/awesome-sgx

178. van Liesdonk P, Sedghi S, Doumen J, Hartel PH, Jonker W (2010) Computationally efficient searchable symmetric encryption. In: Secure Data Management, 7th VLDB Workshop, SDM 2010, Singapore, September 17, 2010. Proceedings, Springer, Lecture Notes in Computer Science, vol 6358, pp 87–100

179. Lindell Y (2016) How to simulate it—A tutorial on the simulation proof technique. IACR Cryptology ePrint Archive p 46

180. Linoff GS, Berry MJ (2002) Mining the Web: Transforming Customer Data into Customer Value. John Wiley & Sons, Inc., USA

181. Liu C, Zhu L, Li L, an Tan Y (2011) Fuzzy keyword search on encrypted cloud storage data with small index. In: 2011 IEEE International Conference on Cloud Computing and Intelligence Systems, CCIS 2011, Beijing, China, September 15–17, 2011, IEEE, pp 269–273

182. Liu Z, Lv S, Li J, Huang Y, Guo L, Yuan Y, Dong C (2022) EncodeORE: Reducing leakage and preserving practicality in order-revealing encryption. IEEE Transactions on Dependable and Secure Computing 19(3):1579–1591

183. Lu D, Yurek T, Kulshreshtha S, Govind R, Kate A, Miller AK (2019) HoneyBadgerMPC and AsynchroMix: Practical asynchronous MPC and its application to anonymous communication. In: Proceedings of the 2019 ACM SIGSAC Conference on Computer and Communications Security, CCS 2019, London, UK, November 11–15, 2019, ACM, pp 887–903

184. Lu R (2019) A new communication-efficient privacy-preserving range query scheme in fog-enhanced IoT. IEEE Internet of Things Journal 6(2):2497–2505

185. Lu W, Huang Z, Hong C, Ma Y, Qu H (2021) PEGASUS: bridging polynomial and non-polynomial evaluations in homomorphic encryption. In: 42nd IEEE Symposium on Security and Privacy, SP 2021, San Francisco, CA, USA, 24–27 May 2021, IEEE, pp 1057–1073

186. Mattson T, Gadepally V, She Z, Dziedzic A, Parkhurst J (2017) Demonstrating the BigDAWG polystore system for ocean metagenomics analysis. In: 8th Biennial Conference on Innovative Data Systems Research, CIDR 2017, Chaminade, CA, USA, January 8–11, 2017, Online Proceedings, www.cidrdb.org

187. McKeen F, Alexandrovich I, Berenzon A, Rozas CV, Shafi H, Shanbhogue V, Savagaonkar UR (2013) Innovative instructions and software model for isolated execution. In: HASP 2013, The Second Workshop on Hardware and Architectural Support for Security and Privacy, Tel-Aviv, Israel, June 23–24, 2013, ACM, p 10

188. Mechalas JP, Odom BJ (2016) Intel® software guard extensions tutorial series: Part 1, intel® sgx... Online at https://www.intel.com/content/www/us/en/developer/articles/training/intel-software-guard-extensions-tutorial-part-1-foundation.html

189. Microsoft (August 2007) OneDrive. Online at https://www.microsoft.com/en-ww/microsoft-365/onedrive/online-cloud-storage

190. Microsoft (2010) Microsoft azure SQL database. Online at https://azure.microsoft.com/

191. Microsoft (April, 2022) SQL server transparent data encryption (TDE). Online at https://docs.microsoft.com/en-us/sql/relational-databases/security/encryption/transparent-data-encryption?view=sql-server-ver16

192. Microsoft (June, 2022) Azure Data Encryption at rest. Online at https://docs.microsoft.com/en-us/azure/security/fundamentals/encryption-atrest

193. Miers I, Mohassel P (2017) IO-DSSE: Scaling dynamic searchable encryption to millions of indexes by improving locality. In: 24th Annual Network and Distributed System Security Symposium, NDSS 2017, San Diego, California, USA, February 26–March 1, 2017, The Internet Society

194. Mishra P, Poddar R, Chen J, Chiesa A, Popa RA (2018) Oblix: An efficient oblivious search index. In: 2018 IEEE Symposium on Security and Privacy, SP 2018, Proceedings, 21–23 May 2018, San Francisco, California, USA, IEEE Computer Society, pp 279–296

195. MongoDB (June, 2022) Encryption at Rest. Online at https://www.mongodb.com/docs/manual/core/security-encryption-at-rest/

196. Natarajan A, Mittal N (2014) Fast concurrent lock-free binary search trees. In: ACM SIGPLAN Symposium on Principles and Practice of Parallel Programming, PPoPP '14, Orlando, FL, USA, February 15–19, 2014, ACM, pp 317–328

197. Naveed M (2015) The fallacy of composition of oblivious ram and searchable encryption. IACR Cryptology ePrint Archive p 668

198. Naveed M, Kamara S, Wright CV (2015) Inference attacks on property-preserving encrypted databases. In: Proceedings of the 22nd ACM SIGSAC Conference on Computer and Communications Security, Denver, CO, USA, October 12–16, 2015, ACM, pp 644–655

199. Networks IS (2021) Skyhigh for salesforce. Online at https://www.mcafee.com/enterprise/en-us/products/mvision-cloud-salesforce.html

200. Ning J, Huang X, Poh GS, Yuan J, Li Y, Weng J, Deng RH (2021) Leap: Leakage-abuse attack on efficiently deployable, efficiently searchable encryption with partially known dataset. In: CCS '21: 2021 ACM SIGSAC Conference on Computer and Communications Security, Virtual Event, Republic of Korea, November 15–19, 2021, ACM, pp 2307–2320

201. Nowak D, Zhang Y (2010) A calculus for game-based security proofs. In: Provable Security—4th International Conference, ProvSec 2010, Malacca, Malaysia, October 13-15, 2010. Proceedings, Springer, Lecture Notes in Computer Science, vol 6402, pp 35–52

202. van Ooijen C, Ubaldi B, Welby B (2019) A data-driven public sector: Enabling the strategic use of data for productive, inclusive and trustworthy governance. OECD Working Papers on Public Governance (33)

203. Oracle (June, 2022) Oracle Transparent Data Encryption (TDE) Technology. Online at https://docs.oracle.com/en/cloud/saas/marketing/responsys-user/EncryptionAtRest.htm

204. Orenbach M, Lifshits P, Minkin M, Silberstein M (2017) Eleos: ExitLess OS services for SGX enclaves. In: Proceedings of the Twelfth European Conference on Computer Systems, EuroSys 2017, Belgrade, Serbia, April 23–26, 2017, ACM, pp 238–253

205. Osborne C (June, 2022) Trend micro reveals rogue employee sold data of up to 120,000 customers. Online at https://www.zdnet.com/article/trend-micro-reveals-insider-threat-exposing-customer-data/

206. Oya S, Kerschbaum F (2021) Hiding the access pattern is not enough: Exploiting search pattern leakage in searchable encryption. In: 30th USENIX Security Symposium, USENIX Security 2021, August 11–13, 2021, USENIX Association, pp 127–142

207. Oya S, Kerschbaum F (2021) IHOP: Improved statistical query recovery against searchable symmetric encryption through quadratic optimization. CoRR abs/2110.04180, 2110.04180

208. Pagh R, Rodler FF (2004) Cuckoo hashing. Journal of Algorithms 51(2):122–144

209. Paillier P (1999) Public-key cryptosystems based on composite degree residuosity classes. In: Advances in Cryptology—EUROCRYPT '99, International Conference on the Theory and Application of Cryptographic Techniques, Prague, Czech Republic, May 2–6, 1999, Proceeding, Springer, Lecture Notes in Computer Science, vol 1592, pp 223–238

210. Palutke R, Neubaum A, Götzfried J (2019) SEVguard: Protecting user mode applications using secure encrypted virtualization. In: Security and Privacy in Communication Networks—15th EAI International Conference, SecureComm 2019, Orlando, FL, USA, October 23–25, 2019, Proceedings, Part II, Springer, Lecture Notes of the Institute for Computer Sciences, Social Informatics and Telecommunications Engineering, vol 305, pp 224–242

211. Pandey O, Rouselakis Y (2012) Property preserving symmetric encryption. In: Advances in Cryptology—EUROCRYPT 2012—31st Annual International Conference on the Theory and Applications of Cryptographic Techniques, Cambridge, UK, April 15–19, 2012. Proceedings, Springer, Lecture Notes in Computer Science, vol 7237, pp 375–391

212. Papadopoulos D, Papamanthou C, Tamassia R, Triandopoulos N (2015) Practical authenticated pattern matching with optimal proof size. Proceedings of the International Conference on Very Large Databases 8(7):750–761

213. Papamanthou C, Tamassia R (2007) Time and space efficient algorithms for two-party authenticated data structures. In: Information and Communications Security, 9th International Conference, ICICS 2007, Zhengzhou, China, December 12–15, 2007, Proceedings, Springer, Lecture Notes in Computer Science, vol 4861, pp 1–15

214. Papamanthou C, Tamassia R, Triandopoulos N (2016) Authenticated hash tables based on cryptographic accumulators. Algorithmica 74(2):664–712

215. Pappas V, Krell F, Vo B, Kolesnikov V, Malkin T, Choi SG, George W, Keromytis AD, Bellovin SM (2014) Blind seer: A scalable private DBMS. In: 2014 IEEE Symposium on Security and Privacy, SP 2014, Berkeley, CA, USA, May 18–21, 2014, IEEE Computer Society, pp 359–374

216. Patel S, Persiano G, Yeo K (2018) Symmetric searchable encryption with sharing and unsharing. In: Computer Security—23rd European Symposium on Research in Computer Security, ESORICS 2018, Barcelona, Spain, September 3–7, 2018, Proceedings, Part II, Springer, Lecture Notes in Computer Science, vol 11099, pp 207–227

217. Patel S, Persiano G, Yeo K, Yung M (2019) Mitigating leakage in secure cloud-hosted data structures: Volume-hiding for multi-maps via hashing. In: Proceedings of the 2019 ACM SIGSAC Conference on Computer and Communications Security, CCS 2019, London, UK, November 11–15, 2019, ACM, pp 79–93

218. Patel S, Persiano G, Seo JY, Yeo K (2021) Efficient Boolean search over encrypted data with reduced leakage. In: Advances in Cryptology—ASIACRYPT 2021—27th International Conference on the Theory and Application of Cryptology and Information Security, Singapore, December 6–10, 2021, Proceedings, Part III, Springer, Lecture Notes in Computer Science, vol 13092, pp 577–607

219. Pavlo A, Aslett M (2016) What's really new with NewSQL? SIGMOD Record 45(2):45–55

220. Platform SH (October, 2019) SAP HANA client-side data encryption guide. Online at https://help.sap.com/doc/acadad01f5d64f80ae1ff5612487121c/2.0.04/en-US/SAP_HANA_Client-Side_Data_Encryption_Guide_en.pdf

221. Poddar R, Boelter T, Popa RA (2019) Arx: An encrypted database using semantically secure encryption. Proceedings of the International Conference on Very Large Databases 12(11):1664–1678

222. Poh GS, Chin JJ, Yau WC, Choo KKR, Mohamad MS (2017) Searchable symmetric encryption: Designs and challenges. ACM Computing Surveys 50(3):40:1–40:37

223. Popa RA, Zeldovich N (2013) Multi-key searchable encryption. IACR Cryptology ePrint Archive p 508

224. Popa RA, Redfield CMS, Zeldovich N, Balakrishnan H (2011) CryptDB: protecting confidentiality with encrypted query processing. In: Proceedings of the 23rd ACM Symposium on Operating Systems Principles 2011, SOSP 2011, Cascais, Portugal, October 23–26, 2011, ACM, pp 85–100

225. Popa RA, Li FH, Zeldovich N (2013) An ideal-security protocol for order-preserving encoding. In: 2013 IEEE Symposium on Security and Privacy, SP 2013, Berkeley, CA, USA, May 19–22, 2013, IEEE Computer Society, pp 463–477

226. Powers R, Beede D (July 2014) Fostering Innovation, Creating Jobs, Driving Better Decisions: The Value of Government Data

227. Priebe C, Vaswani K, Costa M (2018) EnclaveDB: A secure database using SGX. In: 2018 IEEE Symposium on Security and Privacy, SP 2018, Proceedings, 21–23 May 2018, San Francisco, California, USA, IEEE Computer Society, pp 264–278

228. Ren K, Guo Y, Li J, Jia X, Wang C, Zhou Y, Wang S, Cao N, Li F (2020) HybrIDX: New hybrid index for volume-hiding range queries in data outsourcing services. In: 40th IEEE International Conference on Distributed Computing Systems, ICDCS 2020, Singapore, November 29–December 1, 2020, IEEE, pp 23–33

229. Rivest RL, Shamir A, Adleman LM (1978) A method for obtaining digital signatures and public-key cryptosystems. Communications of the ACM 21(2):120–126

230. Roche DS, Aviv AJ, Choi SG (2016) A practical oblivious map data structure with secure deletion and history independence. In: IEEE Symposium on Security and Privacy, SP 2016, San Jose, CA, USA, May 22–26, 2016, IEEE Computer Society, pp 178–197

231. Rompay CV, Molva R, Önen M (2015) Multi-user searchable encryption in the cloud. In: Information Security—18th International Conference, ISC 2015, Trondheim, Norway, September 9–11, 2015, Proceedings, Springer, Lecture Notes in Computer Science, vol 9290, pp 299–316

232. Rompay CV, Molva R, Önen M (2017) A leakage-abuse attack against multi-user searchable encryption. Proceedings of Privacy Enhancing Technologies 2017(3):168

233. Rompay CV, Molva R, Önen M (2018) Fast two-server multi-user searchable encryption with strict access pattern leakage. In: Information and Communications Security—20th International Conference, ICICS 2018, Lille, France, October 29–31, 2018, Proceedings, Springer, Lecture Notes in Computer Science, vol 11149, pp 393–408

234. Rompay CV, Molva R, Önen M (2018) Secure and scalable multi-user searchable encryption. In: Proceedings of the 6th International Workshop on Security in Cloud Computing, SCC@AsiaCCS 2018, Incheon, Republic of Korea, June 04–08, 2018, ACM, pp 15–25

235. Sallam A, Bertino E (2019) Result-based detection of insider threats to relational databases. In: Proceedings of the Ninth ACM Conference on Data and Application Security and Privacy, CODASPY 2019, Richardson, TX, USA, March 25–27, 2019, ACM, pp 133–143

236. Sander T, Young AL, Yung M (1999) Non-interactive cryptocomputing for nc^1. In: 40th Annual Symposium on Foundations of Computer Science, FOCS '99, 17–18 October, 1999, New York, NY, USA, IEEE Computer Society, pp 554–567

237. SAR HK (December 1996) The personal data (privacy) ordinance. Online at https://www.pcpd.org.hk/english/data_privacy_law/ordinance_at_a_Glance/ordinance.html

238. van Schaik S, Minkin M, Kwong A, Genkin D, Yarom Y (2021) CacheOut: Leaking data on intel CPUs via cache evictions. In: 42nd IEEE Symposium on Security and Privacy, SP 2021, San Francisco, CA, USA, 24–27 May 2021, IEEE, pp 339–354

239. Schuster F, Costa M, Fournet C, Gkantsidis C, Peinado M, Mainar-Ruiz G, Russinovich M (2015) Vc3: Trustworthy data analytics in the cloud using SGX. In: 2015 IEEE Symposium on Security and Privacy, SP 2015, San Jose, CA, USA, May 17–21, 2015, IEEE Computer Society, pp 38–54

240. Schwarz M, Weiser S, Gruss D (2019) Practical enclave malware with intel SGX. In: Detection of Intrusions and Malware, and Vulnerability Assessment—16th International Conference, DIMVA 2019, Gothenburg, Sweden, June 19–20, 2019, Proceedings, Springer, Lecture Notes in Computer Science, vol 11543, pp 177–196

241. Sergio De Simone (June, 2022) Securing the Open-Source Software Supply Chain. Online at https://www.infoq.com/news/2022/03/securing-open-source-deployment/

242. Sharma D (2022) Searchable encryption: A survey. Information Security Journal: A Global Perspective 0(0):1–44

243. Shi E, Chan THH, Stefanov E, Li M (2011) Oblivious ram with o((logn)3) worst-case cost. In: Advances in Cryptology—ASIACRYPT 2011—17th International Conference on the Theory and Application of Cryptology and Information Security, Seoul, South Korea, December 4–8, 2011. Proceedings, Springer, Lecture Notes in Computer Science, vol 7073, pp 197–214

244. Sidorov V, Wei EYF, Ng WK (2022) Comprehensive performance analysis of homomorphic cryptosystems for practical data processing. CoRR abs/2202.02960, 2202.02960

245. Song DX, Wagner DA, Perrig A (2000) Practical techniques for searches on encrypted data. In: 2000 IEEE Symposium on Security and Privacy, Berkeley, California, USA, May 14–17, 2000, IEEE Computer Society, pp 44–55

246. Song Q, Liu Z, Cao J, Sun K, Li Q, Wang C (2021) SAP-SSE: Protecting search patterns and access patterns in searchable symmetric encryption. IEEE Transactions on Information Forensics and Security 16:1795–1809

247. Stefanov E, Shi E (2013) ObliviStore: High performance oblivious cloud storage. In: 2013 IEEE Symposium on Security and Privacy, SP 2013, Berkeley, CA, USA, May 19–22, 2013, IEEE Computer Society, pp 253–267

248. Stefanov E, van Dijk M, Shi E, Fletcher CW, Ren L, Yu X, Devadas S (2013) Path ORAM: an extremely simple oblivious ram protocol. In: 2013 ACM SIGSAC Conference on Computer and Communications Security, CCS'13, Berlin, Germany, November 4–8, 2013, ACM, pp 299–310

249. Stefanov E, Papamanthou C, Shi E (2014) Practical dynamic searchable encryption with small leakage. In: 21st Annual Network and Distributed System Security Symposium, NDSS 2014, San Diego, California, USA, February 23–26, 2014, The Internet Society

250. Suh GE, Clarke DE, Gassend B, van Dijk M, Devadas S (2003) Aegis: architecture for tamper-evident and tamper-resistant processing. In: Proceedings of the 17th Annual International Conference on Supercomputing, ICS 2003, San Francisco, CA, USA, June 23–26, 2003, ACM, pp 160–171

251. Sun S, Liu JK, Sakzad A, Steinfeld R, Yuen TH (2016) An efficient non-interactive multi-client searchable encryption with support for Boolean queries. In: Computer Security—ESORICS 2016—21st European Symposium on Research in Computer Security, Heraklion, Greece, September 26–30, 2016, Proceedings, Part I, Springer, Lecture Notes in Computer Science, vol 9878, pp 154–172

252. Sun S, Yuan X, Liu JK, Steinfeld R, Sakzad A, Vo V, Nepal S (2018) Practical backward-secure searchable encryption from symmetric puncturable encryption. In: Proceedings of the 2018 ACM SIGSAC Conference on Computer and Communications Security, CCS 2018, Toronto, ON, Canada, October 15–19, 2018, ACM, pp 763–780

253. Sun SF, Steinfeld R, Lai S, Yuan X, Sakzad A, Liu JK, Nepal S, Gu D (2021) Practical non-interactive searchable encryption with forward and backward privacy. In: 28th Annual Network and Distributed System Security Symposium, NDSS 2021, virtually, February 21–25, 2021, The Internet Society

254. Sun Y, Wang S, Li H, Li F (2021) Building enclave-native storage engines for practical encrypted databases. Proceedings of the International Conference on Very Large Databases 14(6):1019–1032

255. Surfshark (April 2022) Data breach statistics by country in 2021. Online at https://surfshark.com/blog/data-breach-statistics-by-country-in-2021

256. Tan S, Knott B, Tian Y, Wu DJ (2021) CryptGPU: Fast privacy-preserving machine learning on the GPU. In: 42nd IEEE Symposium on Security and Privacy, SP 2021, San Francisco, CA, USA, 24–27 May 2021, IEEE, pp 1021–1038

257. Tang X, Guo C, Ren Y, Wang C, Choo KKR (2022) A global secure ranked multikeyword search based on the multiowner model for cloud-based systems. IEEE Systems Journal 16(2):1717–1728

258. Tidy BJ, Molloy D (October 2021) Twitch confirms massive data breach. Online at https://www.bbc.com/news/technology-58817658

259. Tomescu A, Bhupatiraju V, Papadopoulos D, Papamanthou C, Triandopoulos N, Devadas S (2019) Transparency logs via append-only authenticated dictionaries. In: Proceedings of the 2019 ACM SIGSAC Conference on Computer and Communications Security, CCS 2019, London, UK, November 11–15, 2019, ACM, pp 1299–1316

260. Tople S, Jia Y, Saxena P (2019) PRO-ORAM: practical read-only oblivious RAM. In: 22nd International Symposium on Research in Attacks, Intrusions and Defenses, RAID 2019, Chaoyang District, Beijing, China, September 23–25, 2019, USENIX Association, pp 197–211

261. Tramèr F, Boneh D (2019) Slalom: Fast, verifiable and private execution of neural networks in trusted hardware. In: 7th International Conference on Learning Representations, ICLR 2019, New Orleans, LA, USA, May 6–9, 2019, OpenReview.net

262. che Tsai C, Porter DE, Vij M (2017) Graphene-SGX: A practical library OS for unmodified applications on SGX. In: 2017 USENIX Annual Technical Conference, USENIX ATC 2017, Santa Clara, CA, USA, July 12–14, 2017, USENIX Association, pp 645–658

263. Tu S, Kaashoek MF, Madden S, Zeldovich N (2013) Processing analytical queries over encrypted data. Proceedings of the International Conference on Very Large Databases 6(5):289–300

264. Union E (May 2018) General data protection regulation gdpr. Online at https://gdpr-info.eu/

265. Vaucher S, Pires R, Felber P, Pasin M, Schiavoni V, Fetzer C (2018) SGX-aware container orchestration for heterogeneous clusters. In: 38th IEEE International Conference on Distributed Computing Systems, ICDCS 2018, Vienna, Austria, July 2–6, 2018, IEEE Computer Society, pp 730–741

266. Levy-dit Vehel F, Perret K Ludovic, Niederreiter H, Xing C (2004) A Polly cracker system based on satisfiability. In: Coding, Cryptography and Combinatorics, Birkhäuser Basel, Basel, pp 177–192

267. Vertesi J, Dourish P (2011) The value of data: considering the context of production in data economies. In: Proceedings of the 2011 ACM Conference on Computer Supported Cooperative Work, CSCW 2011, Hangzhou, China, March 19–23, 2011, ACM, pp 533–542

268. di Vimercati SDC, Foresti S, Jajodia S, Livraga G, Paraboschi S, Samarati P (2017) An authorization model for multi-provider queries. Proceedings of the International Conference on Very Large Databases 11(3):256–268

269. Vinayagamurthy D, Gribov A, Gorbunov S (2019) StealthDB: a scalable encrypted database with full SQL query support. Proceedings of Privacy Enhancing Technologies 2019(3):370–388

270. Vo V, Lai S, Yuan X, Sun S, Nepal S, Liu JK (2020) Accelerating forward and backward private searchable encryption using trusted execution. In: Applied Cryptography and Network Security—18th International Conference, ACNS 2020, Rome, Italy, October 19–22, 2020, Proceedings, Part II, Springer, Lecture Notes in Computer Science, vol 12147, pp 83–103

271. Vo V, Lai S, Yuan X, Nepal S, Liu JK (2021) Towards efficient and strong backward private searchable encryption with secure enclaves. In: Applied Cryptography and Network Security—19th International Conference, ACNS 2021, Kamakura, Japan, June 21–24, 2021, Proceedings, Part I, Springer, Lecture Notes in Computer Science, vol 12726, pp 50–75

272. Vuppalapati M, Babel K, Khandelwal A, Agarwal R (2022) ShortStack: Distributed, fault-tolerant, oblivious data access. CoRR abs/2205.14281, 2205.14281

273. Wan Z, Deng RH (2018) VPSearch: Achieving verifiability for privacy-preserving multi-keyword search over encrypted cloud data. IEEE Transactions on Dependable and Secure Computing 15(6):1083–1095

274. Wang B, Yu S, Lou W, Hou YT (2014) Privacy-preserving multi-keyword fuzzy search over encrypted data in the cloud. In: 2014 IEEE Conference on Computer Communications, INFOCOM 2014, Toronto, Canada, April 27–May 2, 2014, IEEE, pp 2112–2120

275. Wang C, Cao N, Li J, Ren K, Lou W (2010) Secure ranked keyword search over encrypted cloud data. In: 2010 International Conference on Distributed Computing Systems, ICDCS 2010, Genova, Italy, June 21–25, 2010, IEEE Computer Society, pp 253–262

276. Wang C, Cao N, Ren K, Lou W (2012) Enabling secure and efficient ranked keyword search over outsourced cloud data. IEEE Transactions on Parallel and Distributed Systems 23(8):1467–1479

277. Wang C, Ren K, Yu S, Urs KMR (2012) Achieving usable and privacy-assured similarity search over outsourced cloud data. In: Proceedings of the IEEE INFOCOM 2012, Orlando, FL, USA, March 25–30, 2012, IEEE, pp 451–459

278. Wang J, Chow SSM (2022) Omnes pro uno: Practical Multi-Writer encrypted database. In: 31st USENIX Security Symposium (USENIX Security 22), USENIX Association, Boston, MA, pp 2371–2388

279. Wang J, Ma H, Tang Q, Li J, Zhu H, Ma S, Chen X (2013) Efficient verifiable fuzzy keyword search over encrypted data in cloud computing. Computer Science and Information Systems 10(2):667–684

280. Wang S, Li Y, Li H, Li F, Tian C, Su L, Yanshan Zhang, Ma Y, Yan L, Sun Y, Cheng X, Xie X, , Zou Y (2022) Operon: An encrypted database for ownership-preserving data management. Proceedings of the 48th International Conference on Very Large Databases

281. Wang X, Ranellucci S, Katz J (2017) Global-scale secure multiparty computation. In: Proceedings of the 2017 ACM SIGSAC Conference on Computer and Communications Security, CCS 2017, Dallas, TX, USA, October 30–November 03, 2017, ACM, pp 39–56

282. Wang X, Ma J, Liu X, Deng RH, Miao Y, Zhu D, Ma Z (2020) Search me in the dark: Privacy-preserving Boolean range query over encrypted spatial data. In: 39th IEEE Conference on Computer Communications, INFOCOM 2020, Toronto, ON, Canada, July 6–9, 2020, IEEE, pp 2253–2262

283. Wang Y, Wang J, Chen X (2016) Secure searchable encryption: a survey. Journal of Communications and Information Networks 1(4):52–65

284. Wayne Anderson (June, 2022) Cloud is Ubiquitous and Untrusted. Online at https://www.mcafee.com/blogs/enterprise/cloud-security/cloud-is-ubiquitous-and-untrusted/

285. Wikipedia (October, 2019) List of data breaches. Online at https://en.wikipedia.org/wiki/List_of_data_breaches

286. Wong WK, Kao B, Cheung DWL, Li R, Yiu SM (2014) Secure query processing with data interoperability in a cloud database environment. In: International Conference on Management of Data, SIGMOD 2014, Snowbird, UT, USA, June 22–27, 2014, ACM, pp 1395–1406

287. Wu S, Li Q, Li G, Yuan D, Yuan X, Wang C (2019) ServeDB: Secure, verifiable, and efficient range queries on outsourced database. In: 35th IEEE International Conference on Data Engineering, ICDE 2019, Macao, China, April 8–11, 2019, IEEE, pp 626–637

288. Xu L, Yuan X, Wang C, Wang Q, Xu C (2019) Hardening database padding for searchable encryption. In: 2019 IEEE Conference on Computer Communications, INFOCOM 2019, Paris, France, April 29–May 2, 2019, IEEE, pp 2503–2511

289. Xu L, Duan H, Zhou A, Yuan X, Wang C (2021) Interpreting and mitigating leakage-abuse attacks in searchable symmetric encryption. IEEE Transactions on Information Forensics and Security 16:5310–5325

290. Xu M, Namavari A, Cash D, Ristenpart T (2021) Searching encrypted data with size-locked indexes. In: 30th USENIX Security Symposium, USENIX Security 2021, August 11–13, 2021, USENIX Association, pp 4025–4042

291. Xu P, Wu Q, Wang W, Susilo W, Domingo-Ferrer J, Jin H (2015) Generating searchable public-key ciphertexts with hidden structures for fast keyword search. IEEE Transactions on Information Forensics and Security 10(9):1993–2006

292. Xu Y, Cui W, Peinado M (2015) Controlled-channel attacks: Deterministic side channels for untrusted operating systems. In: 2015 IEEE Symposium on Security and Privacy, SP 2015, San Jose, CA, USA, May 17–21, 2015, IEEE Computer Society, pp 640–656

293. Yao ACC (1986) How to generate and exchange secrets (extended abstract). In: 27th Annual Symposium on Foundations of Computer Science, Toronto, Canada, 27–29 October 1986, IEEE Computer Society, pp 162–167

294. Yaqoob I, Salah K, Jayaraman R, Al-Hammadi Y (2022) Blockchain for healthcare data management: opportunities, challenges, and future recommendations. Neural Computing and Applications 34(14):11475–11490

295. Ye Q, Hu H, Meng X, Zheng H (2019) PrivKV: Key-value data collection with local differential privacy. In: 2019 IEEE Symposium on Security and Privacy, SP 2019, San Francisco, CA, USA, May 19–23, 2019, IEEE, pp 317–331

296. Zeng M, Qian H, Chen J, Zhang K (2022) Forward secure public key encryption with keyword search for outsourced cloud storage. IEEE Transactions on Cloud Computing 10(1):426–438

297. Zhang K, Wen M, Lu R, Chen K (2021) Multi-client sub-linear Boolean keyword searching for encrypted cloud storage with owner-enforced authorization. IEEE Transactions on Dependable and Secure Computing 18(6):2875–2887

298. Zhang M, Chen Y, Huang J (2021) SE-PPFM: A searchable encryption scheme supporting privacy-preserving fuzzy multikeyword in cloud systems. IEEE Systems Journal 15(2):2980–2988

299. Zhang Y, Katz J, Papamanthou C (2016) All your queries are belong to us: The power of file-injection attacks on searchable encryption. In: 25th USENIX Security Symposium, USENIX Security 16, Austin, TX, USA, August 10–12, 2016, USENIX Association, pp 707–720

300. Zhao Y, Wang H, Lam K (2021) Volume-hiding dynamic searchable symmetric encryption with forward and backward privacy. IACR Cryptology ePrint Archive p 786

301. Zheng W, Dave A, Beekman JG, Popa RA, Gonzalez JE, Stoica I (2017) Opaque: An oblivious and encrypted distributed analytics platform. In: 14th USENIX Symposium on Networked Systems Design and Implementation, NSDI 2017, Boston, MA, USA, March 27–29, 2017, USENIX Association, pp 283–298

302. Zuo C, Sun S, Liu JK, Shao J, Pieprzyk J (2018) Dynamic searchable symmetric encryption schemes supporting range queries with forward (and backward) security. In: Computer Security—23rd European Symposium on Research in Computer Security, ESORICS 2018, Barcelona, Spain, September 3–7, 2018, Proceedings, Part II, Springer, Lecture Notes in Computer Science, vol 11099, pp 228–246

Printed in the United States
by Baker & Taylor Publisher Services